DAY OF SHAME

DAY OF SHAME

The truth about the murderous happenings
aboard the Cutter Vigilant during the
Russian-American confrontation
off Martha's Vineyard

By ALGIS RUKSENAS

David McKay Company, Inc.
NEW YORK

To my parents

SECOND PRINTING, MAY 1973

Contents

Charts and Maps

INTRODUCTION

Summary of Facts

On the afternoon of 23 November 1970, near Martha's Vineyard, Massachusetts, a Soviet defector came aboard USCGC VIGILANT from the SOVETSKAYA LITVA. The Coast Guard had notice that he would try to defect, but it did not ascertain and execute that policy of the United States which calls for the retention of political defectors. Pursuant to improper command decision, Soviet crewmen were permitted to come aboard the VIGILANT and forcefully remove and return the defector to the Soviet ship.

The above is a clinical summation of facts in one of the most incredible occurrences in modern U.S. maritime history. They were gathered by a Formal Board of Investigation convened by the United States Coast Guard at the orders of the President following a public outcry over the incident. The summary is cold, detached, professional, but between those lines is a passionate, highly dramatic, and poignant story of one man's meeting with his destiny.

The man was a radio operator named Simonas Kudirka, whose native Lithuania was absorbed by the Soviet Union in 1940. "A man born in a cave does not know what freedom is," he had jotted in a pulpy notebook that he always kept with him, adding: "To die for freedom is worth the risk."

Kudirka took that risk believing that the United States was

a haven for persons seeking refuge from oppression. It was the greatest mistake of his life. His subsequent fate—an aberration —became the most bizarre incident to occur in U.S. territorial waters.

Theoretically, the U.S. is, indeed, a haven for the oppressed and that idea is deeply engrained in the American ethos. The Statue of Liberty in New York harbor is a visible symbol of that belief. More importantly, U.S. policy favorable to refugees and defectors is solidly based in the law. Title 8 of the United States Code deals with Aliens and Nationality and section 1153 (a) (7) specifies that the Attorney General may prescribe immigrant visas "to aliens who satisfy an Immigration and Naturalization Service officer at any examination in any non-Communist or non-Communist-dominated country, (A) that (i) because of persecution or fear of persecution on account of race, religion, or political opinion they have fled (I) from any Communist or Communist-dominated country or area . . . and (ii) are unable or unwilling to return to such country or area on account of race, religion, or political opinion."

The Code of Federal Regulations by which appropriate agencies implement the law is even more specific. Part 253 of Title 8 instructs the Immigration and Naturalization Service—a part of the Justice Department—on "Parole of Alien Crewmen." Under section 253.1 (f), a crewman "who alleges that he cannot return to a Communist, Communist-dominated, or Communist-occupied country because of fear of persecution in that country on account of race, religion, or political opinion shall be removed from the vessel or aircraft for interrogation. Following the interrogation, the district director having jurisdiction over the area where the alien crewman is located may in his discretion authorize parole of the alien crewman into the United States . . ."

Based on its own laws, the United States has over the years, especially after World War II, accepted many defectors and refugees into the country. However, until 1951, the U.S. had never signed any international accord defining the concept of political asylum and thereby recognizing its validity in international law. It did accede in 1951 to a convention relating to the status of refugees done at Geneva, Switzerland, under the auspices of the United Nations. That convention was updated in 1967 as a multilateral Protocol Relating to the Status of Refugees and signed by the United States in November of 1968. The Soviet Union also signed the Protocol.

Underlying the treaty was the Charter of the United Nations and the Universal Declaration of Human Rights approved by the General Assembly in December of 1948 which "affirmed the principle that human beings shall enjoy fundamental rights and freedoms without discrimination." Article 33 is most relevant in the case of the *Vigilant* incident. It states: "No contracting State shall expel or return ('refouler') a refugee in any manner whatsoever to the frontiers or territories where his life or freedom would be threatened on account of his race, religion, nationality, membership of a particular social group or political opinion."

Precipitated by unawareness of U.S. policy, the incident demonstrated the viciousness inherent in a totalitarian regime and official American passivity in the face of it, pinpointed ignorance in high places in the government bureaucracy, shattered a sacred U.S. maritime tradition, assailed the public morality of the American people, and jarred the United States Coast Guard to its foundations.

This book is a factual account of that affair. It consists of two parts: the incident and an analysis of the aftermath and its repercussions.

All dialogues and thoughts of the participants are based on their memories and were gleaned from interviews with them or from official transcripts of the U.S. Coast Guard's Formal Board of Investigation. Most telephone conversations in the latter part of the book are verbatim and taken from transcripts of conversations taped in the First District of the U.S. Coast

Guard in Boston. These sources will be noted when appropriate.

Words of Simonas Kudirka and most of the information about him were provided by officers who were in contact with him aboard the cutter *Vigilant* that day. Other information about him was taken from testimony in his reported treason trial in Lithuania six months after the incident.

Since Rear Admiral William B. Ellis, Captain Fletcher W. Brown, Jr., and Commander Ralph W. Eustis were the principals in this incident, they naturally hedged on some questions that might be too embarrassing and did not reveal too much of their inner character. Several other Coast Guard officers involved in the incident were still in uniform when this book went to press and some of their statements were obviously guarded. This, however, did not substantively affect the re-creation of the incident, because their official testimony before the Board of Investigation was revealing enough.

What were a Russian and an American ship doing moored together in U.S. territorial waters in the first place, making a spectacular defection possible? The rendezvous was the result of long-standing bitterness among commercial fishermen of New England over Soviet fishing practices.[1] Local fishermen knew for years that foreign fishing fleets operating off the shores of the Atlantic Coast were violating the few treaties there were to protect certain fisheries. Lobbying in Congress and appeals to the U.S. Department of Commerce to enforce the treaties always met with empty sympathies.

Various nations had made gestures to conservation and by doing so had lulled themselves into a belief that fish were really being conserved. For example, in 1949, mainly through the efforts of the United States, a group of nations formed the International Commission of Northwest Atlantic Fisheries (IC-NAF) to regulate what was then believed to be an increasing exploitation of waters in the Northwest Atlantic. Fifteen nations agreed that fish stocks had to be preserved, but few bothered to take any concrete steps toward that end. During annual meetings that lasted into the 1960s ICNAF conventions centered on regulation of mesh sizes in nets and types of gear. Enforcement of each nation's fleet operations was left to the individual nation and few seemed to care what anyone did in international waters.

The Soviet Union joined ICNAF in 1958 shortly after its massive fleets began operating in waters covered by the commission. It was only in 1962 that the U.S. and Soviet Union began discussing the conflicts of interest between the U.S. fishermen and the Soviet fleets. With their highly sophisticated gear and modern fleets the Soviets—and other nations—were stripping Northwest Atlantic waters of much of their fish life. Soviet marine technology had in fact become so sophisticated that Russian fleets by the late 1960s had depleted up to 95 percent of herring and haddock stocks which were formerly abundant in Northwest Atlantic waters. That prompted U.S. and Canadian authorities to institute seasonal "haddock patrols" to ensure that fishermen of no country take that stock during spawning season.[2]

But according to some biologists this was not enough and they recommended that no haddock be taken anytime so that the species could rejuvenate itself.

Soviet fleets have practiced what is called "pulse fishing"—the taking of certain species of fish almost to a point of extinction, then switching to another species and in turn taking it to a point of extinction and so forth. This practice, called "terrifying" by a member of the House Merchant Marine and Fisheries Committee, continues to be used by Soviet fleets and is not forbidden by any treaty.

In order to protect themselves, local fishermen lobbied in the early 1960s for extension of the territorial fishing zone (contiguous fishing zone) to twelve miles. The U.S. allowed foreign fishermen to fish within three miles—the limit of territorial waters. Other nations had long established a twelve-mile limit for fishing. It would only be in 1966 that the U.S. finally would extend its territorial fishing zone to twelve miles, as most other countries had for a long time. However, New England fishermen continued to feel that if conservation was really to succeed, territorial fishing zones should be extended to either 200 miles or 100 fathoms. They claimed the U.S. would only be doing what other countries with extensive coastal fisheries, except Canada and Mexico, had already done.

But the State and Commerce Departments balked at such suggestions in periodic policy papers. This was not surprising to the local fishermen who believed the government was not working for their interests.

In 1966 local fishermen persuaded the government to ask Russia for talks on fish conservation. According to the knowledgeable New Bedford *Standard-Times,* which in its issues of the late 1960s reads like a chronicle of fishermen's griefs, the Soviets agreed to curb their Atlantic fishing "if necessary." By 1967 at the seventeenth annual meeting of ICNAF the only positive measure taken had been agreement on a minimum mesh size for cod and haddock fishing. But even that could not be enforced. ICNAF was in actuality a lame organization. Meanwhile bilateral U.S.–Soviet talks continued throughout 1967, and in November the Soviet Union agreed to curb fishing off the east coast by signing a pact to that effect. However, the treaty was more indicative of what it excluded than what it included. Excluded were Georges Bank, fishing grounds off Cape Cod, and the waters off Martha's Vineyard and Nantucket Island. Most fish were located in these areas, but the areas were excluded on the grounds that they were covered by previous ICNAF agreements.[3] But the bilateral pact had been sought by local fishermen because they were convinced the ICNAF agreements were inconsequential—it was a merry-go-round.

The U.S. government claimed progress was being made and in policy papers cited the various agreements, but the fishermen continued to haul in smaller and smaller tonnages.

Meanwhile, reports that Soviet fishing fleets were also carrying out spying operations added to the problem. In May, 1966, a U.S. Senate subcommittee was closely studying reports that Soviet trawlers were dropping homing devices that could direct missiles to many of the nation's urban centers.[4] Trawlers were perennially sighted near submarine lanes leading in and out of bases in Connecticut and Virginia. In early 1969 twenty vessels of a fleet of a hundred violated the twelve-mile territorial fishing zone off Virginia. The trawlers were operating near a NASA rocket center at Wallops Island. The rest of the Soviet fleet ranged from twenty-five to forty miles off Hampton Roads, one of the largest naval installations on the east coast. Coast Guard cutters sometimes intercepted intruding vessels and warned Soviet captains that repeated offenses could mean "possible seizure." But no countermeasures were taken.

The major concern for New England fishermen, however, remained the fish harvests. Commercial fishermen of New Bedford had been noticing that since the mid-1960s their catches of yellowtail flounder—the flat, ugly, yet succulent money fish of New Bedford—were dwindling. They suspected that the Soviets, having fished other species to excess, were encroaching on flounder. When local fishermen reached yearly quotas for yellowtails, the government would dutifully order them off the fishing grounds, but would allow fleets of other nations to remain, because the other nations claimed they were after fish other than yellowtail flounder. This, to some extent, was true, but local fishermen knew, and U.S. fisheries officials conceded, that yellowtails were being caught illegally as well.

Hoping to alleviate part of the problem, fishing industry representatives of New Bedford in February of 1969 urged the Commerce Department to raise the cull on yellowtails from one-half to three-quarters of a pound in order to allow the fish to grow and reproduce better. This was a stopgap measure in view of their continued suspicion that the Soviets were violating a recent agreement on yellowtail flounder. An ICNAF treaty allowed the Soviets to pick up one percent in "accidental" catches, but local fishermen knew, and the Soviets had admitted, that they caught large numbers of yellowtail flounder beside the herring, mackerel, and hake which they sought.

At a meeting in Halifax, Nova Scotia, in the summer of 1969 the Soviets had made a "gentlemen's agreement" to use larger mesh nets and keep away from yellowtails, but the decreasing catches by New Bedford fishermen indicated to them that the Soviets were reneging on their agreement. The fishermen were not surprised and complained vainly to the Bureau of Commercial Fisheries in Washington that Soviet fleets were fishing the grounds so clean that local fishermen could not even find "monkey fish"—the term they used for rejects.

"They fish so clean, even the sea gulls don't follow their ships," a New Bedford fisherman cynically told a reporter inquiring into the problem.

For its part the Bureau of Commercial Fisheries, on the basis of aerial photographs, insisted there was no problem with the Soviets concerning yellowtail flounder.

Representatives of the New Bedford fishing industry were not satisfied and early in 1970 filed a complaint with the National Marine Fisheries Service (NMFS) within the Department of Commerce, accusing the Soviets of violating the agreement made in Halifax the previous year. Local fishermen wanted to meet with the Soviets to discuss the problem. They wanted to inspect Soviet trawlers to see for themselves what the Russians were actually hauling in. NMFS passed that request along to the State Department.

Initial soundings were made on an ambassadorial level and both governments agreed to let their representatives meet. This was not to be an official meeting between governments, but a meeting of interested parties. The Soviet side, however, by its nature, was an arm of the Russian government since the *Kombinats*—the fleets—were wholly government-owned and operated. On the U.S. side, the parties interested were members of the New Bedford fishing industry. They would be accompanied by an official of the National Marine Fisheries Service who would act as the nominal head of the delegation. Present also would be an interpreter who happened to be an official in the foreign fisheries bureau of the Commerce Department, and an observer from the U.S. Coast Guard.

The meeting was to be informal, and one of the American officials even refrained from calling the group a "delegation," but rather a "team."

Arrangements on the U.S. side were then relegated to agencies directly involved: the Regional Office of the National Marine Fisheries Service (NMFS) in Gloucester, Mass.; the New Bedford fishing industry; and the First District of the U.S. Coast Guard, headquartered in Boston.

The Coast Guard's role was twofold. First, it had a legitimate interest in the meeting because the enforcement of fishing agreements was within the jurisdiction of its Office of Law Enforcement. Second, the Coast Guard would transport the U.S. delegates to the Soviet fleet and back. Since the meeting was strictly for purposes of observation, the Coast Guard's primary role was that of transportation.

Because the meeting was to be informal, no member of the U.S. delegation had authority to make agreements or take any action on the yellowtail problem. The Americans would simply go wherever the Soviet fleet happened to be fishing, board a working trawler, see what the Soviets were catching, discuss the problem and go home. This type of arrangement was considered typical by representatives of the New Bedford fishing industry, who expected little from the meeting.

After several delays the meeting was set for November 23, 1970, in international waters off the island of Martha's Vineyard.

CHAPTER

1

A steady whine, at first barely audible, then increasing to a high pitch, sounded throughout the U.S. Coast Guard Cutter *Vigilant* as she prepared to slip from her moorings at New Bedford's State Pier. Over the loudspeakers a voice pierced the misty, late November morning. "Take in one, two, three. Take in four, five, six." Mooring details responded and started taking in lines.

Commander Ralph W. Eustis, Captain of the *Vigilant,* stood at the coaming of the starboard bridge wing watching the preparations. In the wheelhouse the helmsman manipulated the levers controlling the pitch of the propellers driven by two turbo-charged diesel engines and eased the ship astern from the pier. Eustis leaned over the coaming and saw the pier recede from the hull. When the bow cleared the end of the pier the cutter turned slowly to port and made her way southward through the harbor. Satisfied, Eustis went back inside to be with the five civilians he had aboard together with a lieutenant from Coast Guard Headquarters in Washington. They were the American representatives to the meeting.

The chalk-white cutter rolled slightly because she was tall and lean and had only a ten-foot draft, but she glided as effortlessly through the water as the screeching sea gulls did above the surrounding wharves. She was a medium endurance cutter,

210 feet long, used for search and rescue operations on the high seas and for law enforcement within territorial waters. Her life's role was symbolized at the base of her orange mast where an eagle in flight with binoculars in one talon and a salvaged ship in the other was painted over a light-colored diamond background.

This trip, however, was for an entirely different purpose. The *Vigilant* was on her way to rendezvous with a Russian factory trawler in the Atlantic.

They would sail nine miles south of Gay Head at the southernmost tip of Martha's Vineyard where a Soviet vessel would be waiting in international waters for a meeting on fisheries problems.

Commander Eustis and his Executive Officer, Lt. Commander Paul Pakos, chatted with the fisheries representatives. Eustis knew most of them from mutual interests in the sea and in New England fisheries. As the delegates exchanged small talk and speculated about what the meeting might accomplish, his mind drifted to the rendezvous area and he wondered if the meeting could take place at all. Weather for the previous several days had been stormy, and Eustis sensed that a rendezvous could not easily be accomplished in rough seas. He figured he might just have to escort the Soviet vessel to the lee of Martha's Vineyard and hold the meeting in sheltered waters. This, of course, would mean getting permission to bring a foreign vessel into territorial waters.

He interrupted his conversation to ask his Operations Officer, Lt. (jg) Douglas Lundberg, to contact the Coast Guard Station at Woods Hole to find out the exact location of the Soviet ship.

Lundberg, third in command, was feeling a little crowded in the wheelhouse among all the officers and guests. He could sense an undertone of excitement generated by everyone's anticipation of a rare meeting with the Russians. Lundberg stood next to a small P-58 transmitter aft of the helm holding a microphone in his left hand and leaning that elbow on a platform supporting the transmitter. He was moon-faced and youthful-looking, but just a bit heavy for his thirty-one years. Lundberg was dressed in khakis, without the customary black tie, and he wore a dull-green foul-weather jacket.

Woods Hole had just reported that the Soviet ship was already waiting for them, anchored in the vicinity of Martha's Vineyard. Jotting down the call letters UBMD, he paused, looked idly at the people in the wheelhouse, then spoke into his microphone.

"UBMD. This is Cutter *Vigilant.* Over."

Three of the civilians talking with Eustis were in business suits and the other two were dressed casually in half-coats for the winter weather. The lieutenant from Washington stood near the Captain. Like Eustis, he wore a dress-blue uniform and a white officer's cap.

"UBMD. This is Cutter *Vigilant.* Over," Lundberg repeated, noticing that some of the men in the wheelhouse had stopped talking and were listening to him. "UBMD. This is Cutter *Vigilant.* Over."

Several long moments went by, then: "*Eta* UBMD *zapryba Kaliningrad.*" Lundberg couldn't understand the voice that crackled through his receiver. He asked for an interpreter.

Alexis Obolensky, an official from the Division of Foreign Fisheries of the U.S. Commerce Department, came to the transmitter. He was a Russian himself and from a noble family. His grandfather had served in the czarist government and his father was an officer in the Russian Army during World War I. Even after fleeing Russia in 1918, following the Bolshevik takeover of the previous year, the family retained the title of "Prince" and was prominent in social circles. Alexis Obolensky was fifty-one, of medium height and build, his black hair combed straight back over his head. His hair was full and long, draping the back of his neck and flaring at the ends. A black mustache matched his deep, dark eyes.

Obolensky was born in Germany in 1919, a year after his

parents fled Russia, and he lived there until 1929. Then the family moved to Italy, where Alexis studied politics at the University of Milan. He came to the U.S. in 1959 with his wife and family and moved to Washington four years later. He had been in his position with the Department of Commerce for two years and had made official visits to the Soviet Union. His astuteness could only be gleaned from conversations, but even on sight he seemed more than the man in the street. Obolensky wore several rings on his fingers and had a thin gold chain hanging from his neck. It crossed his chest and disappeared into his shirt pocket. The sweep of his hair resembled that of a concert pianist. This, plus a hint of an aristocratic English accent mixed with an East European one, immediately set him apart.

Lieutenant Lundberg gave him the microphone, while Commander Eustis relayed a question.

"Kokaja pogoda?" ("How is the weather?") he asked after Lundberg showed him how to operate the microphone.

"Pogoda haroshaja." ("The weather is good.")

One of the other civilians listened closely to the radio conversation. He was Robert Brieze, President of the New Bedford Seafood Producers Association, who knew Russian and translated the words to his friend John Burt, port agent of the New Bedford Fishermen's Union. Both were dressed in half-coats, work slacks, and caps—workman-like, but warm.

John Burt was the embodiment of the image of the independent, self-made fisherman who had long ago come to terms with the sea. His parents were from Newfoundland where his father was a fisherman before him. His father had sailed from New Bedford, then gone to Boston after business slackened in New Bedford in 1942. He was lost at sea in a storm. Now Burt was following his father's footsteps: scalloping, dragging, fishing. He had been in the business twenty-three years.

Robert Brieze was a former refugee who had fled his native Latvia in 1944 when the Soviets had overrun the country for the second time in four years. While the Obolenskys had earlier escaped the Soviets unscathed, Brieze's family had not been so fortunate. The Soviets had deported his father, mother, a sister, and a brother-in-law to Siberia.

A short, paunchy man of fifty, he spoke with a heavy European accent enunciated through a slightly prominent lower jaw. But his nondescript features enveloped a determined soul. Brieze had surmounted extremely trying situations after he fled his country. The most harrowing had been an uncertain passage across the Atlantic Ocean in an old, converted British minesweeper. He sailed with about one hundred other refugees from neutral Sweden, where he had sought refuge. Fear of being returned by the Swedes to Russian rule had been too terrifying, and the refugees had risked the open sea in an illegal passage to America rather than take even the remotest chance of being forced back to Soviet territory.

In January, 1945, Brieze, then twenty-four, had managed to get passage on a transport ship headed for Germany. He often remembered the perilous passage among mines in the Baltic Sea, so perilous that the ship had to turn back and try again after a week. He eventually found himself in East Prussia with his wife and a surviving sister. Brieze finagled a truck ride to Danzig in nearby Poland, a precious ride paid for by some bacon and a bottle of vodka that he had brought from Latvia. He found a job on a tugboat operating out of the port of Danzig, and from that day Brieze's life had been inextricably linked with the sea.

He was then near the Baltic Sea, a natural escape route to points unknown, but the specter of Soviet rule and its long grasp still plagued him. Russian armies were pressing westward, blazing a trail of destruction. Most foreboding to Brieze was the blood lust of the NKVD, the Soviet secret police. Within two months the Russian front had advanced dangerously close, and Brieze, with his wife and sister, together with other refugees, made his way to Bornholm, a Danish island,

and then to Sweden where he was granted permission to stay. Still, the specter of the Soviets haunted him, and for the next two and a half years Brieze lived a gypsy-like existence in Sweden accompanied by the fear that the Soviets would persuade the Swedes to return refugees who had escaped to that country.

Hundreds of thousands of refugees seeking asylum all over Western Europe were a profound humiliation to the Soviets and their role as "liberators," and the Western Allies, in a bloated spirit of generosity, agreed to send back thousands of them. This secret project was called "Operation Keelhaul."[1] Fear of being caught up in the operation prompted Brieze to join with a group of other refugees in a plan to escape from Sweden to the United States, where they would hope for the best.

Pooling meager resources, more than a hundred refugees bought an old British minesweeper, rummaged around for a serviceable engine, and after two years were ready to make a perilous journey across the Atlantic.

One hundred fifty men, women, and children from Latvia, Lithuania, Estonia, and the Ukraine—without registration papers or a flag—stealthily left the harbor at Falkenberg on the night of August 4, 1950. Their odyssey ended after seventeen days at sea climaxed with a ramming by an American fishing trawler in a fog off Boston. Brieze and the rest of the refugees subsequently spent six months in the U.S. uncertain whether they would be allowed to stay. Finally, by special act of the U.S. Congress, all the refugees were allowed to remain and they dispersed to all parts of the country.

Brieze moved to New Bedford with his wife and sister. There he found work on the waterfront, saved his money, eventually bought a trawler, and became a successful fisherman. Now he had two boats—one of them among the largest in the New Bedford fleet. This day, as President of the New Bedford Seafood Producers Association, fortified with U.S. citizenship and all its juridical protections, he was nonchalant about going aboard a Soviet vessel and meeting with men whose leaders had subjugated his country.

Listening also to the radio conversation was William Gordon, Associate Director of the NMFS in Gloucester. As head of the delegation, he was the senior civilian aboard. Gordon listened intently to the Russian words to see how much he could understand. He had spent brief periods in the Soviet Union on fisheries matters and had learned enough of the language to get by with little need of an interpreter. Gordon was in his early forties, about five feet eight and just a little bit round, with blondish hair receding from his forehead.

Commander Eustis was asking Obolensky to get the coordinates of the Soviet ship.

The voice reported they were anchored at 41° 22' N and 70° 46.9' W.

The Captain went to his chart table, leaned over it, and automatically looked for the coordinates somewhere south of Martha's Vineyard near a buoy off No Man's Land. He was surprised that the actual position was much farther north. In fact, it was in Menemsha Bight, about a half mile off Tissbury Beach at the southwestern end of Martha's Vineyard.

The Soviets, without permission or escort, had anchored in territorial waters.[2]

Eustis had sailed the area since childhood and knew the bight was an ideal anchorage against bad weather, but no one had authorized the Soviets to enter territorial waters, much less the bight.

Eustis took a pencil and put a dot with a circle at the position on the chart. He was not particularly concerned that the Russians had anchored in U.S. waters, but a diplomat would have had fits.

Weather for the last several days had been rough, forcing even the New Bedford fleet to stay home. But this morning the sea had calmed, swells were no more than three feet, and temperatures were already reaching into the fifties and were ex-

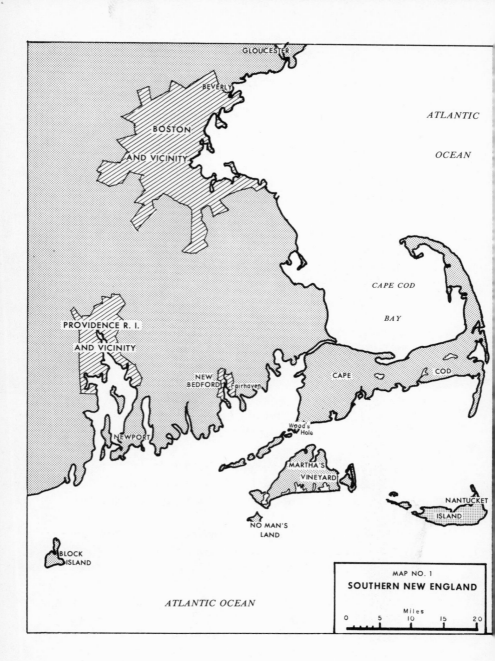

ATLANTIC

OCEAN

GLOUCESTER

BEVERLY

BOSTON
AND VICINITY

CAPE COD

BAY

PROVIDENCE R. I.
AND VICINITY

NEW
BEDFORD   Fairhaven

CAPE   COD

Wood's
Hole

NEWPORT

MARTHA'S
VINEYARD

NANTUCKET

ISLAND

NO MAN'S
LAND

BLOCK
ISLAND

ATLANTIC OCEAN

MAP NO. 1

SOUTHERN NEW ENGLAND

Miles
0   5   10   15   20

8

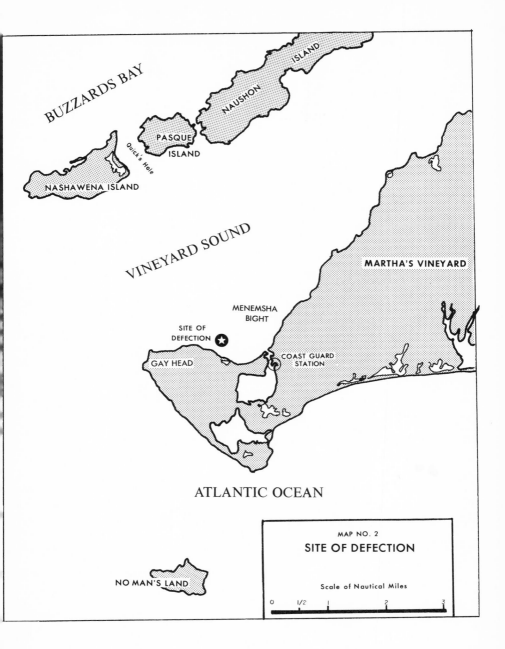

BUZZARDS BAY

NAUSHON ISLAND

PASQUE ISLAND

Quick's Hole

NASHAWENA ISLAND

VINEYARD SOUND

MARTHA'S VINEYARD

MENEMSHA BIGHT

SITE OF DEFECTION

GAY HEAD

COAST GUARD STATION

ATLANTIC OCEAN

MAP NO. 2

SITE OF DEFECTION

Scale of Nautical Miles

0   1/2   1   2   3

NO MAN'S LAND

9

pected to go higher. The Soviets really had no need for such sheltered anchorage. Their trawlers were so sophisticated and seaworthy that most of them could operate in storms of Force 8—winds of up to forty and fifty miles per hour. They had another reason for coming so near to shore, a reason that would soon become obvious to the American delegates.

Vigilant took a course for Menemsha Bight some twelve more miles and a little more than an hour ahead.

During that time Eustis divided his attention between navigating the cutter through Buzzard's Bay and entertaining his guests. This was typical, for he was naturally friendly. Commander Eustis was a "fine, gutsy officer" and had a keen sense of duty. He was a graduate of the Coast Guard Academy and had been in the Coast Guard seventeen years. At thirty-seven he was an experienced seaman and administrator. He had served on various ships, commanded a LORAN (Long Range Navigation) Station in the Far East, studied in the U.S. Naval Postgraduate School, and had a degree in economics. Eustis specialized in fiscal matters and had spent time in the Allowances Branch of Coast Guard Headquarters.

He had a grass-roots air about him that endeared him to practically everyone he met. His dress-blue uniform showed rank and prestige, but he was still the boy next door. In fact, his big round eyes, round nose, and reddish hair suggested the look of a mischievous altar boy. The only betrayal of his age was slightly jowled cheeks that accentuated a generous downturned mouth.

In the year and a half since July, 1969, when he took command of the *Vigilant,* Eustis had gained a reputation as one of the most admired skippers in the First Coast Guard District. So it was not surprising that whenever prestigious assignments were handed out, Commander Eustis usually got them. The *Vigilant* had most recently monitored the Bermuda Races and the vaunted America's Cup Race, serving in both as a front row seat for various dignitaries and the press.

This rendezvous with the Soviets was also a plum. It was rare, meant a change from tedious routine patrol, and was a chance to take part, if in even a small way, in "international affairs."

Eustis piped a piloting detail to stations when the cutter approached Quick's Hole within sight of the anchorage. *Vigilant* passed through the channel between Pasque and Nashawena islands.

Then they saw her.

Most of the men in the wheelhouse walked out to the bridge wing and gazed ahead. In the distance, outlined by the green-gray waters of the bight and the low, gray stratus clouds, was a ship that looked massive even from a distance.

"He sure did come in close," Lieutenant Lundberg thought to himself when he saw the behemoth's proximity to land.

A voice crackled over the receiver and Obolensky repeated in English that the Soviets wanted the *Vigilant* to moor alongside.

Commander Eustis hesitated. He remembered reading a report of a previous Soviet-American meeting in the Fifth District. Delegates there had been ferried back and forth by launch. He conferred briefly with his Executive Officer, deliberating whether to moor alongside. Without much ado he decided it would be safer and more convenient for the delegates to board the other ship if the two were rested together. He ordered preparations for mooring.

Lieutenant Lundberg was surprised by this order, since mooring had not been contemplated. He speculated that once the ships were lashed together a lot of people could be jumping aboard. He remembered the Latvian woman and her father who had lived next door to him when he was stationed in New London. They had told him stories of humiliation, brutalism, and murder perpetrated by the Soviets in Latvia before their escape after World War II. Seeing the ship made that seem real to Lundberg.

As the *Vigilant* approached the Soviet ship Lt. Commander
Pakos, the Executive Officer, wondered if someone might try to
defect. Vague memories of stories of the Hungarian Revolt of
1956 and escapes over the Berlin Wall stirred his mind as he
looked at the ship.

Outside, leaning on the bridge wing by John Burt and Robert
Brieze was a short, slim, hawkish-looking man in a business suit
and long overcoat. He was Howard Nickerson, Executive Director of the New Bedford Seafood Dealers Association.

"I sure hope we don't get a defector," he said. "It would
cause a lot of problems."

Nickerson was known by colleagues as very talkative and
something of a fussbudget. A month earlier when Commander
Eustis and another officer had met with representatives of the
New Bedford fishing industry to prepare for the meeting, Nickerson had made it a point to mention that one of the delegates
to the meeting would be a former refugee—Robert Brieze. But
Eustis and Commander John F. Curry, Chief of Intelligence
and Law Enforcement in the First District, had seen little
reason to worry, especially since Brieze himself seemed uncon-
cerned.

Now Brieze stood by Nickerson watching the Soviet ship
loom nearer. He too wondered if someone would try to defect.

"Even Lenin escaped from Russia at one time and sought
political asylum," he mused to himself.

John Burt looked out over the water toward the gray-hulled
vessel. He had stopped smoking more than a month earlier and
his lungs felt fresh as he breathed in the windy, salty, air. By
midnight, he would be a chain-smoker again.

Inside the wheelhouse Obolensky was telling Lieutenant
Lundberg that the Soviets wanted them to moor on their
"right" side.

"What does he mean right side?" Lundberg asked. He was
used to the conventional terminology of "port" and "starboard" and did not know if the Russians spoke of left and right
in the same way.

Obolensky checked while Lundberg's oval face retained its quizzical look. "Right side to his bow," the interpreter said.

Vigilant drew nearer and the Russian ship grew. She was a giant rising almost 66 feet out of the water, 500 feet long, and displacing 14,000 tons. A yellow, cream, and white, three-decked superstructure amidships was bordered fore and aft by triangular masts, each of which had four booms extending from the base. Two fenders suspended from the hull extended all the way to the water amidships while two others hung short from the bow.

A cone-shaped net hung seemingly useless from a winch at the stern, dangling at a level even with the stern anchor housing. Just above the housing in Cyrillic was the name *Sovetskaya Litva (Soviet Lithuania)*. Below the Cyrillic notation in Roman letters was the word Klaipeda, a city in Lithuania on the Baltic Sea and home port of the ship.

Her superstructure was capped with a tapered smokestack, red and blue, and embellished with a large, red hammer and sickle—the emblem that for half a century has symbolized Soviet Russia.

None of the officers aboard the *Vigilant* bothered to check the name of the Soviet ship with the Cyrillic alphabet–Roman alphabet key posted on the wheelhouse bulkhead in front of the helm. The watch had written "*Zapryba Kaliningrad*" in the log when the Soviet radioman had described the ship as "*zapryba Kaliningrad*"—meaning "from the fishing fleet of Kaliningrad." None of the officers would know the name of the ship until much later. Some of them didn't even know the name of the alphabet posted on the bulkhead in front of the helm, even though they often ran across Soviet ships with Cyrillic notations and had to transcribe them in their reports. The officers referred to the foreign alphabet in various terms including "Gaelic" and "acrylic." The Soviet presence off U.S. shores was a routine irritant, outside their personal curiosity or interest.

The *Vigilant*'s turbines were already winding down as "mooring stations" were piped over the loudspeakers. Crewmen were standing on the decks, many with hands in the pockets of their foul-weather jackets, their shoulders hunched up against the brisk northeast wind. Most were wearing watch hats or baseball caps, the utility headgear aboard ship. They quietly watched crew members lining the rails of the *Sovetskaya Litva*. Sailors at mooring stations heaved lines to Soviet deckhands, who fastened them to bollards hidden by the railings of the Russian vessel. The mooring detail heaved fenders over the side of the *Vigilant* to ensure against damage as the ships came together. Ship's lines were then tightened by winches that drew the *Vigilant* sideways to the *Sovetskaya Litva*. Bumpers touched, and she came to an abrupt halt, swaying slightly back and forth while water trapped between the hulls lapped at them with hollow splashes. The hulls were about fourteen feet apart.

The watch noted in the log: "1030 moored port side to Soviet vessel 'Zapryba Kaliningrad' in posit 41° 22′ N 70° 46.9′ W." This was also sent as a message to the First District.

On the flight deck, crewmen, mostly in their late teens and early twenties, were coming alive. "Hey, there's women aboard!" "Hey, girls!" They saw pretty, babushka-covered heads looking towards them from portholes in the superstructure and noticed some women were lining the rails as well. This was a pleasant surprise, that women took part in the arduous jobs at sea. Several whistles pierced the air, but they were quickly muffled by the wind. The day would not be dull after all. They waved at the women and murmured impishly to one another. Some of the people aboard the other ship waved back.

Four officers, accompanied by the delegates, filed out of a hatchway just in front of the *Vigilant*'s launch two levels below the wheelhouse. They walked along a narrow space past the launch and into a large open area which was the flight deck. It was painted a dark, reddish-blue with purple markings to guide in helicopters. The colors contrasted sharply, almost psychedelically with the white of the cutter.

The *Vigilant* was only two-thirds the size of the mother ship, but her tall superstructure, high mast, and lean, streamlined afterdeck which extended to the rear mast of the *Sovetskaya Litva,* tended to put the Soviet vessel into somewhat more tolerable proportions.

Brieze noticed the three long, canvas-covered lifeboats hanging from davits on the third deck of the ship. Above them he saw what looked like some sort of utility deck with vents and air intakes. Partly obscured by the forward lifeboat and attached to a grid railing on the top deck was a sign in Roman letters: SOVETSKAYA LITVA. No one had to transliterate the Cyrillic to know the name of the ship; it was posted for everyone to read. But no one bothered to do so and put the correct notation in the log.

"Soviet Lithuania," he pondered. With a grudging admiration, Brieze conceded to himself that the Soviets were experts at propaganda. The United States did not recognize the Soviet annexation of Lithuania, Estonia, and his native Latvia, yet here were the Soviets flaunting "Soviet Lithuania" right in Menemsha Bight. He wondered if any of the officers aboard ship knew that the prewar Baltic Republics still had legations in Washington and whether anyone would contact Washington and tell them the Soviets were insulting the United States by bringing a ship named "Soviet Lithuania" into U.S. waters. Brieze harbored a long-standing bitterness against the Soviets and felt they were always getting the best of the United States, even in seemingly minor points of principle.

Indeed, arrangements for the meeting had stipulated that the Americans would go out to the Soviet fishing fleet on the open sea and board the vessel *Nikolai Danilov* to see what the Russians were catching.[3] But the Soviets had abrogated that by sailing right into Menemsha Bight with the *Sovetskaya Litva* and no one seemed concerned.

Brieze suspected that the State Department was playing around with the Kremlin and he was not the only fisherman who believed that. Many New Bedford mariners felt so, and

Brieze had stated as much in an official letter to Secretary of State William Rogers the previous month, accusing the State Department of "some hidden bureaucratic policy" that was counter to the interests of New England fishermen. The letter had even suggested that the U.S. pull out of ICNAF.[4] Consequently, New Bedford representatives were approaching this meeting somewhat casually. They knew nothing good would come of it. John Burt's boss was supposed to be there, but had relegated the job to him. Howard Nickerson was a reluctant participant and only came because the regular delegate could not. A representative of Boston fishermen had not even bothered to show up. For the fishermen, the meeting was little else than a public relations gesture by their government. Meeting in Menemsha Bight rather than the fishing grounds was the first proof of their skepticism, because it meant the Soviets were reluctant to show them a working trawler as they had agreed.

Before Commander Eustis and the Officer of the Deck (OOD) could decide how to get the delegates aboard the other ship, a large boom swung over the *Vigilant*'s flight deck. An old truck tire suspended by cable from the boom and enmeshed in a cargo net landed with a dull thud on the deck. Controlling the winches near the aftermast of the Soviet ship was a man in a turtleneck sweater, suit jacket, and visored seaman's hat. His slim features and goateed face gave him a distinctly Mephistophelean look. He manipulated the lift, sitting on a bulkhead above everyone.

Noticing the wire was greasy, Eustis instructed a crewman to get gloves for each of the delegates. Then he turned to his Executive Officer.

"No cross-visiting at this time, Paul. We'll see how things are later."

"Okay, Captain," Pakos replied.

When the crewman returned with gloves, William Gordon, Robert Brieze, John Burt, and Alexis Obolensky each put on a pair, stepped onto the rim of the tire, and were lifted into the air. A young Soviet deckhand guided the tire with a rope, while a crewman from the *Vigilant* held another rope to help stabilize the rig so the four men clinging precariously to it would not sway dizzily above the short stretch of water between the two ships.

The transfer was watched by a group of official-looking Soviets standing in an open space on the third deck of the *Sovetskaya Litva*. Another group looked on from an open area one deck below.

Watching also was a solitary figure standing near a lifeboat on the third deck.

The rig came down slowly, touched the rust-colored main deck, and the four stepped off looking toward the Soviet officials filing down ladders to greet them.

Obolensky walked toward them, while Gordon and the others stood where they landed. A short, ruddy-complexioned man with a broad face, large, hooked nose, and wavy, black hair met Obolensky and the two started smiling and talking. He was Ivan Burkal, Acting Commander of the Soviet fleet. He and Obolensky had met a year earlier in a seminar on international fisheries at the University of Rhode Island. They had roomed together and were casual friends. Several more officials fanned out around the two, while others went toward the delegates farther down the deck. The Soviets stopped short when they came near Gordon, Burt, and Brieze, uncertain whether to initiate conversation. The Americans stood idly in the shadow of the aftermast, looking around and occasionally exchanging words. It was a moment of mutual uncertainty.

Meanwhile, the rig came across a second time with Commander Eustis, Howard Nickerson, and the lieutenant from Washington. The lieutenant was Leo Morehouse, Jr., from the Office of Law Enforcement at Coast Guard Headquarters. He and Eustis were the only two uniformed men in the U.S. delegation. Morehouse had been an enlistee who had showed promise and was sent to the Coast Guard Academy for officer training.

He was a new staff member in the Office of Law Enforcement, having assumed his duties just three months earlier. He had no instructions for the meeting, just to "get the feel" of what was going on in the area of law enforcement. It was an orientation trip.

When the rig touched the deck the Americans and Soviets grouped together. Introductions were brief and names were soon forgotten, although the delegates did recognize Burkal in his waist-length officer's jacket. Gordon, Brieze, and Burt had also met him in the University of Rhode Island seminar and each wondered if Burkal remembered them. He gave no sign that he did. Burkal apologized through his own interpreter that the Fleet Commander was ill and could not be present. He would act in his place.

Burkal and Vladimir Popov, Captain of the *Sovetskaya Litva*, then led the delegation toward the ladder leading to the upper decks. Except for his heavier build, Popov was of the same mold as Burkal. He had jet-black hair, a broad face, and reddish complexion. Both were jovial as they led the Americans up the ladders and through a bulkhead door on the third deck.

CHAPTER

2

When the delegates disappeared into the Soviet ship, Lt. Commander Pakos turned to one of the petty officers on the flight deck and said lightly: "No one is allowed to come aboard— except defectors." They both laughed, then Pakos and some other officers headed back toward the bridge. Crew members of both ships began lining the rails and exchanging polite smiles.

Pakos and Lieutenant Lundberg returned to the wheelhouse. This is where Lundberg felt most comfortable because he had an unobstructed view of everything going on aboard the *Vigilant* and a large portion of the Soviet ship. Pakos stayed with him briefly, then went out to the forward bridge wing.

Pakos was a short, light-framed man of thirty-two. His round face with close-set eyes was accented by a handsome, full, brown mustache and he wore the standard, dull-green foul-weather jacket and khaki uniform. Lettered on the back of his jacket in black were the words "Executive Officer." A dark blue baseball cap with the word "VIG" on the forehead and an insignia of a lieutenant commander below the "I" sat squarely on his head. His rank was somehow reflected in the crispness of his uniform. He was an ambitious officer and his associates knew he would make admiral with no difficulty. Pakos looked assured, unassuming, and usually hid his innermost thoughts behind a friendly smile. He leaned on the coaming in front of the wheelhouse and looked over the Soviet ship.

Several crew members had also come to the bridge wing to get a better view of the Soviet vessel. They gathered on the port wing opposite the *Sovetskaya Litva*. After several minutes Lieutenant Lundberg noticed the crewmen were laughing and talking boisterously. Beyond them, standing at the railing of the other ship's bridge, was a man.

"I'd better go out and take a look," he thought, suspecting the crewmen might be poking innocent fun at him. Lundberg came out of the wheelhouse and leaned on the coaming next to Seaman John Fowlie.

The man on the *Sovetskaya Litva* was no more than eight to ten feet away. He was framed on his right by one of the vessel's bulky spotlights clamped to a railing and on the left by two white containers of inflatable life rafts. The rudder of one of the long lifeboats was several feet above his head and a high railing in front of him completed the visual frame.

The man was dressed in a dark blue flannel sport shirt with sleeves rolled up just above his elbows revealing his muscular arms. He was good-looking, his face slightly pointed, with brown hair combed straight back in the East European fashion. His hair was slightly receding and tended to accentuate a prominent forehead. A small wisp of hair hung down over his left eyebrow, suggesting he had been doing something intently and could not bother to brush it back into place. The man appeared to be in his thirties.

He looked at Lundberg, turned his head to either side of him, vaguely aiming toward half a dozen shipmates farther down the deck, then turned again, facing his body directly toward Lundberg. In a slow, heavily accented and deliberate voice he said: "I want political asylum."

Lundberg was taken aback, not sure if he heard right. "What did he say?" he asked, turning to Seaman Fowlie.

"I don't know, Mr. Lundberg, but I think it sounded like he wants political asylum."

The man kept looking at Lundberg. "I want political asylum," he repeated, then jerked his head toward his right and left shoulder, each time intoning, "Gestapo. Gestapo." Lundberg knew the man's gestures were aimed at the Soviets farther behind him. The sudden excitement brought a surge of blood to his head as he hurried the few steps around the wheelhouse to where the Executive Officer was looking out over the bow.

"Mr. Pakos, you aren't going to believe this, but this guy says he wants political asylum."

"What?" Pakos asked, only mildly surprised.

"This guy says he wants political asylum."

They walked back and joined the other crewmen. The man again looked behind him, then turned toward Lundberg. "I will go with you."

"He's Exec. I'm second mate," Lundberg said as inconspicuously as he could. The man did not understand and continued addressing him.

"I'm second mate. He's first mate," Lundberg repeated as he pointed to himself and Pakos. "He's my boss." He wondered why the man would not address Pakos, then realized that Pakos was wearing a baseball cap, while he himself had the more formal officer's hat. "He must think I'm the Captain," he said. Pointing to his hat, then to Pakos, he repeated, "I'm second mate. He's first mate."

The man's face finally indicated recognition and he repeated his request to Pakos. Neither of them replied and both went into the wheelhouse to consider their predicament, leaving Seaman Fowlie and the other sailors in quiet curiosity on the bridge wing.

"I think we ought to get a message out right away," Lundberg suggested, but he did not press the point, knowing the Captain was the releasing officer for all messages and he was aboard the other ship. He was not even sure the man was serious. Lundberg did not want to act too hastily and "end up rattling empty cages."

Pakos, on the other hand, was certain the man was serious

and suspected he might jump across any moment. He was ready to let it happen and, without saying anything more to Lundberg, went back to the bridge wing.

The time was shortly after 11 A.M., a half hour since the *Vigilant* had tied up to the *Sovetskaya Litva.*

Pakos stood at the rail, his hands in his jacket pockets. The man was still there. Each looked at the other in silence, waiting for a sign, a gesture. Pakos was worried. What would he do if the man jumped? He didn't know, but at the same time he was confident he could handle whatever happened. A group of shipmates walked toward the man. He raised his hand in a half wave and walked off. The Executive Officer remained where he was, looking casually over the other ship as the Soviets passed by on the opposite deck. Were they suspicious?

Several moments later the man came back. He leaned into the rail, facing Pakos. "Not too cold. I swim," he said, placing his hands just in front of his chest and making a small swimming motion. He kept staring at Pakos, then abruptly walked away along the deck.

Pakos stepped back into the wheelhouse where Lundberg was telling Lt.(jg) John Burke, the Communications Officer, what had happened. "I think he's going to jump," Pakos interjected. "We'd better rig up a Jacob's ladder just in case."

Crewmen hung the ladder on the starboard side out of view of the Soviet ship. The man could easily be guided to it.

"We'll set up a watch," he continued. "Mr. Lundberg, you take the forecastle. Mr. Burke, you take the fantail and inform the OOD to watch for the man from the flight deck."

Each officer then went to his station, each spending anxious moments waiting for the man to slip into the water and swim the short distance to the *Vigilant.*

As the initial excitement wore off, Pakos grew more worried. The Captain and the others were still aboard the Russian ship. What if the man jumped now? Could the Russians hold them hostages? He was back on the bridge wing waiting and wondering. Again the man appeared and moved opposite him. He gazed intently at the Executive Officer with an expectant look on his face.

"Swim?" the man asked.

Pakos did not want to influence him, especially while the Americans were on the other ship. Nor did he want to ward him off. He slowly shrugged his shoulders. As he did so he sensed the man realized the situation and would not make his move hastily. Pakos casually walked away to the forward bridge wing and summoned Lieutenant Lundberg from the forecastle deck.

"Take my place on the bridge," he told Lundberg when he walked into the wheelhouse. "I'm going to send a message to the District."

He hurried to the radio room on the 02 level, went to a desk cluttered with various routine messages and quickly printed the word "Immediate" with a double underline on top of a piece of yellow, legal-size paper. He knew from his friendship and professional relationship with Eustis that he could write a message on his own initiative and tell Eustis later, because Eustis had absolute confidence in him. Normally, a captain would have to authorize a message first. Pakos collected his thoughts, then printed the following message, crossing out and modifying several words as he went along:

Fm Vig
To CGDONE
A. MY———

Secret

1. Situation: Alongside Soviet mother ship as per Ref. A. Estimate with 80 percent probability that one crewman from Soviet mothership will attempt defection to Vigilant. Defection was not enticed. Crewman spoke in broken English to Operations Off. that he wished asylum. Same man later indicated to Executive Off. that water not too cold

and that he would swim. CO and other visitors still aboard and unaware of situation. Will attempt to advise CO.

2. If escape is undetected, plan to recall entire delegation under false pretenses and depart. If escape detected, foresee major problems if delegation still aboard. Req. advise.

3. Plan to . . .

Plan to what? There was nothing more he could do. He crossed out "Plan to" and wrote: "Plan no action pending further developments."

Pakos reread the message and gave it to the radioman. "Make sure this gets out immediately," he said and left.

As Lundberg held the watch for the Executive Officer, a lieutenant walked into the wheelhouse. He had noticed the extra watch and declared, jokingly, "Hey, what you got, a defector coming?"

"Yes, we do," Lundberg replied seriously. The lieutenant looked at him a moment, uncertain whether Lundberg was joking, then walked out with a question mark still on his face.

Pakos returned, told Lundberg the contents of his message to the District, and that he was going to call Commander Eustis back from the Soviet ship.

"How are we going to get him back without arousing suspicion?" Lundberg asked.

Pakos wondered himself. They discussed several possibilities and decided the most likely would be a search-and-rescue ploy. They would call the Captain back on the pretense of some ship needing assistance.

"What if he should jump now?" Lundberg continued. "They might open fire on him. The hull of the *Vigilant* is only three-eighths of an inch thick and if they don't kill or hurt him, they might hit somebody down below. Bullets could go right through the hull."

"Yeah, maybe you're right," Pakos told him.

An incident of several years previous was in both their minds. Some Cubans in a small boat had tried to defect from their ship off Norfolk, Virginia, and were fired upon while a Coast Guard cutter stood nearby. The incident had occurred in international waters.

Neither of them put it past the Soviets to try the same.

"Maybe you'd better go look around their ship. See if they have any ready boxes or guns they could break out," Pakos instructed the Operations Officer.

Lundberg left for a visit to the Soviet ship.

Pakos glanced at the green wall-to-wall carpeting in the wheelhouse, then glanced out toward the *Sovetskaya Litva* and wondered what was going to happen. He called in the quartermaster and asked him to get some old SAR (search and rescue) messages from the Communications Room.

When the quartermaster returned, he took the messages, quickly looked them over, then walked down the aluminum stairway leading to the boat deck hatch and went aft onto the flight deck.

The tire rig lay unused near a rail. Crewmen stood around throwing cigarettes, American change, and other items to small groups on the deck of the other ship. Several crew members were serenading each other with guitars and balalaikas, while both American and Soviet bystanders laughed approval. The atmosphere seemed lighthearted, and temperatures, which had reached into the pleasant sixties, added to the cordial mood. Only one man, somewhere else on the Soviet ship, was engaged in more serious matters, contemplating his life and death move.

Pakos noticed a Russian officer and called across to him to summon Commander Eustis. He nodded that he understood and hurried up the ladders to the top deck. Pakos waited, hiding his concern behind an outer calm. Had they observed the man's activities on the bridge? Could he really call back Eustis without evoking suspicion?

CHAPTER

3

Aboard the *Sovetskaya Litva* Commander Eustis and the others had been given a quick tour of the pilothouse and then taken to a large stateroom adjoining Captain Vladimir Popov's cabin. Ivan Burkal, the Assistant Fleet Commander, was officiating. He had seated the guests at two heavy wooden tables heaped with food and drinks. Various kinds of sausages, a hard, white European farmer's cheese, dark and light heavy-crusted bread, and caviar graced the tables, together with prominently placed tins of fish—the center of the controversy. Bottles of brandy and vodka were placed strategically among the dishes. Next to them were bottles of carbonated mineral water and jars of Instant Sanka coffee.

Smiling demurely, several pretty women had come into the room to the pleasant surprise of the Americans. They were among the forty or so women aboard and were chosen as hostesses for the meal.

"We will now have lunch," Burkal said offhandedly in Russian. His interpreter, a large, neatly dressed man in a gray suit, translated.

"Lunch?" Commander Eustis thought to himself. "It looks more like a full-course meal."

Eustis sat together with Gordon and Obolensky. Facing them were Burkal and several other Soviets. The other Americans were at a second table off at an angle near a wall. Brieze, Burt, Nickerson, and Lieutenant Morehouse were being entertained by Captain Popov. Brieze was at the end of the table and next to him and at an angle were two officers who spoke with him in his native Latvian. They were pleasant, animated.

Burkal introduced his associates. "Valentin Shennikov, Commander of the Kaliningrad Fleet . . . Vasili Poletaev, Chief Inspector for Safety and Navigation . . . Vsevolod Morozov, Chief Technologist . . . Emilis Grušauskas, First Mate of the *Sovetskaya Litva* . . . Lev Gartman, Chief Master Catcher of the Fleet . . . Genrikas Baltrunas, interpreter." The guests forgot the names as they were mentioned, but Obolensky jotted them down on a piece of paper for the record.

One man in the room was not introduced. He was short and chunky, with a red face, broad nose, and straight, black hair combed back over his head. He wore a gray, button-up sweater and walked around the room chain-smoking. The man in the gray sweater said nothing, but moved all the time, first to one table, then the other. His name was Zabiela and he had recently been assigned to the *Sovetskaya Litva* as "Captain's Assistant for Political Affairs."[1] His presence was noticed by everyone, Soviet and American alike.

Zabiela may have been casually dressed, but it was obvious that he outranked all the other Soviets, regardless of uniforms or positions. He was in charge—the Commissar—on the sidelines, yet supreme.

"I'm William Gordon. I'm the Associate Director of the National Marine Fisheries Service, Region Three in Gloucester," Gordon said when the Soviets were finished. He had been trained in zoology and had joined the Commerce Department as a fisheries biologist in 1955. Beginning in the Great Lakes region he worked his way up to fisheries administrator, then went to Washington as a program planner for NMFS. He had taken over his duties in Gloucester only four months earlier.

Commander Eustis introduced himself next.

"Obolensky," the U.S. interpreter intoned after Eustis. The international flavor of his background imparted to him a distinct continental air.

In turn, delegates at the other tables introduced themselves. John Burt spoke in his gruff, matter-of-fact voice. Lieutenant Morehouse followed, then Nickerson.

Farther down from Nickerson was Brieze who was chatting with the Latvian officers. He stopped briefly to introduce himself. Brieze and Obolensky, among the U.S. delegates, were the two most familiar with the Soviet system, and Brieze still bore painful memories of the Soviet occupation of his country. The meeting that morning had a significance for him that went beyond the fishing problems. He was curious about recent conditions in his homeland and continually asked the Latvian officers about them.

The men started eating and toasting and before long small talk filled the room as they felt more and more at ease in each other's presence.

Obolensky was feeling a certain rapport with Ivan Burkal. They had roomed together for three days at the University of Rhode Island seminar and had little difficulty communicating. Where Brieze was naturally suspicious of the Soviets and their intentions, Obolensky was tolerant and took them at face value. Brieze, for example, believed that the Commander of the Fleet was not really ill, but only chose not to attend the meeting in order to snub the Americans. Obolensky had no reason to doubt that the fleet commander was ill. Brieze suspected the Soviets would torpedo the meeting. Obolensky believed they were sincere and wanted to solve the fisheries problems.

There had been a single barrel of herring placed on deck when the delegates came aboard. Brieze believed it was put there on purpose, as a taunt; they had come to see what the Soviets were catching, but the decks of the giant mothership were empty except for that single barrel of herring. It seemed too conspicuous to Brieze. Obolensky thought nothing of it.

Brieze's attitude was molded by harsh experiences under Soviet rule, while Obolensky's came from a more equal, diplomatic contact with the Soviets. He had never been subject to them. Still, Obolensky knew the system well and was acutely aware that they used repression as a common political tool.

Commander Eustis had no preconceptions about the Soviet Union. The meeting for him simply reflected a person-to-person contact: men of the sea talking about common problems and experiences. He sampled some canned herring and found it delicious. "If my native state of Maine could can herring this good, we would be in pretty fine shape," he said politely to a large Russian in a business suit across from him. "I'll have to tell my friend the governor."

Before the translator could open his mouth, the man beamed and replied in Russian, "We'll make sure you get some before you leave."

Eustis grinned. He knew the Russians understood more English than they admitted. Often in his overseas assignments, he had met people who knew more English than they pretended. But this little game did not bother him. He continued sampling the food, talking occasionally to Gordon next to him.

At the other table Captain Popov was looking across at Burt and engaging him in boisterous talk. Popov seemed a jolly man. "How old are you?" he asked Burt. Someone translated.

"Forty-nine."

"I am forty-eight," Popov said, then pointed to himself and Burt and in English declared: "Robust, robust." He began laughing.

"Yeah," said Burt with a chuckle.

"You will ship with me?" the Captain continued in Russian, his broad face beaming.

"Who me? No, no," Burt chimed after the translation.

Popov continued in Russian, but Burt sensed he could understand English. He had a distinct feeling the Soviets were finding it hard not to drift into English, as if they had instructions to speak only in Russian. He could tell by their eyes—signs of recognition.

Nickerson listened to Burt and the Captain and added an occasional word, but for the most part he remained silent. He was mainly wondering when they were going to see the Russian trawlers.

At the end of the table Brieze and the Latvian officers were continuing their friendly conversation. The young officers told him they knew fellow-Latvians were fishing out of New Bedford, but they were surprised that one of them would be a member of the U.S. delegation. Was he a high-placed official in the U.S. government? they asked.

Meanwhile, the man in the gray sweater noticed how well Brieze was getting along with the Latvian officers. He purposefully walked by the group several times. Each time the Latvian officer who was speaking would stop short and look vacantly at the table. When the man in the gray sweater passed, he would again start talking.

"We would like a loading place near here and a fueling place in Boston," the officer said at one point. "Why the hell are you afraid to let us get some groceries and supplies?" Brieze did not answer. He noticed the officer was already a bit tipsy.

"How are conditions for you in Latvia?" Brieze asked.

The officer replied that members of the fleet were relatively well off. The work was hard, very hard, but they received good wages—up to 800 rubles per month. That was, indeed, high for Soviet wages, but by U.S. standards would be about $200 per month.

"There's a decline of religion in Latvia," the officer continued in a different vein. "Young people are not going to church as much as they used to."

Brieze had heard and believed the reverse was true, but did not want to argue the point.

The first mate of the *Sovetskaya Litva,* Emilis Grušauskas, sat at an angle from Brieze and listened in. He was a Lithuanian and could understand the language of neighboring Latvia, which has a similar linguistic base. Now and then he joined in the small talk (in Russian) which was made ever smoother by the flow of vodka and brandy.

As he got drunker, the young officer next to Brieze became more and more talkative. He leaned over, draped his arm across Brieze's shoulder, and started muttering something to him.

Suddenly the man in the gray sweater was standing in front of him. "Come!" he said. The young officer looked up at him in fright and obeyed. He left the room with the man in the gray sweater, and when the man in the gray sweater returned he was alone. The others at the table noted the scene with some uneasiness.

The luncheon continued for over an hour, cordial, but marked by moments of suspicion. Brieze noticed it most when unidentified men he took to be security officers followed him and the others whenever they went to the ship's head. They were not allowed to be alone, not even for the most private matters.

But this did not dismay Brieze; he expected the Soviets to be like that. His mind was on more pleasant things. He had met one of the hostesses and she had asked him if he could arrange for her to see the *Vigilant.* He said he would. The officers and the hostess, Skaidrite, who also happened to be Latvian, gave him a postcard with a view of the Moscow Prospekt in Leningrad. The colors were bland, almost pink, but that was unimportant, for the crew members had signed the back as a memento of that day: "From the Latvian sailors, Lidums"; "E. Grušauskas," the first mate; a scribbled name that Brieze soon forgot; "Very happy to meet all men of the sea," signed by another man whose name was soon forgotten; "From the Latvian girls, Skaidrite 23.11.70."

How enigmatic they all were: outwardly jovial, friendly, yet at the same time fearful.

It was nearly noon when the man in the gray sweater went

up to Burkal and whispered something in his ear. Burkal had just been asking Commander Eustis if he and some of his officers could visit the American cutter and Eustis had agreed. Now Burkal stood up and smilingly suggested that the men end their meal and go on to the conference which would be held in another room.

The Americans were still wondering when they would get to see the trawlers.

Burkal led the way to another stateroom where tables had been placed end to end for the talks. The room was appointed with dark, wood paneling and heavy-legged tables; it appeared to be a recreation room. Several television sets were placed along the walls, and corner tables had books. A stern Lenin looked down on the scene from his picture frame placed prominently on a wall.

Delegates seated themselves around the tables, the Americans and Soviets mingling informally with each other rather than taking opposite sides.

The man in the gray sweater sat alone by a small table with a telephone.

After seating himself, Commander Eustis pushed his chair back from the conference tables so he would not give undue importance to his presence. The civilians were conducting the meeting and he was serving only as a transporter of the delegation. He had no stake in the proceedings. Little did he know that he would soon be burdened with the most crushing responsibility of all.

When everyone was settled, silence fell over the room. Gordon motioned to Obolensky that he was ready, then began speaking. He thanked the Soviets for agreeing to the meeting and stated the case of the local fishermen.

"We are interested jointly in conservation of resources, but we are concerned about the presence of your fleet and the hardships it brings to the New Bedford fishing industry, which does not fish in the fashion that the Soviet fleet fishes."

Obolensky was giving a running translation.

"Our fishermen are small-boat owners who use short-term departures from home port, while your fleet is capable of sustained operations on the high seas. Your fishing practices are such that they possibly could endanger the well-being of the stocks and, certainly, your presence and competition on the fishing grounds imposes hardships on our fishermen."

The Soviets listened politely as Obolensky translated.

"As you know," Gordon continued in his soft, even voice, "the port of New Bedford is totally dependent on fishing for its economic livelihood and our people and we and the federal government are concerned about the future well-being of the stocks. We are gathered here to discuss with you the various ramifications of the fleet operations, and, hopefully, get your assurances that it is not your intent to harm the stocks."

He concluded: "We hope that through mutual exchange of information and perhaps additional visits of this nature to some of your actual fishing fleets, you will be able to show us by word and by deed that you are not endangering the stocks."

When Obolensky finished translating, Burkal rose and smilingly responded. He spoke briefly, giving assurances the Soviets were not depleting the stocks. "We do not wish to endanger the stocks or to harm your fishermen," Burkal said. "We are fishing for stocks that you do not traditionally use, such as herring, hake, and mackerel."

As he observed Burkal speaking, John Burt recalled the time they met at the international fisheries forum the previous summer. Burkal evidently did not recognize Burt now, but Burt recalled vividly how the Acting Fleet Commander had spoken then. Burkal had admitted then that the Soviets fished for yellowtail flounder as well as other stocks. Now he was saying the Soviets fished for species not "traditionally" used by the U.S. fishermen.

"What are you fishing for?" Burt had asked him then.

"Yellowtails, mackerel, and alewives," Burkal had replied in English.

"What are you going to fish for after that?" Burt had asked.

"Yellowtails, mackerel, and alewives," Burkal repeated.

"Yeah, but what are you going to fish for when they're all gone?" Burt remembered pressing.

"Yellowtails, mackerel, and alewives," Burkal had said again.

"Geez, he sounds strange," Burt remembered commenting to himself. "He sounds just like a robot."

But now, it seemed, Burkal was telling the U.S. delegation what it wanted to hear: "We will do everything possible to avoid endangering the stocks."

His interpreter, Baltrunas, translated the statement but faltered, and Obolensky interjected with appropriate English words. He had to interject several times during the meeting to correct the Soviet interpreter's translations.

Gordon then explained that the U.S. delegates would like to ask some questions. Burkal agreed.

"Are you catching yellowtails for market?" Burt asked to see if Burkal would repeat his statement of the previous summer.

The Chief Master Catcher, Lev Gartman, replied. "No. We catch them for meal. The flounder we catch we feed to the fleet."

This was incredible to the Americans. No fleet could gobble up more than twenty-seven million metric tons of yellowtail flounder in a year, the amount the Soviets had admitted catching the previous year. Local fishermen suspected the amount was even higher.

Just then the telephone rang and the man in the gray sweater quickly picked it up. He listened a moment, put it down, then hurried to Burkal and whispered something in his ear.

"The Executive Officer of the *Vigilant* would like to see Captain Eustis," Burkal announced.

It was nearing 1 P.M.

The Americans looked at each other with quizzical expressions. What could have happened? Brieze became a little nervous. He knew there was something wrong. There had to be something wrong.

Commander Eustis left the room, escorted by the first mate.

Meanwhile, several doors away, Lieutenant Lundberg, who had come aboard the Russian ship to check for weapons, had been sidetracked by several persistent crew members. No sooner had he come aboard when the second and third mates grabbed him and Ensign John Hughes and took them to the chart room. Ensign Hughes knew nothing of Lundberg's purpose and was actually aboard for a tour. But the mates would not allow Lundberg or Hughes to leave. Determined, persistent, staggering, and smelling strongly of alcohol, the mates insisted on a visit with the American officers. Lundberg would recall several months later: "You could tell some of them looked like regular, devout alcoholics. Their eyes were all red, noses bulbous . . . a lot of them were half-lit."

He wanted to get away to see the ship, but the mates would have nothing of it. Ensign Hughes, on the other hand, took their hospitality at face value and this encounter would later prove for him a minor blessing. Lieutenant Lundberg was stymied. Trying to be polite, he responded to their questions, but was itching to see other parts of the ship, especially along the starboard side facing the *Vigilant.* He was hoping too he might run into their man, but the mates were ruining everything.

Still, they were friendly and likeable, and Lundberg began feeling a little guilty that he was aboard on false pretenses. He imagined himself a character from a spy film while the mates talked about charts on the table. He recognized the Massachusetts coastline and was fascinated by the familiar features noted in a strange alphabet.

The third mate spoke no English, so the second mate officiated. "What is the current here—in Vineyard Sound?" he asked with a heavy accent as he pointed to a spot on the chart.

"Four knots," Lundberg replied.

"And what is the current here?" he asked, pointing to Quick's Hole.

"Four knots," Lundberg said, unwittingly giving the tipsy mate information about territorial waters that the Soviets would otherwise have to somehow learn for themselves.

"Is your ship a military ship?" the mate inquired with seeming concern. "We are peaceful. We do not want to tie up with a military ship."

"No. The *Vigilant* isn't a military ship. We only go out to save lives," Lundberg explained.

"Then what is the gun doing on your ship?" the mate challenged.

"The gun? That's uh, like for police," he replied, referring to the forty millimeter piece on the forecastle deck. "That's to make ships stop if they're breaking the law."

The mates seemed to understand and went to another subject. Both of them were large and heavy-built with what Lundberg thought were characteristic ruddy complexions.

They spoke proudly of their chart room, pointing out features that were familiar to Lundberg and Hughes. It was like any chartroom on any ship, except this one evoked a sense of the past. The tables were heavy-legged in typical marine style, but the light fixtures seemed old and cabinets had seen better days. The *Sovetskaya Litva* was only ten years old, but her appointments predated her.

Soon a short, burly man with blond, curly hair walked in. He was "smashed out of his mind," as Lundberg was to recall. He introduced himself as one of the engineers and his jacket indicated he was an officer. The second mate translated his thick-tongued jovialities and presently suggested they all go for some refreshments. The three Soviets agreed and led Lieutenant Lundberg and Ensign Hughes into the passageway. They were friendly, outgoing, but there was something more here, a hint of fear lurking about them. Lundberg felt it when he saw them gazing suspiciously up and down the passageway looking for unseen eyes. As they passed a closed door with large Cyrillic lettering Lundberg stopped. "Hey, what d'ya got in there?" he asked baitingly as he reached for the handle.

"No! No! No!" the second mate exclaimed as he waved his hands and blocked the door. All three took on concerned, frightened faces.

"Hmmm, that must be their secure room or something," Lundberg wondered to himself. The Soviets were drunk, but still cautious. Lundberg kept hoping he could get away from them and look around the ship for signs of small arms. At the least, the mates could take him around for a tour, but they did not. He would recall later: "We don't think like they do at all. To me that was plain that day . . . it's nothing you could put your finger on . . . it was just an atmosphere."

They came to a small stateroom and went in, with the second mate stopping at the door, looking up and down the passageway, then closing and locking it. Lundberg and Hughes were offered seats and the Soviets immediately broke out sandwiches and a bottle of vodka. They offered some to the Americans and engaged them in small talk that was limited by the mates' ignorance of English, Lundberg's and Hughes's ignorance of Russian, and the persistence of the mates in toasting whatever subject crossed their minds.

The visit was pleasant enough, but it was not getting Lundberg what he wanted. Somewhere along in their conversation there was a knock on the door. One of the men unlocked it and in walked the first mate, the man who had escorted Commander Eustis from the meeting. As Lundberg looked him over he wondered how he knew they were in the stateroom. There had to be eyes in the passageway.

The first mate was about thirty-five, tall with a sturdy build. His black hair contrasted handsomely with his trim gray business suit. In accented English he told Lundberg that the Captain of the *Vigilant* had just been called back to his ship. Suddenly, Lundberg saw his chance to get away and see more of the Soviet ship. He was still mistakenly convinced that they might let him wander at will around the vessel. "Well, it's time for us to get back to our ship," he declared and stood up. Hughes also rose.

With broken English and sign language, the Soviets insisted the Americans stay, but this time Lundberg persisted. The Soviets gave in and indicated they would accompany them to the deck. Smiling and talking, the group left.

Lundberg was even more frustrated. How could he check out their ship if these guys shadowed him like that? On deck, he started climbing onto the tire rig, then hesitated. He had not yet accomplished his mission. "Well," he said in a drawn out manner, "maybe we don't have to go quite yet." As long as they were on deck he figured he could wander around a little. But the mates beamed at his reconsideration and immediately escorted the two officers straight back to their stateroom to continue the visit.

Back in the room the group chatted some more and exchanged American quarters and dimes for Russian kopeks and other small items. The mates offered the officers some gloves and packages of their cigarettes. Lundberg gave them a pack of his Camels. Then one of the mates offered them the bottle of vodka. Lundberg looked at it. There was just a small amount left, probably meant for them to finish off. He said "thank you" and indicated they would finish it later. Actually, Lundberg would end up keeping the bottle and what remained inside as a memento—a memento of those same officers whom he would meet again that night, but in a totally different guise.

CHAPTER

4

Commander Eustis emerged from a hatchway on the *Sovet-skaya Litva* and came toward the ladder. His hands swung purposefully as he walked and his gait was deliberate, reminiscent of a march. He descended the ladder and walked toward the boom, escorted by the first mate. As he waited for the rig to swing over from the *Vigilant,* he looked inquisitively at Lt. Commander Pakos.

"We have a potential SAR case developing, sir," Pakos called out loudly as he held up the old messages. The Soviet officer looked on impassively as Eustis acknowledged. Pakos's ruse seemed to be working.

Eustis jumped off the tire just before it touched the *Vigilant*'s flight deck and took one of the messages. "What's this, the *Nancy Jane* sinking again?" Some of the ancient New Bedford trawlers were often in trouble, but he remembered towing the *Nancy Jane* just recently.

Pakos urged him toward the bridge and started explaining the real reason for calling him. They entered the hatchway by the launch, walked down a narrow, carpeted passageway and into the Captain's cabin. Eustis was listening intently. His Executive Officer told him about the seaman's overtures and the contents of the message to the District.

When he finished, Eustis spoke. "Do you think the man is serious?"

"I think he is."

"Well, any man that would make a decision like this must be ready to go through with it. We'd better be ready with some possible courses of action if he does defect."

"We already have a Jacob's ladder rigged on the starboard side and several of the officers are standing watch. If he jumps and isn't seen, he can be guided to the ladder. Mr. Lundberg is on their ship now to see if they have any ready boxes."

Pakos's preparedness was typical and was one of the reasons Eustis had unreserved trust in his Executive Officer. They were old friends and had served together several times before. Pakos had reported aboard the *Vigilant* at the same time Eustis took command. He had graduated from the Coast Guard Academy in 1959, served on an ocean station vessel for two years, then as commanding officer of a ninety-five-foot patrol boat in New York. From 1962 to 1963 Pakos was commanding officer of a remote LORAN Station in northern Japan and the following year enrolled at the Massachusetts Institute of Technology to get a master's degree in electrical engineering. After graduation in 1965 he went to the Electronic Engineering Division of Coast Guard Headquarters, where he stayed until his assignment to the *Vigilant* in July, 1969.

Fellow officers considered Pakos "not just smart, but brilliant" and Eustis thought him outstanding "both as a professional and as a member of the community." He had what he termed a "unique" relationship with Pakos. They did not operate as Commanding Officer and his subordinate, but as a "team." They conferred on all crucial matters and Eustis put high value on all of Pakos's advice.

Their relationship had deep, personal roots. Eustis and Pakos had met about ten years earlier when both were stationed in Japan. Eustis then was a lieutenant and Pakos a lieutenant, junior grade. Pakos took to Eustis immediately. He would remember long after the incident: "Ralph has no airs about him —he is deeply interested in the well-being of other people and he is 'approachable,' as opposed to a superior who dictates orders and expects immediate compliance with no question. It was this attitude of friendliness and cooperation which enhanced our relationship at the time."

Later they served together in Washington and were overjoyed when they learned they would be serving together aboard the *Vigilant.* Eustis was never afraid to delegate authority and, after spelling out general policies, let subordinates take care of all details without interfering. This was a rare quality and instilled self-confidence in subordinates. Pakos was particularly happy with the relationship, because Eustis left the running of the ship to his Executive Officer. "It allowed me to make many independent decisions without first checking with him, because I knew it was consistent with his general feelings on the subject," Pakos would recall.

Eustis and Pakos were neighbors in the small New England town of Mattapoisett near New Bedford, jointly owned a small sailing boat, and raced it on alternate weekends at the Mattapoisett Yacht Club.

They acted as two civilian friends would, but aboard the *Vigilant,* in spite of their unique CO/XO relationship, there was no question that Eustis was still Captain and Pakos his Executive Officer. They were "Ralph" and "Paul" to each other, but "Captain" and "Mr. Pakos" in the presence of the crew.

They considered now the possibility of preventing the defection, but both were sensitive, compassionate men and neither felt the moral right to interpose himself one way or another. They would leave the crucial decision to the man himself.

"Well, anyway, if he jumps now, his chances of getting away are pretty slim, because our delegation is still there and they might keep them as hostages," Eustis speculated, "but if he jumps when the conference is over, his chances of escape seem pretty good. We can easily outmaneuver their ship to get him.

I think he's smart enough to know that it would be unfeasible for him to jump until we're ready to depart."

Pakos agreed.

"Keep meeting the man, but don't try to influence him. I'm going back to the meeting so they won't get suspicious."

"Okay, Ralph, but why don't you come up to the bridge for a minute and maybe you can get a chance to see the man," Pakos suggested.

"All right, but we can't do anything else without giving the impression of trying to entice him."

As they went to the bridge the two officers felt confident that they would be controlling the situation.

Pakos scanned the bridge of the *Sovetskaya Litva* and discreetly indicated to his Captain that the man standing near the railing and looking down at the bow of the *Vigilant* was the would-be defector. The man noticed the two officers and walked along the rail until he was opposite them. He looked silently at Eustis, knowing his formal blue uniform meant he was the Captain. Eustis gazed at the man a moment, then remembering his own admonition to Pakos, turned abruptly and walked into the wheelhouse. He did not want to give the man any kind of communicative look. But regardless of stares or the lack of them, the very presence of the officers and their curiosity was already encouragement to the anxious figure on the opposite deck.

"We'd better not let the crew know of this situation, Paul. Only the officers immediately concerned should be kept informed so they can take the necessary action if something develops."

Eustis had no qualms about leaving the ship as long as Pakos was in charge, so he headed back for the conference. He stepped onto the tire rig. The operator with the Mephistophelian face drew back the levers of his winch and lifted Eustis back to the deck of the *Sovetskaya Litva*.

Some minutes later Lieutenant Lundberg returned to the *Vigilant* holding a pair of gloves and the nearly empty bottle of vodka given him by the mates. He reported his little misadventure to Pakos, adding that he saw nothing suspicious. "I didn't see any ready boxes or guns, Mr. Pakos, but I'm sure they got 'em."

Pakos just smiled at Lundberg's predicament and told him the chances looked good for an escape. He told him he had informed the Captain and that both officers believed the man would only jump when the conference was over.

"Yeah, that would be the sensible time," Lundberg agreed.

He put away his gifts, then went to the bridge wing, leaving Pakos in the wheelhouse with Lieutenant Burke, the Communications Officer. Burke had come up to snap some pictures of the man with his Instamatic camera and discreetly did so whenever the man was in the proximity of the *Vigilant*'s bridge. Within a week those photographs would become sensational and be requisitioned by the Commandant. Lieutenant Burke would not have a chance to see what he snapped until months later.

Outside, Lundberg lit a cigarette, holding it about waist-high between puffs, his left hand (as habit dictated) stuck in his pocket. He looked down toward the deck of the *Sovetskaya Litva* and saw three men and two girls standing near the rail posing for a *Vigilant* crewman with a camera. An old tiger tomcat sat on the rail. One of the girls, a pretty blond, held a mongrel puppy, while two officers and the bushy-haired deckhand who helped with the transfer that morning looked on and smiled. Lundberg recognized one of the officers. He was the curly-haired engineer he had just met in their chart room. The engineer patted the puppy, murmured softly to it, then smiled for the camera, revealing the dimples in his cheeks.

Crew members nearby were tossing cigarettes to each other. Lundberg took a few more drags of his own cigarette, tossed the butt into the sea, then went below to his stateroom where he got several more packs. He went onto the flight deck and tossed them to some people lining the rails.

The solitary figure on the top deck of the Soviet ship watched the scene.

Soon Lundberg returned to the bridge wing. The man he wanted to see was still there, leaning on a rail farther down the deck. He was staring intently at the bow area of the *Vigilant,* but when he noticed Lundberg he walked along the rail to the spot where he first encountered the officer. They stood facing each other, searching each other's eyes.

"*Sprechen Sie Deutsch?*" Lundberg suddenly asked on an impulse.

"*Ja! Ja!*" the man replied and his eyes opened wider. He began speaking in German.

"Wait! Wait! Not me!" Lundberg cried as he put up his hands. "*Habla español?*" he tried, drawing on his rudimentary knowledge of Spanish picked up while on duty with the army in Panama. He had spent two tours in the army before making a career of the Coast Guard.

"*Poquito,*" the man answered and held up his thumb and forefinger in front of his face, signifying "a little."

An image of one of the Cape Verdian crew members acting as a translator crossed Lundberg's mind, but he immediately dismissed the idea as too obvious a move.

Several Soviets then walked onto the deck behind the man. He quickly turned his head, then walked forward along the rail and stopped again at the spot from where he had been staring at the *Vigilant*'s bow. Lundberg's eyes followed. He thought again of his former Latvian neighbors, their sufferings under Soviet rule, and wondered what tribulations drove this solitary figure to take the desperate move he was contemplating: who in fact this man could be.

CHAPTER

5

He was a Lithuanian crewman named Simonas Kudirka and an unwilling subject of the Soviet Russian government which ruled his native land. He was not much different in dress and appearance from the other sailors aboard ship and was typical of many Baltic nationals in the Klaipeda fleet. He was an Everyman and his background was the background of many Lithuanian, Latvian, and Estonian contemporaries.

Robert Brieze shared Kudirka's background, yet Brieze at that moment was a guest aboard the Soviet vessel, while Kudirka envisioned himself a prisoner. That paradox mirrored not only their personal destinies, but the ill-fortunes of their countries which had cast differing fates for their people in the tumultuous years after the Soviets swept into the Baltic States.[1]

Now, finally, fate seemed ready to smile on Kudirka, known to his friends and shipmates as Simas.

At a very youthful-looking forty-one he was theoretically one of the vanguard of Soviet ideology. He had witnessed the death throes of the old order in his country and watched the Soviets build a new one. Simas matured while being nourished with rigid Communist interpretations of the world and was expected under threat of severe penalties to withstand and conquer all antitheses of its logic. But his soul was with another cause, the cause of that old order which he had seen destroyed in his homeland.[2]

Kudirka felt smothered.

Staring at the gray-painted steel decks of the *Vigilant,* he brooded over his lot and knew that by touching them he could change it—change it miraculously. All he would have to do would be to jump from one deck to another, a leap of fourteen to sixteen feet over chilly water. The jump would be difficult, but not impossible. The act itself, however, would have to be the most daring move of his life.

Simas Kudirka was a highly trained seaman. He had studied to be a radio technician, knew four languages, was in a profession that was well paid by Soviet standards, and had the rare privilege of leaving the boundaries of the Soviet Union. But this was not enough to mollify his urge for liberty. Political commissars knew this and in recent years had been slowly and deliberately disparaging him. It was too obvious to Kudirka, who was an intense, emotional man prone to bare his soul when silence would have been wiser.

He had come to grips with his dilemma and decided to settle it in his own way. He stared from the rail and waited anxiously for a signal from the Americans, waited for his one and only chance to escape.

To understand what, besides immediate, secret thoughts motivated him, one has to retrace more than thirty years of Kudirka's life. They are years filled with gaps which make him much of a mystery to this day, but they are also years known intimately to history as times of repression, horror, frustration, and widespread despair in the Baltic States.

Simas was eleven, living in his home village of Griškabudis in central Lithuania when the Soviet army marched into his country on June 15, 1940. His parents and their friends were bewildered, uncertain. Lithuania had been a sovereign, neutral country having cordial relations with its neighbors and suddenly found itself a slave nation. Terror seeped into the marrow

BALTIC AREA

NORWAY

FINLAND

SWEDEN

Tallinn

ESTONIA

*NORTH
SEA*

Riga

LATVIA

UNION OF SOVIET

DENMARK

Moscow

LITHUANIA

Klaipeda

Kaunas

Vilnius

BELORUSSIA

POLAND

SOCIALIST REPUBLICS

W.   E.
GERMANY

CZECHOSLOVAKIA

UKRAINE

ANCE

SWITZ.

AUSTRIA

HUNGARY

ITALY

RUMANIA

km.   100

YUGOSLAVIA

BLACK SEA

of the country's social, political, economic, and religious life, and would remain there in its most savage forms until the death of Josef Stalin thirteen years later.

Young and impressionable, Simas Kudirka was struck with the awesome changes in his life. He would declare at his secret trial: "I had grown up in a very poor family and was familiar with social injustice. In 1940, when the Red Army occupied Lithuania, social injustice was increased, because national injustice was added to it."

He survived a massive purge in July, 1940. He survived another massive purge in June, 1941. Both had claimed between 50,000 and 60,000 of his countrymen. No one knew who would be next, but everyone feared it might be himself. Indeed, Soviet plans called for the annihilation of 700,000 persons in the Baltic States.[3]

Inevitably, there were rumblings of revolt and Simas's older schoolmates and students in the universities secretly formed underground groups. The young, especially, swelled with patriotic feelings taught by their elders, conspired with them for revolt. The nation did rise up on June 22, 1941, at the time of the German attack on the Soviet Union. But the nation's proclamation of reestablishment of liberty and independence was short-lived, for a Nazi occupation descended over all of Eastern Europe and much of the Soviet Union. Starting in mid-1944 with the Nazis in retreat, the Russians again swept through the Baltic States, this time to stay.

Simas Kudirka turned fifteen during the transition and was surely mature beyond his years, having experienced the end of his childhood under two similar forms of oppressive alien rule, and aware of brutal and insidious realities that clashed sharply with his Roman Catholic upbringing. He referred to that time during his trial: ". . . Rumors began that the Soviet system had changed, but if it did, it changed for the worse . . . One again saw deportations of innocent people to Siberia, one again saw mass murders."

During his first two years of gymnasium [high school], older schoolmates had participated in a national revolt. Others had been involved in clandestine activities against the Nazis. Now he himself was old enough to seriously consider the dangerous craft of patriotism. Many of his friends—fifteen, sixteen, seventeen years of age—were joining anti-Soviet partisans, but Simas never developed courage enough to follow their example.

He moved to Vilnius, the capital, probably boarding with relatives, where he continued his schooling under the new and strange system. Cities were generally safer than the countryside, where battles raged between Soviet security forces and Lithuanian partisans. Fighting would continue for eight years after the war and keep the Soviets on a war-footing in Lithuania long after other battle-weary armies of the world had demobilized. By 1952 more than 50,000 partisans would die, including many of Kudirka's friends.

Although he never joined his friends in the woods, he supported their ideals by shunning membership in the Communist Youth Movement (*Komsomol*) and the Communist Party. Membership was a key to advancement, and non-membership was routinely suspect as a sign of sympathy for the nationalist cause.

In 1948, at the age of nineteen, Kudirka finished gymnasium and pupils were then selected for additional training depending on talent, capacity for learning, and, most of all—discipline. Kudirka had apparently applied himself well and was chosen to go on, but only to technical school rather than the university, most probably because he was not a member of *Komsomol*.

He was fortunate in avoiding another massive purge that year, the biggest since the Soviets first took over in 1940.

Kudirka decided to become a sailor and explained why at his trial: "My grandfather was a sailor and I've been drawn to far-away countries. There was the wish to see the world, and besides, I thought that at sea I would forget the tragedy of my people. I wanted to flee the strange scene. Not a week went by

that in various Lithuanian towns the disfigured bodies of Lithuanians [partisans] weren't stacked up in the marketplace. I
wanted to flee the hunger which reigned in the *kolkhozes* [col-
lective farms] at that time, the total lack of rights."

Balts were allowed to train as sailors because of the phenome-
nal shortage of manpower, much of it due to the purges and the
number of able-bodied men in partisan formations. However,
the non-Russians were obviously not trusted. Virtually all avenues of advancement were by and through the Communist
Party, but seamen were among those excepted within certain
limits. The regime found it expedient not to put obstacles in the
way of a profession that was by its nature arduous, lonely, and
boring.

Incentives to be a seaman were attractive to any young man.
Various assignments brought from 800 to 1,000 rubles per
month. To Baltic seamen, however, the profession had a particular lure—the lure of leaving the boundaries of their Russian-
occupied countries, the lure of possible escape, which many
would do in the ensuing years.

By twenty-one he was an apprentice seaman, specializing in
radio technology. Two years later, in 1953, Stalin died and
more uncertainty followed as his heirs groped for power.
Kudirka recalled the transition during his trial: "I remember
that when I studied in Vilnius, instead of the two prisons which
were there under the Germans, there were seven under Soviet
rule in which there were about 20,000 prisoners. They were
overfilled until 1955. Already in 1950 waves of Lithuanians
with their young went to the concentration camps . . . The death
of Stalin saved my people from physical extermination. However, the essence of the policy remained the same. Now we are
destined to die a much slower death—assimilation. However,
we don't want to die. For ten years our brothers in the woods
[partisans] fought believing that in the West our struggle was
known and supported, even morally. Those who died in battle
or in the concentration camps believed it as well. The Atlantic

Charter, which promised the enslaved nations freedom, was an empty promise, costing my people 50,000 dead and 400,000 deported, of whom 150,000 found their graves in the earth of Siberia."

The situation improved somewhat by the 1960s with occasional retrenchment in the hard line. The best way to survive was to apply oneself as wholeheartedly as required to ideological and social precepts. Outwardly, Kudirka had, no doubt, done this. In 1960 he was an experienced seaman of thirty-one. But he was feeling the results of his determination not to join the Communist Party. His application for advanced training in the merchant marine had been rejected. He moved to Klaipeda, the major seaport, where he was extremely fortunate to find living accommodations, because housing was one of the most scandalous rarities with upwards of three or four families living in minuscule apartments.

He sailed from Klaipeda on small coastal freighters.

Kudirka had married and lived unobtrusively with his wife Genele, raising two children—two-year-old Lolita and newborn Evaldas. He would tell the Soviet court: "I categorically deny . . . that my behavior was instigated by family troubles. I love my wife and she is faithful to me . . . I hoped from America to help my family more than with the slave wages I receive here. Besides, I hoped to bring them abroad." Kudirka made 500 rubles per month which was 200 below the average for his type of work, but he got by. Most other jobs did not pay even 100 rubles per month.

After serving on the freighter *Petras Cvirka* throughout the mid-sixties, he requested transfer to the *Boyevaya Slava* [*Battle Glory*]. He had a difficult time obtaining the transfer, and when he did get it, he was assigned ordinary seaman's tasks instead of being allowed to work in the radio room.

Life at sea is hard, but life in the Soviet fleet was made even worse by the addition of totalitarian repression. Kudirka was only to reveal general symptoms of his hardships in the fleet, but composite accounts of other defectors certainly apply to him as well.[4] Fleet members—who could not have relatives abroad—went to sea for six months at a time without a single weekend, holiday, or free day. Hours were long, often going into two shifts depending on the type of work. The labor was backbreaking, especially on working trawlers that fed the mother ships. Nerves were invariably strained.

Overseeing everything were the political commissars. They gave lectures over loudspeakers and during political indoctrination sessions. Everyone had to attend the sessions given in each ship's "red corner." There was no rule that stipulated it, but anyone not attending was singled out and harassed. Some crew members had radios, but could only listen secretly to the American coastal radio stations which beamed as far as 800 miles out to sea. There were televisions aboard ships, but no one was allowed to look at them when in range of American stations.

Upon returning to port, each of the crew members was replaced, but it sometimes happened that replacements did not show up, which meant the hapless man or woman had to go out again for another six-month stint—a full year at sea with no days off. In port the Russians were put up in special hotels. Balts were not. If they lived in the port city they were fortunate, if not they had to remain aboard ship. Two-week vacations were offered sailors of the fleet, but this, too, was generally reserved for Russians.

Seamen had a right to quit, but other jobs were scarce and the pay dismal. What was worse, quitting meant giving up whatever living accommodations a sailor had and finding others which were virtually non-existent.

To remain a sailor meant hardship, but to look for another type of work meant even greater hardship.

Alcoholism, not surprisingly, was rampant in the fleet, because it was an illusory escape. Lieutenant Lundberg had noticed it almost as soon as he had put foot aboard the *Sovetskaya Litva* earlier.

In this social and political atmosphere Kudirka felt disparaged and openly began to mention his disdain for Soviet rule.

"He always listened to foreign broadcasts," a fellow-sailor told a Soviet journalist preparing an article about the defection for émigré consumption.[5] "He always confronted us with anti-Soviet arguments and criticized our system."

This was a grave offense bordering on treason.

Kudirka had a voracious appetite for news from abroad and was politically aware. Having read Marx and Lenin, he was convinced their theories were not being practiced in reality. There only existed for him what he termed a "parody of socialism." He collected foreign magazine clippings, mainly from satellite countries, and compared everything to the situation in Lithuania. He complained about various shortcomings.

It was not long before Kudirka's anti-Soviet sentiments became known to security organs, which immediately diagnosed a pattern of deviant political inclinations. Commissars badgered him during indoctrination sessions in the "red corner." He had not joined the party. Why? He was maligning the system. Why? This was a particularly sensitive subject since some of the partisans had survived and melted back into the population. The commissars routinely suspected that Kudirka knew something about the underground. He disclaimed such knowledge and at the same time refused to denounce the partisan movement.

Kudirka was a likely "enemy of the people," but the regime was no longer as paranoid as under Stalin. Instead of arresting him, the political commissars started pressuring him psychologically. He was not allowed shore leave that he could normally expect when time came for the *Boyevaya Slava* to put into a West German port for refitting. The action grieved him; it was an obvious punishment.

Early in 1970, Kudirka was transferred to the *Sovetskaya Litva,* one of the mother ships of the Klaipeda fleet. The fleet was making ready to sail for the area of Georges Bank and

would be at sea for six months. Kudirka was assigned to clean-
ing heads, handling garbage, and doing other menial tasks unrelated to his training as a radio technician. This was no bureaucratic slipup. Simas Kudirka was an ideological liability,
distrusted, and being made an example for others.

The badgering continued. He complained to his court: "The
atmosphere became more heavy when Zabiela was appointed
the Captain's Assistant for Political Affairs. He's a typical
hoodlum and he hated me the most." The man in the gray
sweater.

Kudirka remained bitter, knowing he was being punished for
his beliefs and his background. During his trial, Kudirka said:
"It's a shame, but even in the fleet I found injustice and national
discrimination . . . In the press I read about the great Lithuanian fleet, but in reality there is no Lithuanian fleet. It's
Lithuanian only insofar as some of the ordinary sailors are
Lithuanian. Lithuanians command this fleet only in exceptional
cases. The majority doesn't even know the Lithuanian language. The top leadership of the so-called Lithuanian fleet lives
in Moscow and doesn't trust us Lithuanians. Permission to sail
abroad and go ashore is, in general, not granted us Lithuanians."

Throughout the fishing season of 1970 the fleet ranged from
Grand Banks off Nova Scotia to Block Island, northeast of New
York City. The hours were long and diversions few. Kudirka
grabbed whatever hours he could, making notations in his notebook, reading and re-reading romantic poems and sayings he
had copied from various books, and listening to U.S. coastal
radio stations.

On October 15 he and his friends most probably heard a U.S.
news report over the radio that a Lithuanian father and his
fifteen-year-old son had hijacked a Soviet airliner and diverted
it to Turkey where they asked for and received political asylum.
It was the first successful hijacking of a plane from the Soviet
Union and would be followed soon by an unsuccessful attempt.[6]

"I wanted to raise my son in an atmosphere of freedom," the father was quoted in a newscast several days later.

If Kudirka heard this broadcast, and it is likely that he did, he felt perhaps a tinge of envy and an underlying fear that his own intransigence might lead to more severe consequences for himself. He probably dreamed of escape often as he watched the U.S. coastline from afar, little realizing that in just over a month he himself would have a chance to make a similar choice.

CHART NO. 1

DEPARTMENT OF TRANSPORTATION
U.S. COAST GUARD ORGANIZATION

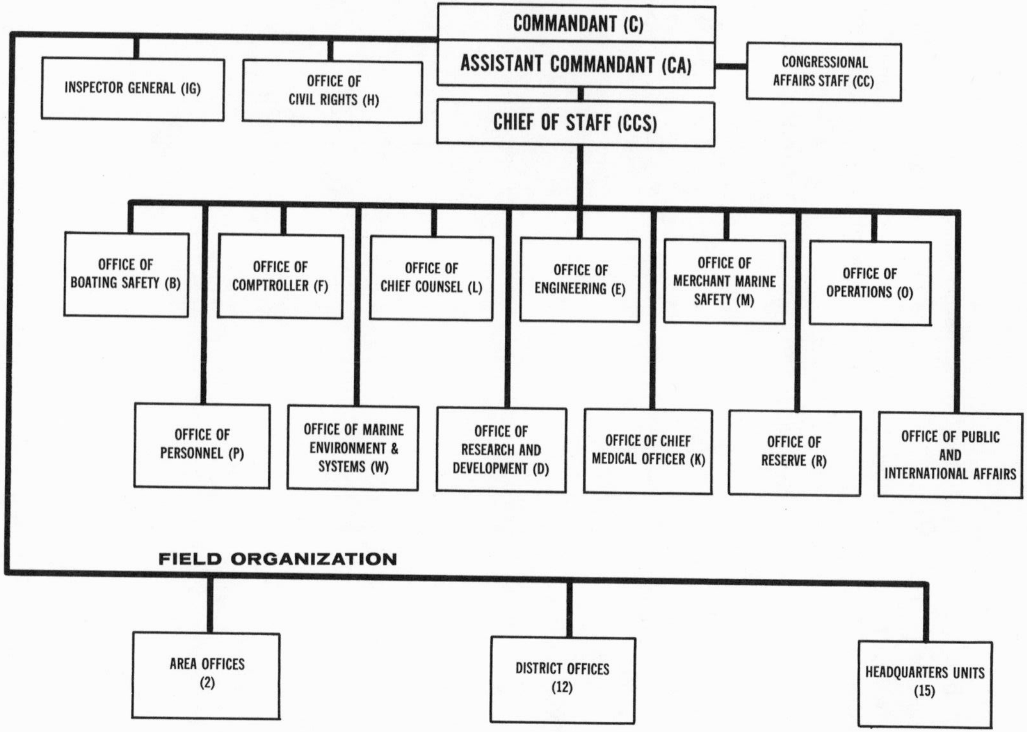

COMMANDANT (C)

ASSISTANT COMMANDANT (CA)

CHIEF OF STAFF (CCS)

CONGRESSIONAL AFFAIRS STAFF (CC)

INSPECTOR GENERAL (IG)

OFFICE OF CIVIL RIGHTS (H)

OFFICE OF BOATING SAFETY (B)

OFFICE OF PERSONNEL (P)

OFFICE OF COMPTROLLER (F)

OFFICE OF MARINE ENVIRONMENT & SYSTEMS (W)

OFFICE OF CHIEF COUNSEL (L)

OFFICE OF RESEARCH AND DEVELOPMENT (D)

OFFICE OF ENGINEERING (E)

OFFICE OF CHIEF MEDICAL OFFICER (K)

OFFICE OF MERCHANT MARINE SAFETY (M)

OFFICE OF RESERVE (R)

OFFICE OF OPERATIONS (O)

OFFICE OF PUBLIC AND INTERNATIONAL AFFAIRS

FIELD ORGANIZATION

AREA OFFICES (2)

DISTRICT OFFICES (12)

HEADQUARTERS UNITS (15)

56

CHART NO. 2

U.S. COAST GUARD ORGANIZATION
DISTRICT OFFICE

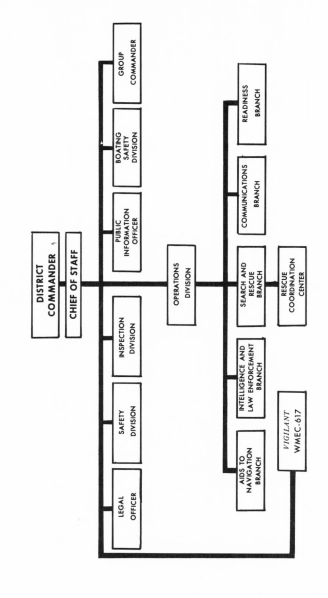

CHAPTER

6

Imperceptibly, far from the decks of the *Vigilant* and the *Sovetskaya Litva,* the sealing of Kudirka's fate began. It began not at the scene where men were face to face with a situation and instinctively seemed to do the correct thing.

It began in District One, in a complex of offices at the John F. Kennedy Federal Building in downtown Boston. It began within the system of administration universally known as "the bureaucracy," be it military, civil, or political. It began in that huge, impersonal, confusing, inflexible, and lethargic bureaucracy that everywhere seems to have a life of its own.

District One was one of twelve field offices of the U.S. Coast Guard, and the *Vigilant* was one of a number of cutters assigned to the District. District offices, headed by a District Commander, were operational commands that reported directly to the Commandant of the U.S. Coast Guard at Headquarters in Washington. Headquarters, too, was made up of component offices and the entire setup was part of the U.S. Department of Transportation. The accompanying charts illustrate the organization of the U.S. Coast Guard and a typical District such as the First.

Since all twelve District Commanders were admirals and reported directly to the Commandant's office or that of the Assistant Commandant, they were technically equal to the heads of other offices at Headquarters and sometimes even outranked them. Even though in day-to-day affairs District Commanders or members of their staffs dealt directly with the various component offices at Coast Guard Headquarters, they were ultimately responsible only to the Commandant, unless the Commandant chose to give official instructions through a staff office at Headquarters. Generally, when District Commanders dealt with staff offices at Headquarters they would use the encompassing term "Commandant" and say: "I called Commandant" or "I have advice from Commandant," even though the Commandant himself might not have anything to do with the business at hand.

This system worked well for established policies and procedures, leaving routine matters in the hands of subordinates. There were standing instructions from the Commandant, however, which stated that he "be informed immediately of transportation-related incidents which have potential national, international, or widespread local significance."*

The message *Vigilant*'s Executive Officer sent to District One was definitely in this category.

It was printed out at 120 words per minute on one of the light-green teletype machines at the Communications Center on the tenth floor of the JFK Building. The secret message was transmitted in the space of six minutes, but was to be the only one completed before technical failures crippled the system and caused up to four-hour delays on subsequent messages.

Lieutenant Kenneth L. Ryan, Duty Officer at the Rescue Coordination Center (RCC) for the twenty-four-hour period, was sitting behind an epoxy-finished, brown counter shaped like a horseshoe. It extended the entire length of the RCC room, which was next to the Communications Center. RCC occupied the southwest corner of the tenth floor and was an assemblage of electronic equipment, telephones, sophisticated tape record-

*See Appendix A.

ers, and charts and wallboards indicating the location, size, and capabilities of all ships and planes in the District. RCC was the District's nerve center and coordinated all ships and planes within it. It was manned twenty-four hours a day and relayed information of important developments to relevant offices within the District and to Headquarters in Washington. Two figures pinned side by side near Martha's Vineyard on a map of the Massachusetts coastline represented the *Vigilant* and the Soviet ship, still incorrectly identified as *Zapryba Kaliningrad.*

All the equipment around Lieutenant Ryan seemed a little out of place in a downtown office building and would have been more appropriate in some underground bunker of a spy thriller.

At 12:50 p.m. an enlisted man came from the Communications Center next door and handed Lieutenant Ryan *Vigilant's* message. The barrel-chested controller read it and immediately gave it to the Chief of the Communications Branch, who read it and ordered Ryan to contact the District Commander; the Chief of Intelligence and Law Enforcement; and the Chief of Search and Rescue, who was also Acting Chief of Operations.

The officers were still at lunch, so Ryan left word that they contact RCC as soon as they returned.

At several minutes past one, Captain Fletcher Brown, Jr., walked into his office after a leisurely lunch. He was Chief of Staff of the First District and second-in-command, but for the past three weeks had been Acting Commander in the place of Rear Admiral William B. Ellis, who was home on convalescent leave. When his secretary told him of Lieutenant Ryan's call, Brown personally went the short distance to RCC to see what had occurred.

"Oh, my God," Captain Brown muttered upon seeing the message. "It's a good thing Ralph Eustis is down there."

The problem was "a beaut." It was something Brown had never encountered before. Never in his thirty years in the Coast Guard, most of them as an aviator, had he had to deal with a defection. Its nuances were somehow too complex to fit into the

standard practices with which he was accustomed. He had
flown in helicopters in storms, in the dead of night, rescuing
people from disasters and shipwrecks. These acts took tremendous courage and nerves of ice, but they were standard procedure for him. No matter what the risk, you pull a victim out
of the sea and the case is closed. A defection, however, was
different; it had implications. As he scanned the message,
Brown conjured up visions of Russians and Americans competing to get the man out of the water. What would happen if both
sides went for the man? Would they start shooting? He would
need advice.

"Doublehead this message to the Commandant," Brown said
curtly to Commander Smith, the Communications Chief, "and
get me a copy." He then told the assistant controller of RCC
personally to summon Commander John Curry, the Chief of
Intelligence and Law Enforcement.

Captain Brown hurried back to his office and asked his secretary to place a call to Washington to the Chief of Law Enforcement at Headquarters. This was a logical place to call, since the
Office of Law Enforcement (OLE) often dealt with foreign
vessels in transit through U.S. waters and had routine experience in fisheries problems. In fact, one of OLE's men, Lieutenant Morehouse, was at that moment with the delegation aboard
the *Sovetskaya Litva.*

"Captain Hayward is in Cleveland," Brown's secretary replied after placing the call. "Is there anyone else there you
would like to talk to?"

"No. In that case I'll call Admiral Hammond." Brown went
into his inner office and started dialing the number himself.
Meanwhile, an enlisted man came in with a copy of *Vigilant*'s
message. Brown looked at it, then handed it to Commander
Curry who had just come into the office.

Captain Brown was calling the Chief of Operations, Rear
Admiral Robert E. Hammond, an old friend. The Office of Law
Enforcement, whose Chief he could not reach, was a division

within Operations, so Hammond was a proper officer to call. His office dealt with short- and long-range planning for all activities of Coast Guard units. As the name implied, it coordinated operations.

The ensuing conversation is a composite of Brown's recollections in interviews and testimony both he and Admiral Hammond gave the Board of Investigation.[1] Hammond, whose role remains a subject of controversy among some officers and former officers, refused to say anything outside of his testimony.

"Admiral? Fletcher Brown here. Admiral Ellis is still on the inactive list."

"Yes, I know," a voice replied over the line. Hammond was aware that the District Commander was on sick leave and that Captain Brown was in charge of the District.

"Bob, we have a problem. We just received a message from the *Vigilant* saying a Russian seaman will try to defect from a Soviet fishing vessel. The two ships are in conference about a half mile off Gay Head. I suggest that you go personally to the Comm Center so that you can see this thing as it comes over the wire."

Hammond was an old friend of Brown's from their aviator days and he never hesitated to call the admiral "Bob," even though Hammond was his senior.

Brown continued. "Some of our people are aboard their ship and they might be held as hostages if the man jumps. We're really concerned about how much force to use to get him out of the water." He asked Hammond what the District should do if both the Russians and Americans went for the defector at the same time. He speculated they might open fire on the man. "Bob, we're going to need some help on this one," Brown concluded.

Hammond replied that he could not easily give an answer and cautioned Brown he could not advise what action to take if the Soviets opened fire.

This consideration of force was extreme, but not unprecedented in the Coast Guard's experience. Most officers were aware of the incident where Communist Cubans opened fire on refugees in international waters. The *Sovetskaya Litva,* however, was in territorial waters and under the jurisdiction of the United States.

"This is pretty big. I'm going to call Admiral Ellis and tell him about this," Captain Brown said.

"Well, there's no sense in our sitting here and discussing this further," Hammond replied. "I'll hang up and we'll go to the State Department and try to get guidance from them. I'll be in touch with you."

Brown heard the click of a disconnecting line. His inability to reach the Chief of the Office of Law Enforcement at Headquarters and his alternative call to Admiral Hammond marked the beginning of the dispersal of responsibility in Washington and thereby the dilution of that responsibility—the classic "passing of the buck."

He waited several seconds for a dial tone, then dialed again, this time the home of Rear Admiral William B. Ellis in Beverly, Massachusetts.

Rear Admiral Ellis had been at home almost two weeks following corrective surgery on a recurring hernia condition. He was Commanding Officer of the First District, and his convalescent leave was due to end within a week. Meanwhile, he was off-duty.

The telephone rang as he was finishing a sandwich and a glass of milk in his upstairs sitting room. At fifty-seven Ellis was at the peak of his career. He had served thirty-four years and seven months in the Coast Guard. Five more months and he would retire after a career of thirty-five years of distinguished service. When Admiral Chester R. Bender, his friend and classmate at the Coast Guard Academy, became Commandant, Ellis asked that he be left where he was as Commander of the First

District. He was happy in Boston and felt a move to a new duty at such a late stage in his career would be inconvenient. Bender happily accommodated him.

Ellis looked fit for his years. His hair, cropped close around his ears, was sprinkled with gray, giving him the standard dignified air. He was five feet ten inches tall, solidly but trimly built, and spoke in a soft, pleasant voice through somewhat thin lips framed by facial lines. The wrinkles under his eyes and furrows in his forehead suggested a man who often made important decisions.

Ellis was known as a man who got things done. He was known as a man who made quick decisions and stuck by them —sometimes doggedly.

The Admiral picked up the telephone.

"Hello, Bill, this is Fletcher." The call was not out of the ordinary. Even though Captain Brown was technically the Commanding Officer, he called the Admiral up to three times a week to inquire about his health and bring him up to date on District matters. They were good friends, having gotten to know each other over the past two years.

Brown was Acting District Commander, but knew it was important to keep Ellis informed of business so he would not be swamped with work when he returned to duty the following week. Brown would say later: "I felt obligated—it was essential that I call him as my immediate designated superior."

He told Admiral Ellis the situation, his call to Washington, and his conversation with Admiral Hammond in Operations. "The Admiral said they'd work on it and get back to me. Commander Curry is with me now."

Ellis had been aware of the scheduled meeting with the Russians, but because of a change of date while he was on sick leave, he was not aware it was that day.[2] He asked Brown for details and was surprised at some of what he heard. He thought the meeting would be at sea as intended and did not expect the Russians to be in territorial waters. And he was surprised the ships were anchored and that the *Vigilant* was moored along-side the Soviet vessel. "They shouldn't have tied up in the first place," he declared.

"What do you think we ought to do about the defector?" Brown asked after explaining that a U.S. delegation, including Commander Eustis, was aboard the Soviet ship.

"Deserter!" shot through Ellis's strict military mind. He made an immediate decision. "Fletcher, we've gotta do it this way. Tell the *Vigilant* that they should not, in any way, indicate that we will grant him . . . the *Vigilant* will grant him refuge. If the man goes in the water he should be saved. If the Russians go after him, let them. If not, we should go get him. And if we do we should give him back to the Russian ship. And tell them to get Commander Eustis back aboard ship."

"Okay, Admiral. I'll keep you informed," Brown replied and put down the phone.

Ellis went back to munching his sandwich, leaving Captain Brown with indecision. "I was surprised that he made the decision. I had already told him that we had called Washington," Brown would say months later. "I could not in my own mind feel that a man under these circumstances should be summarily returned. And I was quite disturbed."

Admiral Ellis was his designated superior, but Captain Brown was Acting District Commander. He could technically override Ellis, but what would happen if he bucked his Admiral? He sensed he would be in hot water when Ellis returned.

In thinking back on the incident months afterward Ellis would say: "We were going to have to, under any rules of decency, send him back." He admitted, though, that at the time he was totally unaware of accepted national policy regarding defectors or of the principles and procedures inherent in the concept of asylum. Ellis would say: "He's a deserter no matter what he is and I don't think I really thought about . . . I didn't think of any political overtones." Ellis saw the entire matter strictly in military terms and made no distinction between a common deserter and a man seeking refuge from oppression. He took for granted that Washington would advise the same thing. The Admiral's decision was quick, simplistic, and, barring extraordinary new facts, irrevocable.

Captain Brown knew the man must be very desperate and should not be automatically returned, yet Admiral Ellis's reasoning sounded logical and gentlemanly. Brown would explain six months after the incident: "Our ship was invited alongside their ship. We invited them into our waters. You might say to a certain degree that [keeping the defector] is a breach of trust."

The Coast Guard would have to be a good host if it wanted to maintain a respectable image in the eyes of the Soviets. But the ship that day had not been invited into U.S. waters; the Soviets had steamed in on their own. In any case, that was irrelevant, for the U.S. still had complete authority, legal and physical, over the situation. Never before had the government or any of its representative agencies considered abrogating sovereignty over a question of politeness, until Admiral Ellis unknowingly did.

Brown was still wavering. There was something that did not settle right. "Here was a man and a human being. Here was a guy. He was in trouble. I was for him." Brown knew that as Acting District Commander he could run the day-to-day affairs of the District, but he could not authorize a change in policies of the District. And the Admiral's policy toward the defector seemed clear. Unknown to Admiral Ellis, a defection case was for neither of them to decide.

Commander Curry looked at Brown as he put the phone down. "What are we going to do?"

"The man is to be returned."

"Why?"

"Because that's the decision that was made."

"I don't know," the Intelligence Chief said. "I don't think we have to make that decision. The State Department has to make that decision."

Brown sensed Curry was right and it unsettled him, but the knowledge that Headquarters was working on the problem soon eased his mind. He was confident that Headquarters would relay a decision which would override Admiral Ellis's opinion. Arguing with Ellis was useless without the weight of higher authority, because Brown knew his Admiral as "a stubborn man who stuck to his guns." His doggedness had already caused Commander Eustis some embarrassment only four months earlier.

Eustis in July of 1970 had spotted a West German trawler, the *Konrad,* poaching in territorial waters and had asked for instructions. The First District quickly contacted Headquarters. The Commandant had been unavailable, the Assistant Commandant and the Chief of Staff had been unavailable and the Chief of Operations had been unavailable, so the responsibility of what to do had fallen on Captain Wallace C. Dahlgren, Chief of the Intelligence Division at Headquarters. Dahlgren had immediately called the Office of Law Enforcement and asked them to get advice via the State Department. Law Enforcement quickly called its contacts in the State Department and then relayed word to Captain Dahlgren that the State Department had authorized seizure.

Dahlgren called the First District saying the *Konrad* could be seized. The order was buttressed by a written message confirming the telephone authorization. It was a rare instance of U.S. willingness to seize a foreign fishing trawler. Admiral Ellis had then relayed the advice to Captain Brown and Commander Curry and ordered them to tell the Commanding Officer of the *Vigilant* to board the *Konrad* and take her to port. Such a move was demeaning to a captain of a ship and was always carried out by subordinates, but Ellis had not thought of it. His order was unprecedented. Commander Curry indirectly reminded the Admiral of that.

Captain Brown was to recall the exchange: "And Curry said, 'You want the CO, you want Eustis to go aboard and take it?'

And Ellis said 'God damn it! What do I have to do, spell it out for you!' Now, Jack Curry and I picked up our hands, shrugged, and looked at each other, and said, 'Yes, sir.' And as we got outside his office we said, 'Well, okay, the man says to do it, so we do it.' "

Eustis did board the *Konrad* and personally seized her, causing a minor flap within the District that soon died down.

Now Brown again began taking steps to carry out a decision neither he nor Commander Curry agreed with. At this point, however, Brown was still confident of other sources of advice, sources higher than Ellis. He started for the Communications Center and formulated the essence of Admiral Ellis's instructions along the way. Upon arrival he quickly sent the following message:

0231830Z Nov 70
FM CCGDONE
TO CGCVIGILANT
BT
SECRET

FROM DCS

A. YOUR 231743Z NOV 70
1. (S) TAKE NO DIRECT OR OVERT ACTION. HOWEVER BE PREPARED TO LAUNCH SMALL BOAT IMMEDIATELY.
2. (S) GET CDR EUSTIS BACK ABOARD USING ANY PRETEXT.
3. (U) COMDT NOTIFIED OF SITUATION.
4. (S) IF MAN GOES IN WATER GIVE USSR EVERY OPPORTUNITY TO RECOVER.

The message was a paraphrase of what Admiral Ellis told Brown over the telephone. Brown here was not acting as Acting District Commander, but was relaying instructions as Chief of

Staff. Significantly, his message was headed "From DCS," from District Chief of Staff. No matter what Brown was technically, he was operating in spirit and in fact as Admiral Ellis's subordinate. Technically, Brown had solid ground to argue with Ellis as an equal, but Brown simply did not see it that way. His respect for authority, for the chain of command, had been deeply ingrained over a period of thirty years. A technicality like a sick leave did not make any impression on Brown's image of his own status. He saw himself as Acting Commander in name only, and when he called Ellis he was calling the real District Commander. Now he was relaying the District Commander's instructions, regardless of what he himself thought of them. It was a typical reaction of a military man and had been enacted thousands of times, in thousands of places, over thousands of years. But here was a situation that develops now and then to test an officer's true mettle.

"See that this gets to the *Vigilant* as fast as possible," Brown told the Communications Chief as he handed him the message. He then started back for his office.

A clock on a hallway wall indicated 1:35 P.M., about an hour since the receipt of the *Vigilant*'s message.

Walking down the hall, Brown noticed Commander Jerome Flanagan. "Hey, Jay," he called out. "Come into my office a minute. It looks like we got a hot one." They went together to Brown's office.

Flanagan was of average build with a slim face and dark hair trimmed closely around the ears. He looked somewhat taller than his five feet nine inches, in his navy-blue uniform. Flanagan was forty and the Chief Legal Officer of the First District.

The Intelligence Chief was still there when Brown and Commander Flanagan walked in. Brown showed *Vigilant*'s message to the District's lawyer. "We doubleheaded it and sent it to the Commandant." Brown then told Flanagan the contents of the reply he had just sent the cutter. "What do you think, Jay?"

"I don't know, Captain," Flanagan replied. "I'd like to think about this for a while rather than give you an answer right off the top of my head. But it seems to me that if we get him, we should keep him. Bring him in and turn him over to State or Immigration."

Brown agreed, and the Legal Officer left the office. Brown then directed Commander Curry, the Intelligence Chief, to keep himself available and returned to the Communications Center to check on the message traffic.

Even though Captain Brown had sent the *Vigilant* a message that directed the ship to "give USSR every opportunity to recover," he still felt the issue was open. He was awaiting word from Headquarters and somehow believed the defection would not occur until Headquarters sent instructions. Unconsciously, he was structuring the case in the way he hoped it would develop.

When he arrived again at the Communications Center, Commander Smith, the Chief, had some disturbing news. "They don't roger for our message. There must be something wrong with their on-line crypto." On-line crypto was a system where tape was punched in ordinary language, automatically scrambled in transmission, then automatically unscrambled at the receiving end.

"We'll have to encrypt it and send it off line," Commander Smith suggested.

"Okay, but get it out as soon as possible," Brown said as he checked his wrist watch.

It was several minutes past 2 P.M.

"Is there anything else from the *Vigilant?*"

"Nothing, sir."

Brown was worried that Commander Eustis was aboard the Soviet vessel. He didn't want anything to happen without Eustis aboard the *Vigilant.* Brown decided it would be good to have some support from another source and went next door to RCC. "Where's the Bravo vessel?"

"That would be the *Decisive* in New Castle, sir," replied

Lieutenant Ryan from his counter, referring to the cutter in a port in neighboring New Hampshire.

"Call them up and put them on Bravo Zero, Ken."

Bravo Zero meant that the cutter *Decisive,* as ready vessel, would be prepared to cast off lines immediately for any assignment.

Captain Brown was getting ready with the reserves.

Meanwhile, Commander Jerome Flanagan had returned to his office and was paging through a reference book, *International Law* by William W. Bishop. Browsing through the book for precedents under "Asylum" and "Refuge" while smoking his pipe, Flanagan looked like a college professor, except that he wore the uniform of a Coast Guard Commander. Flanagan was not just a book man who received a comfortable desk assignment because he was a lawyer. He had served on several cutters as an officer and Executive Officer and knew the ways of men on the line.

Little is written about the concept of asylum that is available for the layman. Even law books contain few references, and Flanagan found no listing under "Asylum" or "Refuge." But this did not bother him, since he knew it was standard procedure to detain defectors, at the very least for routine questioning.

The only references in Bishop's book that were related to the problem at hand were under "Jurisdiction"—the control over foreign vessels in territorial waters—the essence of which Flanagan already knew. There was a section on the United Nations Universal Declaration of Human Rights which sanctioned the right of a person to leave his country. Both the U.S. and the Soviet Union were signatories to the Declaration. Commander Flanagan did not see that section, nor have to read it, to know the defector should be kept as a matter of simple procedure.

He called in two staff lawyers to discuss the problem, and all
three agreed that the man should be brought to Boston and
turned over to Immigration authorities. Captain Brown's earlier statement to him that Headquarters had been notified assured Flanagan that the issue would be referred to the Legal
Office in Washington and to the State Department—as a matter
of simple procedure.

Backed with the unanimous and unwavering opinion of his
staff lawyers, Flanagan returned to Captain Brown's office. He
walked in on an informal meeting that Brown had called about
the anticipated defection. Present were Captain Brown; Commander Curry, the Intelligence Chief; and Captain William
Murphy, the head of Search and Rescue and Acting Chief of
Operations in the District.

Commander Flanagan arrived moments too late to hear
Brown say that he had called Admiral Ellis at home and that
Ellis had advised returning the man to the Russians. Had the
Legal Officer known this, it might have changed the tragic
outcome of the day. As it was, Flanagan believed the case was
coordinated on the District level entirely by Captain Brown, the
Acting District Commander. Flanagan would say after the incident that had he known Admiral Ellis was involved in the
decision-making process, he would have called him personally
and advised him to keep the defector, and he would have called
the Legal Office at Headquarters himself to buttress that advice.
Flanagan often called the Legal Office at Headquarters to check
on advice for Admiral Ellis on various important decisions.

But Commander Flanagan walked into the meeting just minutes late, minutes that would make a fateful difference.

"Sit down, Jay," Brown said. "We just started batting this
thing around a little bit."

Flanagan sat down near Commander Curry.

The officers waited for Brown to proceed. He took a drag on
his cigarette, then said matter-of-factly, "If the man defects, he
is to be returned." Brown was playing the devil's advocate, as

he had done in other conferences on other matters, but this time the issue was not really as open as others might have been. Brown was echoing instructions from Admiral Ellis.

Captain Murphy told Brown he could not think of any precedent that warranted a refusal of asylum. "This has a tremendous potential for reaction," he cautioned. He gave an example of a defection that occurred in his hometown of New York. "There was a woman in New York a couple of years ago who defected from the Soviet Embassy. Someone dragged her right off the Embassy grounds."*

Commander Curry then interjected with another, more recent example. A Czechoslovakian figure-skater performing in the 1968 Winter Olympics had defected and was allowed to remain in the United States. Both officers were hazy on details, but their points were precise and unmistakable. In each case, the person had been kept. The officers told Brown they did not understand why this case should be any different.

"If the man defects, he should be turned over to the State Department or to Immigration in Boston," Commander Flanagan declared. He was reiterating to Brown what he had told him earlier in the hallway, but he did not tell him that opinion was now buttressed by two other staff lawyers from his office. Since the case was secret, he did not want to tell Captain Brown he had taken the liberty to consult two of his staff members.

He used a suggestion made by one of them. "If it happens, we could get a helicopter out there and airlift the guy off. We could tell them he was taken to a hospital for observation." This was one of a number of routine devices used to keep a defector until instructions came from higher authority.

"I don't think it's our job to decide whether to turn him back or not," Flanagan told the others. "This is already in the field of foreign relations and diplomacy."

Flanagan noticed everyone wanted to keep the defector, but

---

* Actually the Soviet Mission with consular offices. The Soviets have an Embassy only in Washington.

that Captain Brown was wavering. He was "straddling a fence." The other officers sensed it too.[3] This seemed natural to Flanagan, since officers sometimes took opposing or neutral views just to get all possible alternatives considered. What the Legal Officer did not know was that Brown was acting on Admiral Ellis's actual instructions to return the man.

Brown and Murphy then began an exchange while Flanagan stood up and walked over to Curry. Curry had just turned toward Flanagan from his chair and was shaking his head from side to side, muttering, "They can't give him back, they just can't give him back."

"What the hell are you worried about? They aren't going to give him back," Flanagan retorted, but out of range of Captain Brown's attention. Commander Curry knew from his earlier conversation with Brown that the man was to be returned. Flanagan could not understand why Curry was upset and Curry did not realize that Flanagan was unaware of Admiral Ellis's instructions to return the defector.

The meeting lasted almost an hour, and each staff officer reiterated his view that the defector should be kept. At one point one of them mentioned the incident of the Cuban refugees who were fired upon by their pursuers and how the Coast Guard's image had suffered.[4]

"Well, this thing is going to move ahead on its own," Brown said. "I hope we get something soon out of Commandant or the State Department."

The statement only reinforced Commander Flanagan's belief that the defector would be kept. Captain Murphy believed the issue was very much alive. But Captain Brown's personal attitude was not clear to the other officers. He seemed to be leaning to one side, then the other.

The officers left Brown's office shortly before 3:30 P.M., having made no contingency plans. Captain Brown had given no further instructions for research or for soliciting opinions; he was waiting for advice from Headquarters. Captain Murphy believed the case was out of his hands, since Brown himself was handling it. Commander Flanagan believed the defector would be kept as a matter of course. But Commander Curry knew the only thing that could save him would be an order from Washington.

CHAPTER

7

Washington had begun working on the case as soon as Captain Brown made his first telephone call to Rear Admiral Robert Hammond at 1:15 P.M.

Hammond, as Chief of the Office of Operations, had been at his post only five months.

His office was in the same white building that housed the U.S. Department of Transportation, of which the Coast Guard was a part. Interspersed along the carpeted, block-length corridors of the eighth floor were the divisions of Law Enforcement and Intelligence, both of which were within the Office of Operations. One of the offices along the corridor was the Legal Office, which routinely gave advice to the Office of Operations on various matters that had legal or international implications.

Admiral Hammond could appreciate the problem formulated by Captain Brown over the telephone. He had come to Headquarters from duty in Alaska, where he was a District Commander. Hammond had been involved in several cases with foreign vessels, particularly Soviet vessels, which abounded in the North Pacific and the Bering Sea.

The issue appeared to him to be one of force. How big a fight could or should the Coast Guard put up with the Soviets to get the man out of the water? Neither Brown nor Hammond had considered the possibility that the defector could leap directly from one ship to the other. That thought simply did not occur to either of them. Nor did either consider the question of whether to keep him—this was understood. (Their conversation had preceded Brown's call to Admiral Ellis.)

Brown had asked Admiral Hammond personally to check the message forwarded to Headquarters and to solicit advice. But Hammond, even though he conferred daily with other officers on various problems, said in testimony he could do nothing himself: "There was nothing I could offer that I felt would be of any help to him."

Instead, Hammond summoned a subordinate, Captain Wallace Dahlgren, who was Chief of the Intelligence Divison within Operations. In the rare instances when advice was needed it was almost always handled by Law Enforcement or Intelligence. So he called in Captain Dahlgren, testifying later: "I felt he knew more about who to contact than I did."

Unfortunately, Captain Dahlgren did not.[1]

Admiral Hammond had sensed an urgency in his friend's tone, but felt, as did Captain Brown, that the defection would not occur immediately. There was time within which to maneuver. Hammond was glad, because he knew from previous experience that the State Department sometimes dragged its feet in coming up with important advice. In fact, sometimes it did not come through at all.

"I just had a call from Captain Brown in the First District," he told Dahlgren when the Intelligence Chief came into the office. "A secret message will be coming in immediately explaining the details. It has to do with the possibility of a Soviet fisherman defecting to the *Vigilant.*" He told Dahlgren the *Vigilant* and a Russian ship were meeting somewhere near Martha's Vineyard.

Dahlgren listened, and, without knowing any details, correctly visualized two ships anchored side by side.

"Why don't you wait until you get the message from the First, then get a hold of someone in the State Department as soon as you can," the Admiral continued. "Then pass the information back to Captain Brown and let me know what occurred."

Captain Dahlgren acknowledged the instructions and left.

Admiral Hammond returned to the administrative duties of his post, satisfied that Captain Dahlgren would take care of the problem. However, there were things in recent memory that Admiral Hammond could have told Captain Dahlgren—things that might have clarified the situation and expedited the search for a solution, things that did not come to mind when Dahlgren was in his office.

While Commander of the Seventeenth District* in Alaska, Admiral Hammond had once kept a Russian captain who had been arrested off one of the Alaskan islands by the Commanding Officer of an icebreaker. Hammond held the Soviet officer in custody until the Secretary of State, Dean Rusk, personally ordered the release. The Soviet captain had been arrested for violating territorial waters, and Hammond's District advised Coast Guard Headquarters that it was holding the officer in accordance with its role of law enforcement.

The captain subsequently was fined in a Federal District Court, but the State of Alaska then wanted to prosecute him under state laws. Hammond refused to release the officer to the State of Alaska unless he received specific instructions to comply.

Coast Guard Headquarters did not reply for hours.

During that time Hammond transferred the Soviet officer to a cutter anchored outside Alaskan waters and told the governor he would do absolutely nothing until he received instructions from Washington.

Only the next day did the State Department come through with advice after the Law Enforcement Division at Headquarters had contacted it. Hammond knew that the search for ad-

*Although the Coast Guard had only twelve districts, their designations were not sequential from one to twelve.

ɛ had gone as high as the White

riately frozen the situation.

ɔ years later, his friend Captain
different situation, but one that
n relations—a situation that was
ʔe Admiral Hammond had faced
aska. Hammond knew the State
ɔt give a fast reply to their inqui-
ain Dahlgren. It simply did not
that the most frequent contacts
ɪrters and the State Department
ement Division and the Legal
e himself contacted the Legal
ly on routine matters. Yet, that
e Legal Office, because he had
ɪ to a subordinate—Captain
about who to contact than I

tion why he did not contact the
ld testify: "I'll tell you exactly,
our legal office. This I realize
ɪg to the State Department we
e and it just didn't occur to me

ɪptain Dahlgren's responsibil-

his way to the Communica-
the message that had been doubleheaded
e was not surprised that he had been delegated
to get advice on the problem. Hammond was his immediate
superior and conferred with him every day. This particular
situation in the First District was in Dahlgren's mind an intelligence matter. The division he headed dealt with personnel
security (background checks), cases of theft, and, in theory,

cases of defection; yet, paradoxically, the Intelligence Division
had no procedural guidelines for one. Dahlgren would explain
to the Board of Investigation: "I was generally . . . I was
certainly aware of what we do in the Cuban area. I know that
we take the Cubans. We will take any Cuban that escapes from
Cuba and offer him asylum. I was aware of the fact there was
a defector policy as far as the people in the intelligence community goes. I knew . . . this committee existed. But at the same
time, I didn't know any way to get in touch with anybody on
that committee; in fact, I didn't know who the members of the
committee were."

Captain Dahlgren knew most foreign vessel cases were handled by the Coast Guard's Law Enforcement Division, which
he had had occasion to contact in other cases, but which in his
search for channels into the State Department he did not think
to call. He had been instructed to "get a hold of someone in the
State Department." Who? Captain Dahlgren, the Chief of the
Coast Guard's Intelligence Division, did not know. His Division in fact did not deal with "intelligence" in the popular sense
of espionage, counterespionage, and foreign intrigue. His Division was mainly a character reference center for Coast Guard
personnel.

Dahlgren's own status as Chief of Intelligence was assailed
in the next few moments when he reached the Communications
Center. He became the victim of a bureaucratic stipulation that
was ludicrous when applied to him.

"Is the secret message from the *Vigilant* in yet?" he asked the
man on watch.

"Yes, sir."

"I want to see it."

"Roger, sir, but we can't give it to you."

"Why not?"

"Because you're not on the cleared list, sir."

Spluttering that he had not been in charge long enough to get
clearance, but that he was still the Intelligence Chief, Dahlgren

nevertheless dutifully returned to his office, because he knew he could not override a strict regulation.

He sent a clerk with security clearance to pick up the message.

While he waited he began a tedious telephone search for the State Department's Operations Center, which relayed problems to all appropriate offices. For someone unfamiliar with its setup, the State Department can be overwhelming. Some idea of its complexity may be conveyed by the simplified, accompanying chart. The State Department was, in fact, so huge that a special "locater" tracked down personnel for people wanting to find them. Many of the offices had overlapping functions as in any bureaucracy, so the case could have been referred to a number of offices: among them were the Bureau of Intelligence and Research, the Office of Refugees and Migration; the State Department's Legal Office, or the Office of Soviet Union Affairs, all of which dealt with defection cases, among other things. It could have been referred also to the Baltic Section, which was a part of the Office of European Affairs, as was the Soviet Desk. But officers involved in the case were oblivious to the distinction between a Russian and non-Russian subject of the Soviet Union. Officers on the *Vigilant,* in Boston, and in Coast Guard Headquarters automatically and incorrectly thought that a "Soviet defector" was by nature a "Russian." They were unaware that the United States did not recognize the Soviet absorption of the Baltic States and did recognize the Baltic republics' prewar legations in Washington.

Captain Dahlgren dialed the office of Captain David Webb, whom he knew casually. Webb was a Coast Guard liaison officer in the State Department assigned to the Bureau of International Scientific and Technological Affairs.[2] Dahlgren was sure that Captain Webb, as a liaison officer with the State Department, could find the appropriate channels for advice.

"We have a possible defector up north," Dahlgren told him when Webb answered the phone. "Who should I contact in

CHART NO. 3

DEPARTMENT OF STATE
ORGANIZATION, DEC. 1969

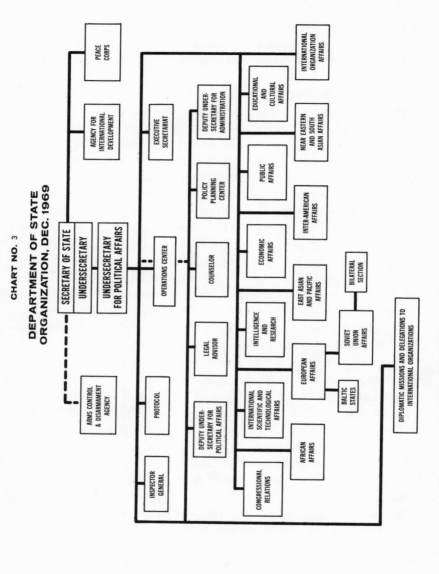

State?" Dahlgren would explain in testimony: "I think perhaps my tone expressed the urgency, but I don't remember whether I said I need it right away. But I am sure that he realized that I needed it as soon as possible."

"Okay, let me find out and I'll call you back," Webb replied. Captain Webb had been at his post just over a month and did not really feel like a liaison officer. Dahlgren's inquiry was only the third he had received. He felt stuck in that billet and figured the job, obscure as it was, would be more appropriate for a junior officer.

Webb would testify: "Well, to the extent that I got . . . tried to get the information that he wanted as soon as I could, yes, I treated the request as an urgent one . . . as far as urgency, yes, but for importance, maybe not."

Captain Webb was not sure himself how to proceed, so he consulted his superior, Dr. Robert Weber, Deputy Director of the Office of Space, Atmospheric, and Marine Affairs within the Bureau to which both were assigned. Weber had had some experience with defections while serving in American embassies as a scientific attaché.

"Try Mr. Gentile. He's the Deputy Assistant Secretary for Security," Weber suggested.

Webb tried Gentile's number and announced himself to the secretary.

"Mr. Gentile is out."

"We received word from one of our Coast Guard districts of a possible defection. Our Headquarters wants to know who they can contact in the State Department for advice," Webb explained.

"You could probably talk to Mr. St. Morris or Mr. Morton. They're in the Special Assignments Desk."

Captain Webb asked for and received the number and dialed it. He asked the secretary if either were in, and, after confirming that they were, he hung up without asking to speak with either of them. He did not find out if the Special Assignments

Desk was the appropriate one for Captain Dahlgren to call.
Within fifteen minutes Webb had returned Dahlgren's call.

By that time Admiral Hammond had got a copy of *Vigilant*'s
message and was starting for the office of Vice Admiral Thomas
R. Sargent, III, the Assistant Commandant. He met Sargent in
the hallway and noticed he too had a copy of the message. As
they walked along the hall he told Admiral Sargent how he was
proceeding in the case, namely, that he had asked Captain
Dahlgren to get advice from the State Department. Since Sargent was on his way to the office of Coast Guard Commandant
Admiral Chester R. Bender, Hammond did not bother to tell
Bender the developments, presuming Sargent would.

Neither Bender nor Sargent acted on the information, nor
inquired about it later in the day. Vice Admiral Sargent himself
would later head a one-man board to investigate the incident.

At about this same time, the military aide to John Volpe,
Secretary of Transportation, called the Coast Guard Operations Center (Flag Plot) located three floors below Volpe's own
office to ask if there was any "hard copy." Important Coast
Guard messages were always forwarded to the Secretary's office
and were handled by his military aide, Lt. Commander Gerald
W. Seelman.

The Duty Officer told Seelman about *Vigilant*'s message and
Seelman asked that it be sent up to him immediately. When he
received it, Seelman thought the message important enough to
inform Secretary Volpe, but Volpe was at a meeting. Lt. Commander Seelman showed him the message sometime after 3 P.M.
and Volpe only said: "Keep me informed."

That was the last either of them knew of the case until the
next day.

Lt. Commander Seelman would tell a House subcommittee
subsequently investigating the incident that the Duty Officer
made no other calls to him and admitted that it never occurred

to him to call the Duty Officer himself as he had done originally.[3]

A clerk with clearance by then had also given Captain Dahlgren a copy of the secret message. When he returned to his office after a brief errand, he found a note with the names "Vern St. Morris, or Mr. Morton" and a number.

He called the number.

It was already 2:30 P.M. when Dahlgren reached the Special Assignments Desk and Morton.

Since the message was secret, he did not read it to Morton over the phone, but only gave him an outline of the problem.

"I don't think that's my job," Morton replied. "I think you should contact the Soviet Desk."

"The Soviet Desk?"

"Yes, Mr. Adolph Dubs is in charge of the Soviet Desk. He should be able to help you out."

Captain Dahlgren was back where he started before his original call to Captain Webb. Webb had fulfilled his duty, but the contacts he had found had been of no help. Dahlgren vaguely knew that the State Department had desks for various countries and could have called and asked for the Soviet Desk directly but, presuming Webb knew more about such things, had chosen to go through the liaison officer.

This roundabout route had taken Dahlgren two hours—two fruitless hours in the labyrinth of the bureaucracy.

But now there was light ahead.

Dahlgren returned to the Communications Center and told the Duty Officer to forward *Vigilant*'s message to the State Department. To play it safe, he ordered the message noted for the attention of Captain Webb; Morton, with whom he had just spoken; and Adolph Dubs, head of the Soviet Desk.

He then returned to his office, called the number given by Morton, and asked for Mr. Dubs. Dubs was not in. His office transferred the call to Edward L. Killham, Officer in Charge of Bilateral Affairs in the Office of Soviet Union Affairs. Killham's office was part of the Soviet Desk.

Captain Dahlgren had finally reached an office that could help.

Killham was in charge of the section that dealt strictly with matters concerning the United States and the Soviet Union. His section reported to the head of the Office of Soviet Union Affairs, who in turn reported to the head of the Bureau of European Affairs. The Bureau of European Affairs was run by an Assistant Secretary of State who reported to the Undersecretary of State and the Secretary of State himself. Not all matters, however, reached the Secretary of State, because the Bureaus and Offices were run by high-ranking foreign service officers who had authority to handle various emerging situations.

Edward Killham had that authority.

He was serving his third tour in the Bilateral Section of the Soviet Desk; for the previous five months as head of the Section. He knew that a meeting had been scheduled between the Soviets and Americans, because arrangements on the diplomatic level had crossed his desk.

Killham listened as Dahlgren explained. "We have a message from one of our cutters off the New England coast saying there is a possibility of a defection. The cutter is meeting with a Soviet fishing vessel and one of the crewmen indicated he wants to defect." He told the State Department official that after a number of false leads and transferred calls he was referred to him and that the message had been forwarded to the State Department.

"Well, wait until I get the message, then I'll call you back," Killham replied.

CHAPTER

8

"Hey! Come to the U.S.! Come on over to the U.S.!" a young crewman called out from the *Vigilant*'s flight deck to two small groups of men standing idly on the main deck of the *Sovetskaya Litva*. There were about fifteen of them, dressed in work clothes; some with sweaters, others with worn suit jackets, and all of them with baggy dark slacks. A few were dragging on cigarettes, others just stood with hands in their pockets.

When they heard the phrase: "Come to the U.S.!" they suddenly stirred, but not in anticipation. Looks of fear crossed their faces and several immediately called back, "No! No! No!" drawing their fingers across their throats in a characteristic gesture of death. The *Vigilant*'s crewman had been joking, but when he saw the reaction, he lowered his own eyes in embarrassment and walked off.

A man standing on a bulkhead by the rear mast of the *Sovetskaya Litva* was silently observing the scene. He was dressed like the rest, with a checkered sweater and gray pants. He did not look like a commissar, but by trying to be inconspicuous he seemed too conspicuous. He had been looking over the deck, holding his hands behind him, feet spread slightly apart—too much like an overseer on an ancient galley.

None of the men on deck looked up to see his reaction. He was a member of the party elite, probably even a member of the secret police, and it was best to remain anonymous before his eyes. The man could cause trouble, he could ask for an explanation of even the most ordinary action, no matter how trivial. And how could one adequately explain a trivial action without belaboring it and thereby making it suspicious?

The men on deck of the *Sovetskaya Litva* kept puffing on their cigarettes, saying nothing, looking vacantly at their feet.

Such omens of a darker truth facing those aboard were the only hints that the people who had sailed into Menemsha Bight in the pre-dawn darkness were not really the same as their American counterparts, even though they smiled and sang and exchanged pleasant small talk with crewmen of the *Vigilant.*

That outward conviviality—those smiles and pleasant phrases—continued into the afternoon.

Meanwhile, in the conference room aboard the *Sovetskaya Litva,* Robert Brieze was questioning Ivan Burkal. "What kind fish you catch?"

"We catch mackerel, herring, and one percent flounder," Burkal said through his interpreter. He told Brieze that according to agreements by ICNAF, one percent of the Soviet catch could consist of flounder. But the Soviets had agreed a year earlier in Halifax that they would not catch flounder at all. Burkal was admitting that the Soviets were not keeping their "gentleman's agreement."

According to Brieze, the most damaging thing to the local fishermen was the fact that that one percent of the Soviet catch amounted to more than the entire quarterly limit set by the U.S. government for its own fishermen. This was feasible for the Soviets to do, because merely two of their huge trawlers were capable of outfishing the entire New Bedford fleet, which consisted of 150 ships.

"What size you catch?" Brieze asked.

Gartman, the Master Catcher, replied they caught fish starting from ten to twelve centimeters. They were catching fingerlings, which indicated to the Americans an obvious disregard for the continued survival of the species.

"The flounder we catch we use for feed aboard ship," Gartman said. He was assuring the delegates that yellowtail flounder did not appear on competitive markets.

But this was not the issue that worried the Americans. They were afraid the Soviet habit of catching fingerlings would deplete the entire stock and there would be no more fish for anyone—for market or for meal.

"What kind nets you use?" Brieze continued.

"Three-centimeter openings," Morozov, the Chief Technologist, told him.

This did not surprise the New Bedford fishermen. They had often found pieces of Soviet nets with one-inch mesh and smaller. ICNAF regulations called for four-and-one-half-inch mesh, which the Americans used conscientiously, but the Soviets were flagrantly and openly violating the provision.

"Our nets are too far off the bottom to catch many flounder," Morozov assured the delegation.

"How deep do you put your nets?" Brieze challenged.

"If we have to, we lower them to within sixteen centimeters of the bottom," the Russian replied through their interpreter.

"This is not right," Brieze retorted. "If you fish in this area you have to be catching yellowtails."

Morozov repeated the Soviet theme of the meeting. "We only fish for mackerel and herring, and any flounder we catch we only feed to the fleet."

"When can we see your trawlers?" Howard Nickerson interjected impatiently.

Burkal looked at him. "The weather is too bad and our trawlers are not fishing today. Maybe it will be possible to visit our trawlers some other time when the weather is better."

This phrase shattered the men from New Bedford, even though they had been expecting as much. Gordon and Obolensky, as representatives of government agencies that the local fishermen suspected of spinelessness, diplomatically accepted the Soviet rationale.

The single barrel of herring on the deck of the mammoth

factory ship was all the Americans would get to see. Burkal's excuse—for the men from New Bedford—amounted to an admission of the Russians' illegal fishing practices. The Americans knew and conceded the weather had been bad a week earlier, but that Monday was ideal for fishing.

"We bargain always in good faith," Brieze would lament in an interview after the incident. "We have not broken any agreements, but the Soviets are always doing so. They make fools out of our government."

The reason for the meeting had evaporated in a phrase, and conversation quickly subsided. But this was really no surprise to the industry representatives. They had sensed earlier that the long luncheon, the drinks, then the question and answer period were delaying tactics. They knew now why the Soviets had sailed into Menemsha Bight. The Soviets had had no intention of showing them their trawlers and had deliberately and illegally sailed near shore to be far away from the fleet. It was now too late to go out twenty miles to see the working trawlers, because the *Vigilant* was due back in port at 6 P.M. Brieze, Burt, and Nickerson facetiously commented to each other that they had expected this. They had been brought here to be mollified, put off. The meeting was arranged to make it appear the government was seriously doing something with the Soviets to solve the fishing problems. It was all just public relations—both on the American and Soviet sides, with the New Bedford fishermen caught in the middle.

After Burkal's statement, the negotiators found little to say and agreed the talks were ended. Burkal then suggested another tour of the ship to be followed by another meal. Gordon, as head of the delegates, agreed. Brieze would remember: "Everything was by grace of the U.S. government and agreement by the Russians. Civilians from New Bedford were only observers. We had no power to say anything, but ask questions."

Burkal and Captain Popov again led the delegation along the passageway and into a large room. "This is a cinema room and recreation hall. It can seat 100 people," Burkal noted.

It was paneled in dark, heavy wood and had a linoleum floor. Pictures of Lenin hung in several places surrounded by slogans printed in Cyrillic extolling the virtues of Communism and urging workers to produce more. Interspersed among Lenin's images were photographs of Soviet fishing vessels and various aspects of fleet operations.

Next door was the "Red Carpet Room." It was the indoctrination center found in every Soviet facility and was filled with books and political posters. Simas Kudirka had no doubt sat in that room countless times answering questions and refusing to denounce compatriots who had fought for the nationalist cause or who sympathized with it now. Grueling sessions there with a political commissar surely had added fuel to his dream of escape. Brieze recognized the room immediately as a "red corner"; the place for thought control. He had had occasion to see "red corners" when the Soviets first took over his country in 1940.

Now Ivan Burkal pointed out the room as a library, a place for quiet contemplation and inspiration.

After quickly perusing the titles of books printed in Cyrillic, the Americans were led farther along the passageway toward the rear of the ship. The area was deserted. There were a number of people on deck, but that was not even half the full complement of 150 persons. Everyone else had to be somewhere below. Brieze made a mental note of the emptiness. Were they forbidden to show themselves? Were only the most trustworthy allowed topside?

They were led to a hospital at the rear of the vessel, where Burkal made some laudatory comments about the ship's medical facilities. After some polite words with the people on duty, the delegation returned to Burkal's stateroom.

A meal even more sumptuous than the first was being served.

It was by then mid-afternoon.

About that same time Lieutenant Lundberg went back to the *Vigilant*'s bridge to resume his watch after a late lunch with Lt. Commander Pakos and several officers who knew of the anticipated defection. They had eased up a little. The District had been notified. Commander Eustis was informed. And all were sure the man would not try anything until the conference ended. Then he would slip away, they would grab him, and that would be that. The officers' anxiety was, in fact, slowly turning to boredom; they were waiting around with little to do. During this interim, most of them had noticed that the ship was named *Sovetskaya Litva,* not *Zapryba Kaliningrad.*

Lundberg stood in the wheelhouse near the shiny brass helm. It was a comfortable place with wall-to-wall carpeting and white bulkheads merging at waist height with large windows. The nerve center of the *Vigilant* was quiet, with only an officer or seaman occasionally coming through for routine business or to see what was happening.

He looked out the port window and wondered what was taking Boston so long to answer their message. It had been almost two hours since Pakos had sent it.

Then he noticed Kudirka standing alone at the rail of his ship. He walked out and leaned on the coaming of the bridge wing, casually looking at him, then elsewhere on the *Sovetskaya Litva.* Kudirka was pointing cautiously to something in the palm of his hand which he held close to his belt. Lundberg recognized a package of cigarettes, but sensed right away there would be something more.

Kudirka pointed again to the package, then to Lundberg. Suddenly Lundberg felt his heart beating fast. The man was going to throw the pack. "What if it hits the sprayshield and bounces back?" he thought. "What if someone sees it?" People had been throwing cigarettes back and forth all day, but not from the open level where the two men faced each other now.

Lundberg knew if the man missed it would be all over. Someone on a lower deck of the Russian ship would get the pack. He tensed and felt his heart banging violently against his chest.

Kudirka suddenly flipped the pack and Lundberg knew instantly it would not clear the sprayshield. He lunged out over the bridge wing just as the pack hit the sprayshield and bounced back. He grabbed wildly, desperately, and felt cellophane in his fist, oblivious to the fact that he himself was hanging precariously over the wing. Seconds later he realized he was staring directly into water thirty feet below him.

He edged back from the wing, stood up straight, adjusted his jacket and hat, and said "thanks" as nonchalantly as he could. His trembling hands felt a bulge as he fumbled for a cigarette in the cranberry pack edged with a yellow border. Kudirka looked at him, his head lowered and eyebrows raised, embarrassed at the effort the officer had made to retrieve the cigarettes.

In his excitement, Lundberg inhaled deeply as he took several drags of the sweet tobacco that emitted a thick smoke. He then casually stepped back into the wheelhouse, closed the hatch, and frantically tore at the pack. Then he saw it—a slip of paper folded tightly and inserted in the bottom between the cellophane and the pack. He pulled it out and unfolded it.

On a paper about two inches square he read the following message printed in a firm hand with a gothic-like, East European style:

> My dear comrade I will
> up down of russians
> ship and go with you
> together. If is a pos-
> sible please give my
> signal I keep a——
> sharp lookout = Simas

On the reverse side, Lundberg read:

> I up down in the time
> when the conference is

end and your delegats
go into your ships
a board!

So his name was Simas, Lundberg mused as he fingered the creased, pulpy slip. Simas's intent to jump when the conference ended seem a wise move. It showed common sense, Lundberg thought. Looking at the slip, he wondered if the back was not written sometime after the first half with the signature. Maybe he added it when he got no positive response from Pakos or himself? Probably. Simas was smart, Lundberg theorized; he knew what he was doing.

He called the Executive Officer, showed him the note, and told him how he got it.

Any lingering uncertainty evaporated as Lt. Commander Pakos read the note. He had thought the man—Simas—would not jump immediately, but now he was certain. He had worried over what to do if Simas came over while the U.S. delegation was still aboard the Soviet ship. That problem had nagged him, because he did not know how to cope with it. Now, in an instant, it had disappeared. He only hoped Simas could get across without being shot at by the Russians.

"We'll have to call the Captain back again," he told Lundberg.

But Commander Eustis was not at the conference. When he returned to the *Sovetskaya Litva* after first learning of the anticipated defection, he could not find his way to the meeting room. The first mate who had escorted him had grabbed him and taken him to his own stateroom.

Eustis had politely said that he had to return to the conference, but the mate would hear nothing of it. Good-naturedly, Eustis had followed the mate. He was huge, about thirty-five, and dressed in a suit. He babbled in Russian and produced some vodka, sandwiches, and pictures of his family. Eustis had kept telling him that he had to return to the conference, but the mate refused to let him go. Feeling helpless, Eustis had politely obliged.

With smiles, hand gestures, and photographs, they talked about each other and their families. The first mate showed Eustis pictures of his wife and children and asked if the Captain had any. Eustis showed him pictures of his own wife and two red-haired sons. Now and then Eustis suggested returning to the conference, but the mate remained adamant.

He had engaged Eustis for an hour when a junior officer knocked on the door. The first mate unlocked it.

"You are wanted aboard your ship," the junior officer announced in English. This surprised Eustis. How did the officer know where he was? The visit was supposed to have been a spontaneous impulse of the first mate. They must be following me around, he thought.

Commander Eustis returned to the *Vigilant* expecting something important and hoping nothing had gone wrong. Pakos and Lundberg showed him the note when he arrived in the wheelhouse.

"Well, that's it. He's definitely going to come." The problem of hostages seemed over, but Eustis now wondered if Simas's actions—his solicitations, the package of cigarettes, the intent looks at the *Vigilant*—were not too obvious. After all, the Soviets seemed to know all the movements of the American officers.

"We'll have to get out of here before it's dark," he said. "It'll be hard looking for a man in the water after dark. Maybe Gay Head could have a boat standing by to pick him up. Any word from the District?"

"Nothing yet, Captain," Pakos replied. Pakos himself had been wondering why Boston did not reply to their message.

"Okay, let's send them another message. Tell them about the note, and ask for a forty-four footer from Gay Head."

Pakos took a legal-size pad from the chart table and wrote the following message:

NMF IDE NHIC
0231923 Z
FM CGC VIGILANT
TO CCGDONE
BT
SECRET

A. My 231743Z Nov. 70

1. Vig CO aware of situation.
2. Note from Soviet crew member of Sovetskaya Litva indicates escape attempt planned when Vigilant is ready to depart.
3. Request Gay Head CG have suitable boat standing by commencing 231530Q. Boat should be instructed to remain far away from Vigilant until Vigilant has departed Soviet vessel. At that time boat should proceed to Vigilant for instructions and be prepared to pick up man in water.

Eustis approved the draft by initialing the bottom. They were no longer asking for advice, but recommending action, because the note had cancelled the problem of what to do if Kudirka jumped while the delegates were still aboard the Soviet ship. Now seamanship would play the major role, and Eustis, Pakos, and Lundberg were experts at it.

Leaving Lundberg on watch, Eustis and Pakos hurried with their new message to the radio room.

CHAPTER

9

Lieutenant Burke was flustered. He had been sitting in the radio room since transmission of the first message an hour earlier. He knew there was something wrong with the on-line receiver, but could not pinpoint the trouble. Boston was sending something, but the copy was garbled.

Burke was a recent graduate of the Coast Guard Academy serving his first tour of duty as the *Vigilant*'s Communications Officer. The visor of his slightly overlarge baseball cap tended to overshadow his pleasant features. His heavy, black mustache made him look older than his twenty-four years. He was an electrical engineer and had been tinkering with the receiver for some time when the Captain and Executive Officer walked in.

"Is there anything from the District yet?" Eustis asked.

"No, sir. There seems to be something wrong with the on-line crypto. The District is trying to send something, but I can't receive it."

"Well, see if you can set up off-line," Eustis told him. "Ask Radio Boston to have the message sent using Adonis."*

"Yes, sir."

Eustis gave him the new message. "Get this out as soon as you can."

*Adonis—another code system that had to be manually ciphered and deciphered.

Together with the Chief Radioman, Lieutenant Burke began
preparations for transmission of the new message. He dated the
copy (2:23 P.M.) and punched it out on tape for an on-line
transmission—the same system that was giving them trouble.
Burke reasoned that even though the *Vigilant*'s on-line receiver
was malfunctioning, her on-line transmitter would be all right.
On-line transmission would save time coding and decoding.
Unfortunately, the District was also having trouble with its
on-line system.

Several minutes past 3 P.M., while Burke was still punching
the tape for the latest message, Boston raised the *Vigilant* using
the Adonis system. However, the operators in Boston were
using the wrong call sign and could not get through. Normally,
the off-line system was a seldom used backup, but now, when
it became a crucial link between Boston and the *Vigilant,* the
men in the District's Communications Center found they were
not quite adept at using it. Within fifteen minutes, however,
they did learn the correct call sign and began sending the message Captain Brown wrote early that afternoon. Lieutenant
Burke rogered for the transmission at 3:36 P.M.—two hours
later.

Lieutenant Burke's new tape was then ready and he signaled
the District to switch to their on-line gear so he could transmit
the latest message from the *Vigilant,* the one about Kudirka's
note and the request for a launch from the Gay Head Coast
Guard Station which was only minutes away from the mooring
site.

At 4 P.M. *Vigilant*'s operator would begin feeding the tape.
It would be the first of eight attempted transmissions of the
same message, eight attempted transmissions that would take
the next three hours to get through to the District—a total
elapsed time from the receipt of Kudirka's note of more than
four hours.[1]

Meanwhile, Eustis was back on the bridge wing with Pakos
and Lundberg looking again for Kudirka.

He saw them and came to the bridge rail opposite the officers. "I will swim," he emphatically told Eustis. The Captain looked at him for a moment then turned and without expression walked into the wheelhouse followed by the other two officers. It was time to set the stage for Simas's escape.

"I'm going back to get the delegation," he said and hurried below.

Minutes after Eustis was lifted aboard the *Sovetskaya Litva*, Lieutenant Burke came into the wheelhouse with the message from the District.

Pakos read aloud from the large telegram-type words pasted together line by line. "One. Take no direct or overt action. However be prepared to launch small boat immediately. Two. Get Commander Eustis back aboard using any pretext. Three. Commandant notified of situation. Four. If man goes in the water give USSR every opportunity to recover."

The words "take no direct or overt action" stuck in Lieutenant Lundberg's mind. "What about the Jacob's ladder?" he asked Pakos.

"Guiding him around the Jacob's ladder isn't overt action. He'll be in the water anyway."

They considered the stipulation about giving the Soviets "every opportunity" to recover Simas, but they tended to downplay it.

They had decided from the start not to entice him, but they wanted him to escape.

"Yeah," Lundberg said. "There are several places he could physically jump across, too, even without going in the water. And once we got him, he's ours."

Lt. Commander Pakos did not want to call Commander Eustis back again, because calling him a third time might arouse suspicion if the Soviets were not already leery of Eustis's movements.

To Lieutenant Lundberg, everything seemed "hunky-dory."

He looked again at the message while Pakos went to the bridge wing to make sure just how Simas would come over.

Lundberg kept thinking about the "overt action" clause and concluded the officers had not taken any overt action. Eustis and Pakos had turned away from the man several times. He himself had caught a package of cigarettes, but then many people were throwing cigarettes back and forth. He wondered if he might have given Simas any sign. No, he concluded, he had not, mainly because he had feared betraying the man. His Latvian neighbors in New London again crossed his mind. Concentration camps. Beatings. Violent death. "How can people live like that?" he wondered.

Lundberg sensed the defection would be a big thing. It would have an impact, be a news story. He had always believed that civilian life was a little monotonous and that military life was where the action was. He did not regret making a career of the U.S. Coast Guard.

Outside, Lt. Commander Pakos was facing Kudirka again. He had to know how this man Simas would come over so he could make preparations. He felt a little torn, not really knowing what he would do if the man jumped in the water in light of Boston's instructions to "give USSR every opportunity to recover." Fellow-officers knew Pakos and his wife Pat as "very concerned with people" and active in social service organizations in communities where they were stationed. In one place they themselves had started an organization that provided transportation to hospitals for the needy, offered them diversions and food. Now his innate compassion was assaulted by instructions which went against his personal inclinations. Luckily, he saw room to maneuver.

Since Simas was determined to escape anyway, Pakos concluded that asking him how would not entice him. Noticing no one within earshot he spoke to Kudirka for the first time. "Water?"

"Which is better?" Kudirka asked.

Pakos was already treading the thin line between "overt" and "non-overt" action, so avoiding insubordination, he very slowly shrugged his shoulders.

Kudirka declared, "I will swim," and walked off along the deck.

As Pakos scanned the other decks for the reappearance of the American delegation, he suddenly saw Kudirka hurrying to the main deck and toward a railing opposite *Vigilant's* flight deck. He had apparently taken Pakos's question as a signal and was coming over. Pakos tensed as he watched Kudirka starting to lift himself onto the rail and stared at him in a frozen gesture. It was too soon!

Kudirka looked up, hesitated a moment, then eased off the rail and hurried back toward a ladder. Some crewmen were still lining the rails. Had they noticed him?

When Commander Eustis returned to get the delegates, the meeting was over and everyone was being treated to another meal. The conferees were grouped at two tables heaped with more food and drink. He noticed Gordon at a table with Burkal, the Soviet interpreter, and Captain Popov and went toward him. Watching closely from the other table was the man in the gray sweater.

Eustis leaned over Gordon's shoulder and whispered something in his ear. Gordon rose and walked several steps back from the table where he huddled with the Captain of the *Vigilant.* "It would be good for us to get back, because I'd like to leave before dark."

"But they asked us to stay for dinner," Gordon replied. "What can we tell them?"

In barely audible phrases, muffled by the conviviality around them, Eustis told him about Kudirka.

Gordon listened intently, then answered, "All right, Captain, I'll tell Alexis to pass the word that we have to leave." He went toward the other table, while Burkal motioned to Eustis to come sit down for some refreshments.

Nickerson and Brieze noticed the activity. Brieze recalled later that he thought Eustis looked pale and worried. Nickerson, disillusioned with the meeting from the start, knew that Eustis had come back to get them, so he automatically stood up to get their coats.

Meanwhile, Gordon had asked Obolensky to step out into the passageway. As they walked through the door, Gordon was overcome with uneasiness. Two Soviet officers were guarding each end of the corridor. "They know something!" he thought and wondered if they would be allowed off the ship. He murmured something about Kudirka and they went back inside the stateroom while the guards observed them.

Obolensky then announced in Russian that the American delegation would like to return home before dark and would be leaving. When he finished, the man in the gray sweater came up to Burkal and muttered something to him. Burkal leaned over to Eustis and said through his interpreter, "You promised us a visit to your ship. We would like to see your ship."

Commander Eustis felt obligated to honor the request. He had earlier invited the senior Soviet officers and now reasoned a visit aboard the *Vigilant* could allay any suspicions the Soviets might have. He could no longer use the search and rescue ploy since Obolensky had announced they were leaving only because of the approaching darkness.

Eustis then joined Burkal in several farewell toasts.

Shortly after that, the Americans returned to the *Vigilant* accompanied by about twenty Soviets and Skaidrite, the blond hostess for whom Brieze had arranged a visit to the cutter with Captain Popov.

The tire rig went back and forth half a dozen times while crewmen of both ships watched. Eight of the Soviets, including Kudirka, stood at a rail on the top deck near the corner where he had first contacted the Americans. They leaned into the rail, their hands clutching it. Kudirka was at a ninety degree angle and his shipmates could only see his back. So it was that only sailors on the *Vigilant* saw Kudirka's hands clenched tightly in prayer just above his chest.

CHAPTER

10

In Boston Captain Brown had finished the informal staff meeting in his office and was dialing the home of Rear Admiral Ellis for the second time. He hoped the weight of the staff officers' opinion would sway him.

It was 3:30 P.M.

When the Admiral answered, Brown reported, "I've heard nothing from the Commandant." He told Ellis there was no additional word from the *Vigilant* and that a message to the cutter had been sent. (The *Vigilant* was only receiving the message as Brown spoke.)

"Some of the staff were discussing this, and there is some point of disagreement with your conclusion," Brown continued. "We don't think the man should be returned without advice from the Commandant."

"Well, you haven't told me anything new that would make me change my mind," Ellis retorted.

Captain Brown did not argue, because he expected an overriding decision from Headquarters anyway. There was no use getting on the wrong side of his Admiral in useless argument.

The situation for Ellis was the same as during his first conversation with Brown two hours earlier. Added only was the fact that some of the staff officers did not agree with the decision, but Admiral Ellis did not need their opinion to know he was right. It was for him a case of desertion, pure and simple.[1]

Admiral Ellis had not asked, nor did Brown say that among those staff officers who disagreed was Commander Flanagan, the Legal Officer. Some briefings and conferences included only people in Operations, and Flanagan was not always present. Ellis would explain long after the incident: "I relied on Flanagan a great deal. I might well have said 'let me talk to him.' I don't know if I'd have listened to Flanagan's advice, but certainly would have given it a lot more thought."

Brown did not tell Ellis which side he favored, but Ellis sensed that Brown was questioning his conclusion by the very fact that he had conferred with the staff officers. This, however, did not faze the Admiral. It was not the first time his conclusions had been questioned, and it was not the first time he had stood firm in his convictions. Admiral Ellis was sure his opinion was correct and gentlemanly, but he would say to the Board of Investigation that he did not consider it an order to Captain Brown, rather an outside opinion to the Acting District Commander.

Captain Brown ended the conversation with a reference to the passing time, telling Admiral Ellis he was going to prod Washington to see what information he could get. "I'll let you know if there is anything further."

"Okay, Fletcher, let me know."

They both hung up their receivers.

Captain Brown's admiration for Admiral Ellis was enormous. In the little more than two years he had known him, Brown had come to believe Ellis was a "very astute" and "discerning" man who could always pierce the heart of an issue. Ellis was "the absolute epitome of guidance."

Ellis's career, indeed, was exemplary. He had commanded a destroyer escort in World War II and before the war ended was a commander of a division of six destroyer escorts. He received a Bronze Star and other medals and commendations for his war-time service. Upon returning to the United States, Ellis held administrative posts in Miami, then went to the Coast Guard Academy as an instructor in gunnery, navigation, and

seamanship. Later he became Commandant of Cadets and pre-
sided over their day-to-day activities, including leadership
training. Ellis then went to Washington for nine years, where
he spent several non-consecutive tours in the Office of Personnel at Headquarters. Two of those years were as Chief of Personnel. He was made Rear Admiral in 1966.

While a cadet, Ellis had specialized in gunnery and seamanship. All courses at the time were technical as most still are. The
exception then was language, and Ellis had elected French. In
1940 he had begun a law correspondence course, but had to
drop it because of long war-time cruises at sea where mail was
irregular. After the war he was told he was "too senior" to
continue the course.

His interests throughout his career remained technical and
administrative, and his decision that Monday reflected them.
Ellis was unaware of the political implications involved in his
decision, which a deeper understanding of politics and history
would have made him conscious of.

The service was deep in the blood of the Ellis family. His son
had wanted to join the Coast Guard, but could not because of
a respiratory condition. His daughter had married a Coast
Guard officer.

When not with his family or six grandchildren, the Admiral
would spend his leisure time woodworking, rebuilding and
refinishing furniture, or constructing stereo sets. He enjoyed
bridge and played it regularly, often with Captain Brown and
his wife. Ellis had to quit golf in 1962 after tearing an Achilles
tendon. In most respects he lived an ordered life closely identified with middle-class values. Some junior officers in the District affectionately referred to him as "a typical son-of-a-bitch
Republican Yankee."

Admiral Ellis had been Commander of the First District
since 1968. He was good at what he did and was a respected
officer who had reached the peak of prestige and power that
went with his rank. One month before that fateful November

day, the Secretary of Transportation, on behalf of the President, had awarded him the Legion of Merit for "exceptionally meritorious conduct in the performance of duty as Commander, First Coast Guard District from June, 1968, to September, 1970. Rear Admiral Ellis has distinguished himself by his dynamic leadership, keen foresight, and unhesitating assumption of a broad spectrum of demanding responsibilities."

Captain Brown certainly agreed, and even though the staff officers had recommended another course of action that Monday, Brown would tell the Board of Investigation that he felt Ellis's decision to return the defector was "a knowledgeable one" and he did not seriously question it. In a subsequent interview, Brown would add: "He is the finest officer I have ever known . . . So when a situation like this comes along to whom do you turn?"

Brown's paradoxical attitude would characterize him throughout the afternoon and early evening. He was wavering, as the other officers had noticed in the staff meeting. He would say in testimony and in interviews that he agreed the defector should be kept and he would also say he agreed that Ellis's opinion to return the defector was "a knowledgeable one." He had sent a message telling the *Vigilant* to "give USSR every opportunity to recover" and at the same time he was waiting for Headquarters to override that very possibility.

Captain Brown's mixed attitude was generated by his inner sympathy for the underdog—Kudirka—and his genuine admiration for Admiral Ellis. And it was generated by his unconscious playing of two contradictory roles—that of Acting Commander and Chief of Staff. He was carrying out Admiral Ellis's wishes, as a Chief of Staff should, and at the same time he was working on his own, as Acting Commander, to solicit different advice from Headquarters. Soon he would become trapped in the middle.

As for Admiral Ellis, he had been commended by the Secretary of Transportation for "unhesitating assumption of a broad spectrum of demanding responsibilities." One high-ranking officer in Coast Guard Headquarters who had once served under Ellis noted that that trait had been with him a long time. He characterized Ellis as a man who would say "give me the facts and let's go." But in this case Ellis was too quick to take on responsibility that was not his to assume. Moreover, his hastily construed and doggedly held opinion of why a man should summarily be refused political refuge was based on a paucity of political and historical facts that he, as a high-ranking military officer whose District for more than twenty years had been in contact with Soviet fleets, should reasonably be expected to know.

Captain Brown pondered the situation awhile after hanging up his receiver. He wondered what was taking Washington so long to respond.

At Coast Guard Headquarters Captain Dahlgren, the Intelligence Chief, was getting impatient while waiting for the return call from the State Department. Five minutes had gone by . . . ten . . . fifteen . . . twenty. He went to several of his staff members and asked if they had ever had any contact with a defection case or knew of any instructions on defectors. No one had.

As he waited for a return call from Edward Killham of the Soviet Desk, he could think of no other way to get advice from the State Department.

But only four months previously Dahlgren had played a very dynamic role in the incident involving the *Konrad*. That case, too, had had foreign policy implications. In the absence of various superiors when the First District had called for advice, Dahlgren had immediately called the office of Law Enforcement and asked them to get advice for the First District. OLE quickly got advice from its contacts in the State Department, and within the hour Dahlgren telephoned the First District with authorization to seize the West German trawler.

Now Captain Dahlgren took a more passive role. Admiral Hammond, the Chief of Operations, had instructed him to get in touch with the State Department and he had. Now it was up to the State Department to act.

Ironically, Captain Brown, Admiral Hammond, and Captain Dahlgren were all aware that the Law Enforcement Division at Headquarters was an appropriate channel for advice, but none of them sought its advice: Brown, because he could not speak with the Chief, even though presumably competent staff officers were on duty; Hammond, because he simply did not think of it at the time; and Dahlgren, because he had been instructed to contact someone in the State Department himself.

At 3:30—forty-five minutes after his initial contact with the case—Edward Killham returned Captain Dahlgren's call.[2] Dahlgren was again out of his office and shortly called Killham back.

Killham told him he had finally received a copy of the *Vigilant*'s [first] message and asked if there was any other information. There was none.

"Nothing should be done to encourage the defection. It might be a provocation." Killham would testify: ". . . I think this is standard operating procedure. When a government official is presented with a potential defector, one of the first things he thinks about: 'Is this guy genuine?'"

Captain Dahlgren did not pursue Killham's line of reasoning and let Killham mention it without comment. He wanted specific advice on a probable defection, what to do when it occurred, not what to do to avoid it. So he presented the problem from another angle. "What if he's already on the American ship? What if he jumps straight from one ship to another? They might be moored together."

"Who says they're moored together?"

"Well, that's just my impression from the message."

They broached the possibility that mutual visits were taking place, that the ships were close together, and that the defector could conceivably come across as one of the visitors.

Killham then made the most specific point in the Coast Guard's search for advice. He said, "Well, if he's on the American ship, let us know immediately and we'll send you further guidance on how to handle the situation."

For Captain Dahlgren that point was already a step beyond what he had been instructed to get, namely guidance on the *actual recovery.* So Dahlgren pressed on. "How about the fact, you have the Coast Guard message now that indicates that the man might try to swim between the two ships. What degree or nature of force is the Coast Guard authorized to use in order to retrieve him if the Soviets are also trying to retrieve him?"

"This is a very sticky question," Killham replied. "I don't think I can answer that question myself and what's more I don't think I can get you a definitive answer to do you any good." Killham was thinking of the political implications inherent in a physical confrontation and feared the defection could occur before he had a chance to "research" an answer.

There was brief silence on the line. Killham sensed that Dahlgren wanted something more definite and was thinking of something firm to tell the Coast Guard Captain.

"You have an immense experience in the field of rescuing people from the sea," Killham finally said. "Certainly, if the man is in the sea he is a mariner in distress and the Coast Guard is perfectly within its rights to go out and rescue him."

Killham was suggesting that the Coast Guard just grab the man as a person in danger of drowning. He was stripping the issue of its cumbersome political overtones.

But Captain Dahlgren did not catch the nuance. "Our traditional role of the Coast Guard," he replied dryly. He had known that much before he called.

"Your traditional role of the Coast Guard," Killham repeated. He was implying that the Coast Guard, with its long tradition of seamanship, would have no trouble getting the man first and avoiding the confrontation the officers involved had come to believe might occur. It seemed strange to Killham, after all, that the Coast Guard should come to the State Department asking how to fish a man out of the water.

"Let me know when he's aboard," Killham repeated, "then we'll be able to provide you with further guidance."

Captain Dahlgren was totally frustrated when he put his receiver down. All Killham had said, it seemed, was if the man was drowning he could be picked up. He realized he would not have much to tell his friend Captain Brown in the First District.

He dialed Boston.

The telephone rang just before Captain Brown could place another call to Washington.

Brown recognized Dahlgren on the line. They had both been aviators together and had known each other for many years.

"Yeah, Wally?"

Dahlgren told him that Admiral Hammond had asked him to get the advice Brown wanted. He reported that he had gone to the State Department. "They've been of very little help. They said we should do nothing to provoke a defection."

"Well, you're not being very helpful to us," Brown replied.

"Yes, I know," Dahlgren admitted. "They only said if the man is in the water we can excercise our traditional role and pick him up."

"Oh, for crap's sake, Wally," Brown said irritatedly. "What do you think we are up here, a bunch of dopes or somethin'. That's our business."

Dahlgren would testify that he was certain he told Brown that the State Department had said: "Call us when the man is on board the *Vigilant.*" He added that he did not tell Brown he himself wanted to know when the defector was aboard. He felt he was only carrying out instructions for his superior, Admiral Hammond.

Brown would tell the board he did not recall Dahlgren saying that the State Department wanted to know when the defector was aboard the *Vigilant.* He would testify he only remembered the Intelligence Chief saying: "We have no instructions how to handle the case from the State Department, but if the man goes in the water, exercise Coast Guard responsibility."

Both, however, did agree at the end of their conversation that the State Department had been of little help to them.

In any event, the misunderstanding over what exactly Dahlgren did tell Brown was overshadowed by a new development. Darkness was enveloping that late November afternoon, the end of the work day was near, and Captain Brown had begun to think that the defection would not occur at all.

He leaned back in his chair, pondering his next move, then picked up the telephone again and dialed through to Admiral Hammond's office at Headquarters.

Commander Flanagan walked in, noticed Brown was busy talking, and walked to a window where he gazed at the Government Center Plaza ten stories below. It was drizzling and the sky was turning dark.

CHAPTER

11

This second telephone conversation between Captain Brown in the First District and Admiral Hammond at Headquarters was the pivotal point in the decision-making process of the *Vigilant* incident.

The conversation occurred at 4 P.M. and was the last contact between high-ranking officers in the First District and Washington, and therefore the last chance for higher authority to override Admiral Ellis's instructions to return the defector, barring, of course, any firm stand by Captain Brown himself, who as Acting District Commander had the legal authority to act independently of Admiral Ellis, as he, indeed, was doing in contacting Headquarters about the case.

But Brown's ambivalence over his role at this point also had its most damaging effect, although that becomes evident only in the light of subsequent events.

Admiral Hammond and Captain Dahlgren were in Hammond's office when Captain Brown called. Dahlgren had just come in to report what he had told Brown in another call several minutes earlier, namely, that the State Department had been of little help.

At the same time the Flag Plot Duty Officer was walking down the carpeted hallway toward Admiral Hammond's office which was several doors away from Flag Plot and the Com-

munications Center. Flag Plot at Headquarters was similar to
the Rescue Coordination Centers in the districts, except on a
larger scale. It coordinated all search and rescue activities in the
districts. Lt. (jg) Wayne Tritbough was Flag Plot Duty Officer
that day and he had seen the first message from the *Vigilant*
early in the afternoon. Tritbough had reacted quickly and told
the Communications Chief he would call Captain Dahlgren
immediately, but the Chief had told him that Dahlgren already
knew about the case.

Now it was 4 P.M. and Tritbough had heard nothing more
about it. He had never come across a defection during the year
that he was assigned to Flag Plot, but he instinctively knew this
case was important enough to warrant further instructions
from his superiors—instructions he had not received up to that
point. As Flag Plot Duty Officer, he would be in a focal position
to pass on information if anything happened, especially after
normal office hours.

When Lieutenant Tritbough walked into Admiral Hammond's office, Hammond was already talking with Brown, and
Captain Dahlgren was listening in on an extension.

Both Captain Brown and Admiral Hammond would tell the
Board of Investigation that they remembered only vaguely
what they said in that conversation, and Captain Brown would
add little more in subsequent interviews.

Hammond stated that he reiterated to Brown the same thing
Captain Dahlgren had told him: the State Department was of
"no help whatsoever." He added: "I asked Captain Brown to
keep us informed. Right. I don't think I said, 'Advise us when
the man comes aboard.' I said, 'Keep us informed of the developments,' or words to that effect."

He said they got into a side discussion, that Captain Brown
was concerned about the attitude of the Soviets. Brown was
afraid the Soviets would become upset if the Coast Guard
grabbed the defector. The Admiral told the board: "At that
point I suggested that if you are able to get him into the boat,

rather than take him back to the *Vigilant,* take him directly to shore and put him on a Coast Guard Station at Gay Head, and then you can tell the Russians that you took him in for medical treatment and let us know, so we can go back to the State Department."[1]

They then broached the possibility of letting the Soviets pick up the man, but Hammond testified he did not agree with that alternative: ". . . We were talking about how we could get him, and the feeling was we would make whatever [attempt] we could to recover him."

To Captain Brown the most important part of the conversation was the question to Admiral Hammond of whether it was all right for him to go home. Brown had begun to think the defection would not occur at all and was anxious to get his regular commuter train to his home in Gloucester. His question to the Admiral seemed uppermost in his mind whenever the 4 P.M. conversation was brought up in testimony before the board and particularly during subsequent interviews.

He told the board: "As close as I can recall, I said, 'Admiral, we're getting very close to the working day up here. We have no further information from the *Vigilant.* If the guy goes in the water and we can get him out, all well and good.' " Brown continued that he told Hammond the sky was dark and rain was falling. He reminded the Admiral that the *Vigilant* had come alongside the Soviet vessel at 10:30 that morning and the meeting should have lasted six hours. He told Hammond that if the *Vigilant* had not already left the Soviet ship, she would be leaving shortly. "I said, 'Do you think I should remain in the office pending some kind of developments or should I go ahead and get my normal commuter service home?' He said, 'I see no reason why you should not go ahead and shove off and keep us up to date if anything further comes up.' "

Although Hammond testified that he did not recall telling Brown to go home, the officers listening in on the conversation corroborated Captain Brown's version.

This, however, did not materially change matters, because just before the end of the conversation Hammond reminded Brown that if the defection did occur, the First District should inform Flag Plot at Headquarters and Flag Plot would pass the information to the State Department. Lieutenant Tritbough, the Duty Officer, heard this and understood it, as did Captain Dahlgren on the extension.

More important, both Captain Brown and Admiral Hammond testified that they agreed this was to be the case.[2] The First District—through Lieutenant Ryan of RCC—would inform Headquarters—through Lieutenant Tritbough of Flag Plot—and Tritbough would pass the information to the State Department.

There was nothing unusual about this arrangement. It was a routine way of communication between the districts and Headquarters after normal office hours.

Brown and Hammond were relegating to routine channels a very irregular potentiality.

Brown had every intention of having RCC inform Flag Plot, therefore he did not tell Admiral Hammond that he had different instructions from Admiral Ellis. He was at this point still behaving as Acting District Commander and did not feel the need to relay Ellis's instructions, because he had every intention of doing what Admiral Hammond at Headquarters had said, thus automatically bypassing Admiral Ellis.

Brown's silence on Ellis's instructions was a fateful error engendered by the ambiguity of his own role as Chief of Staff/ Acting District Commander.

Commander Flanagan was still at the window while Brown talked. He gazed past the brick inlaid plaza of the new city hall toward a clock near Ehrlich's Cigar Store on Tremont Street. A cold drizzle saturated the darkening winter sky as he watched office workers hurrying across the windswept plaza to a subway station blended into it. The face of the blinking electronic timepiece showed 4:15 P.M. and was visible to him more than a hundred yards away.

Brown had just put down the receiver.

"Did you get anything from Headquarters?" Flanagan asked, turning towards him.

"No, Jay. I talked with Wally Dahlgren and Admiral Hammond and they weren't any help."

"Well, I still think if he defects we ought to bring him in to Boston," the Legal Officer said. He looked out the window again. "You know, Captain, if the guy was going to defect, he would be doing it right about now," Flanagan mused. "They've been out there six hours and the ship should be pulling away right about now."

"It's getting dark and I doubt if he jumped," Brown answered.

"Yeah, maybe you're right."

"Headquarters doesn't see any reason for me to stick around, so I'm going to catch my train home," Brown said as he went to a closet where he kept a civilian suit.

Flanagan walked from the window. "I'll be around awhile. And if anything happens later they can call me at home."

Captain Brown changed into his civilian suit and closed his office for the day. Presuming that the defection would not occur, he did not inform Lieutenant Ryan, the RCC Controller, that Headquarters wanted to know when the defector was aboard the *Vigilant*. Ryan had only seen the initial message from the cutter and had received no further instructions on the case. However, as RCC Controller he was normally expected to pass along to Headquarters any important information received by the District.

Commander Flanagan returned to his own office and stayed another hour taking care of some routine business. He would only find out the next morning what happened aboard the *Vigilant* that night.

CHAPTER

12

"Attention to Colors," sounded over the loudspeakers of the *Vigilant* as the sun, hanging low in the sky above Vineyard Sound, edged into the horizon off the starboard beam. Ship's officers and the fisheries delegates were guiding their Soviet visitors through the ship. They stopped whatever they were doing, turned toward the signal bridge behind the wheelhouse, and saluted as a seaman lowered the flag of the United States from its halyard on the orange mast. The visitors watched passively.

Fluttering vigorously, the ensign came down from its perch more than fifty feet above the water. It had flown throughout the day facing the large, red hammer and sickle affixed on the smokestack of the *Sovetskaya Litva*. Now the hammer and sickle remained the only emblem of sovereignty still visible in the growing darkness over Menemsha Bight—a silent premonition.

Vigilant's anchor lights were turned on and lights aboard the *Sovetskaya Litva* began appearing through random portholes.

The Soviets had been aboard nearly half an hour; it was a pleasant interlude. Only for the three top ship's officers and Gordon and Obolensky did it conceal a nervous anticipation. The only sign of that anticipation was on the 02 level behind a closed brown door marked: "Authorized Personnel Only." A radioman was transmitting and retransmitting the message about Kudirka's note and *Vigilant's* request for a patrol boat.

He kept transmitting, but Boston did not roger.

As if the Colors ceremony had been some cue, the officers began leading their guests toward the flight deck. Everyone gathered by the tire rig and Commander Eustis quickly bade his farewells. "Goodbye, goodbye, see you again at sea," he said to them collectively. He then hurried back to the bridge, leaving the Officer of the Deck in charge of the transfers.

Lieutenants Lundberg and Burke were already in the wheelhouse when Eustis arrived. Lt. Commander Pakos stood on the bridge wing next to several other officers and the telephone talker. They were leaning on the coaming, ready to watch the unmooring.

Pakos glanced at the *Sovetskaya Litva* and noticed Kudirka on the bridge opposite him with an excited look on his face. Pakos straightened and stared at Kudirka, who seemed to be looking for some signal. Unable to maintain his neutral pose, Pakos slowly and deliberately aimed his head toward the forecastle deck as a likely spot for him to jump, then turned it slowly and aimed it at the boat deck below him.

Kudirka stared questioningly. Pakos slowly shrugged his shoulders and Kudirka hurried forward along the lifeboats.

"Why are they so slow in leaving?" Eustis thought, peering out a rear window of the wheelhouse at a small group of Soviets still standing on the flight deck. He could not unmoor until all of them were back on their ship. Eustis loosened his black tie, then decided he should change from his dress blues into something more casual.

He hurried below to his cabin where he took off his hat, jacket, and tie. Not bothering to put on his khakis, he pulled a foul-weather jacket over his white shirt.

Lieutenant Morehouse walked in. "You wanted to see me, Captain?" Eustis had not had a chance to speak to the young lieutenant from Washington and now told him about Kudirka.

"Do you have anything to say about it?"

"I think Washington should be made aware of it," More-house replied.

CHAPTER

13

Simas Kudirka climbed onto the forward rail of his ship, balanced himself momentarily, tensed the muscles in his body, and leaped fourteen feet into space toward a wire railing on the bow of the *Vigilant.* He was a shadowy form in the twilight stretching his arms upward to grasp a five-eighths-inch wire running through four stanchions along the bow. In that instant he was rejecting a system he hated, but that rejection had to include everything he was, everything he loved, and everything he had known. In a system that demanded total unanimity he had in that instant become a threat, an outlaw. No matter what happened henceforth, he could never return as the man he had been up to that moment, because his act was a symbol of defiance and demanded punishment. The existence of the system depended on total submissiveness; and in that split second in which he lunged through the fourteen foot distance between the ships, he had committed the greatest sin in a totalitarian system. He had asserted his free will.

Kudirka clambered over the wire, ran through a hatch in the forward bulkhead, into the hatch on the port boat deck, and up the stairs leading to the wheelhouse. He had studied the *Vigilant* all afternoon and knew exactly where he was going. Lt. Commander Pakos, Lieutenant Lundberg, and Lieutenant Burke were startled when he charged up the stairs. He ran up to Pakos, embraced him, and blurted excitedly, "Comrades! Comrades! Thank you!" Then he quickly embraced Lundberg and Burke, each time repeating, "Comrades! Comrades!"

Lundberg grabbed him by the arm and without saying anything led him to the rear of the wheelhouse and opened the narrow door of the "stick." It was an inside ladder leading up the hollow mast to the crow's nest and just barely had room enough for one man. Lundberg shoved Kudirka in backwards and closed the door on his jubilant face. He summoned John Fowlie, a muscular, six-foot two, red-headed seaman, to guard the door. Fowlie was one of the crewmen who had first heard Kudirka ask for asylum that morning.

Meanwhile, Pakos was rushing to the Captain's Cabin, where Eustis had just asked Lieutenant Morehouse what he believed should be done about the defection. Pakos was jubilant as he ran to the Captain's Cabin—jubilant and relieved. Simas was here and he was safe.

Pakos barged into the cabin. "He's here!" he cried excitedly.

"Who's here?" Eustis asked, startled by his Executive Officer.

"The defector!"

"Where is he?"

"In the stick!"

"Did anybody see him jump?"

"I don't know, Captain!"

"Well, you'd better put him out of sight," Eustis replied. "Put him in the Watchstander's Head and don't let anybody near him."

"Yes, sir," Pakos replied. He was bubbling with joy.

"And put a call in to Captain Brown," Eustis added. He felt suddenly relieved, drained. It was over. The whole thing had gone very simply.

Pakos was on his way back to the wheelhouse.

"The Captain says to put him in the Watchstander's Head," he told Lundberg when he returned. "You'd better take him down there out of sight."

The Executive Officer then rushed to the radio room.

"The Captain wants a phone patch with Captain Brown," he told the radioman when he arrived.

He caught his breath while the radioman placed the call.

A telephone patch was a relatively simple, but tedious process by which calls were made directly from cutters to their District or vice versa. The cutters used their radios, while the District received and transmitted via the Coast Guard Radio Station.

Lieutenant Ryan, the RCC Controller, received the *Vigilant*'s request and called Captain Brown. There was no answer. Ryan then dialed the number of Commander Curry, the Intelligence Chief. There was no answer. Both Brown and Curry were en route home.

Brown had not told Ryan that he should contact Flag Plot as soon as he received word that the defector had come aboard the *Vigilant*.

Ryan now informed the *Vigilant* that neither Captain Brown nor Commander Curry were available.

Without hesitating, Pakos asked the radioman to reach Admiral Ellis. It was a fateful decision that Pakos made on his own, knowing, however, that under the circumstances Eustis would approve.[1]

Admiral Ellis was on sick leave, and Pakos would say long after the incident: "I had no inkling of that fact whatsoever, and if Commander Eustis did, he never expressed it."

Little did Pakos know that Admiral Ellis was the man Captain Brown had intended to bypass by dealing directly with Washington.

Since the hookup with Ellis would take several minutes, Lt. Commander Pakos hurried back to the Captain's Cabin.

When he returned he found Commander Eustis telling Gordon and Obolensky what had happened. Pakos listened, still elated over the escape. But then Obolensky—in a phrase—quashed that elation.

"Of course," the interpreter said matter-of-factly, "he will have to go back."

In retrospect it is evident that Obolensky's attitude was temporary, perhaps because of the euphoria surrounding the pleasantries heaped upon the Americans by the Soviets during the day. Later he, and all the civilians, would steadfastly maintain that Kudirka should not be returned.

But now, for the first time that day, Lt. Commander Pakos was stunned. The phrase disoriented him. His mood dampened and he berated himself for being so adolescently joyous. He reasoned his feelings must have clouded some sound logic that had not escaped the fisheries official from Washington. Pakos suddenly felt sheepish over his gladness that Simas had escaped.

"It doesn't seem so obvious to me," Eustis curtly told Obolensky. His words heightened Pakos's mood again.

"We couldn't get through to Captain Brown," Pakos told his Captain as he regained his spirits, "so I asked the radioman to call Admiral Ellis."

"Fine," Eustis replied, unmindful of the fact that Ellis was on sick leave.

Meanwhile, Lieutenant Lundberg had taken a clipboard from the chart table in the wheelhouse and led Kudirka from the "stick" down one flight of stairs to the 02 level. Seaman Fowlie was right behind them.

The Watchstander's Head was in the after part of the superstructure, almost directly under the mast. It was a small toilet similar to one in a typical gas station. Kudirka would spend the next six and one-half hours in that little room with one stool and a washbasin. His only view would be through a porthole directly opposite the *Sovetskaya Litva*, suddenly turned foreboding and threatening.

The passageway on the 02 level was lit, but the head was dark, giving the ensuing conversation between Lundberg and Kudirka inside the head a conspiratorial air.[2]

"How did you come aboard?" Lundberg asked when he led Kudirka inside. "Did you jump?"

Kudirka was still jubilant. He breathed heavily through a wide smile and his chest heaved with excitement. He could not understand what Lundberg was saying.

"Did you jump? Jump?" Lundberg asked. He crouched a little with his hands extended in front of him making a motion with his wrists as if he were grabbing something. "Jump? Jump?"

"Ahhh," Kudirka beamed. "Yes, yes, I jump. I jump. I jump your ship." He had written "up down" in his note because he did not know the word "jump." Now he repeated the new word as he mimicked Lundberg's crouch. "I jump your ship like this," he said and demonstrated a jump.

"I'm Lieutenant Douglas Lundberg. I'm second mate," he said, pointing to himself. "Who are you?"

Kudirka gestured toward his clipboard and Lundberg gave it to him together with a government-issue ballpoint pen. Kudirka held it at an angle above his left shoulder and began writing. Lundberg thought the effort useless; a ballpoint pen could never write upside down, but he was pleasantly surprised when Kudirka finished. On the paper in a firm hand was the notation: "Simas Kudirka," and an address in Klaipeda, Lithuania. Lundberg was fascinated by the East European-style script, which seemed beautiful to him.

With gestures and halting English punctuated by his excited breathing, Kudirka told Lundberg why he escaped. Lundberg recalled that he did not say much at the time: "He told me he came because he had a poor apartment. He got stuck with all the dirty jobs, all the nasty jobs . . . It sounded to me like he was working for someone he didn't like. They were giving him all the trash." Lundberg took a liking to Kudirka immediately: "He seemed intelligent and he was very outgoing."

As they were speaking, Commander Eustis came down with Lieutenant Morehouse. The Captain came up to Kudirka, who embraced him. Eustis was unaccustomed to such a show of affection among men and was momentarily nonplussed. "Oh, Captain, Captain, thank you!" he exclaimed as he held Eustis.

Eustis smiled at him and backed off. He was genuinely happy for Kudirka. Kudirka kept thanking him and they did not say anything more to each other.

The Captain returned to the wheelhouse with Lieutenant Morehouse, leaving Kudirka alone in the head behind a closed door guarded by Seaman Fowlie with Lieutenant Lundberg hovering nearby.

Several doors away from the head a radioman in the Communications Room was still trying to get acknowledgment from Boston of *Vigilant's* 2:23 P.M. message, which was already obsolete. Just as the radioman put the tape into the transmitter for another try, Boston signaled "Wait" and indicated the District had some message traffic of its own. The radioman waited and after several minutes received a routine weather report. He again asked Boston to roger for *Vigilant's* message, but Boston asked him to stand by for some other messages the District had for the *Vigilant*. The radioman waited.

Commander Eustis had just turned the top of the stairway in the wheelhouse when he noticed through the rear window that three Soviets were still on the flight deck. "What's taking them so long?" he wondered and considered for an instant to leave with them on board. But he immediately dismissed the thought. They could be considered hostages and an international incident was the last thing Eustis wanted to risk. The three Soviets seemed ready to be lifted off, but Eustis suspected they knew one of their men had escaped.

He hurried back down the stairway and past the Watchstander's Head to the Communications Room. The phone patch with the Admiral was still not complete, so he went back to see Kudirka again.

Meanwhile, Lt. Ryan in RCC had dialed Admiral Ellis's residence. His wife answered. The ensuing conversation was recorded on magnetic tapes in the District.[3]

"This is Lieutenant Ryan. May I speak to the Admiral, please?"

"One moment, please." Shortly Admiral Ellis was on the line.

"Admiral, this is Lieutenant Ryan in the RCC. I'm sorry to bother you, sir, but I couldn't get through to Captain Brown or to Commander Curry. The CO of the *Vigilant* wants a phone patch with one of the two and I couldn't get through, so now he wants to talk with you direct." Ryan asked the Admiral to stay by his phone while he dialed the Radio Station back to put Ellis on a conference call. He then called the Radio Station.

"This is Mr. Ryan. Are you ready for the phone patch?"

The Radio Station acknowledged.

"All right. I'm going to put it on hold and then I'm going to dial the Admiral," Ryan said.

"Yes, sir, I have a patch ready now," the Radio Station operator said, indicating he had the *Vigilant* in radio contact.

Ryan again dialed Admiral Ellis's number and told him everything was set up.

"Okay," Ellis replied.

Then the relay began.

"Coast Guard Cutter *Vigilant,* this is Coast Guard Boston, over," Ryan said.

"Yes, sir, this is Radio Boston."

"Okay, we're ready for that phone patch," Ryan declared.

"Yes, sir, stand by. Cutter *Vigilant,* Radio Boston."

"Radio Boston, Cutter *Vigilant,*" Lieutenant Lundberg had come to the microphone and responded.

"This is Radio Boston. I have the District Commander on the line. Are you ready for the phone patch? Over."

"Radio Boston. Cutter *Vigilant,*" Lundberg repeated. "My Commanding Officer at this moment is in a position where he can't readily get to the radio. However, I expect his position to be clear shortly so that he will have access shortly. How on that? Over." Lundberg's style of communicating was similar to most military men. It was oblique, had a technical tone, and was filled with redundancies. What he had just said was that Eustis was with Kudirka and would be by the microphone shortly.

"This is Radio Boston. Roger." The operator told Lieutenant Ryan the phone patch would be ready in a minute.

Another exchange followed between Ryan and the radio operator while Lundberg went to get Commander Eustis.

Admiral Ellis interjected. "Cutter *Vigilant,* this is Coast Guard Boston, Admiral Ellis on the line, over."

Eustis had come to the microphone. "Radio Boston. This is Cutter *Vigilant.* Over."

"Ralph?" the Admiral asked.

"This is Cutter *Vigilant.* Go ahead Admiral, over."

"Go ahead Eustis," Ellis countered.

The Captain of the *Vigilant* outlined the situation for Admiral Ellis. "Admiral, we're still alongside the Soviet vessel. We have a man aboard who has defected from the Soviet Union. We believe that they know he has defected."

Thinking the three Soviets had already left the ship, Eustis continued, "They have no men on deck. We are all ready to get away." He repeated Kudirka's request to Pakos and Lundberg earlier in the day and added, "What with the political situation of today has been very successful other than the events that occurred in the last hour, over." In his excitement, Eustis had flubbed the sentence, but meant that, aside from the defection, the meeting had been successful. Actually, Eustis could not know how the meeting went because he had been absent for most of it; he had equated success with the general international conviviality of the afternoon.

"Does the ship know he has come aboard your ship?" the Admiral asked. "If not, I think they should know that, over."

"Radio Boston, this is *Vigilant.* Roger. Understand they

suspect the man has defected the ship and is aboard the *Vigilant*. However, they have expressed no concrete desire to recover the man from the ship, over."

"This is Boston," Ellis said. Then he gave Eustis his reasons for wanting the defector returned. "In view of the nature of the present arrangements with them and in the interest of not fouling up our arrangements as far as the fishing situation is concerned, I think they should know this and if they choose to do nothing, keep him aboard, otherwise put him back, over."

"Boston, this is *Vigilant*. Roger on that," Eustis acknowledged without emotion. "We'll check out further with them as to whether or not they know that man is aboard and desire to return him to Soviet mother ship. If they have no indication that he is aboard or desire to recover him, we'll get underway at this time with man aboard."

He continued, "If they desire to recover him, we'll have them return man to mother ship. If he desires to jump from mother ship to *Vigilant* as we depart, we'll make an attempt to pick him up as he leaves mother ship and recover man and stand by for further instructions, over."

Eustis was already maneuvering around the order.

Ellis agreed with the procedure, but cautioned, "If the man jumps in the water, give the Russian ship the first opportunity to pick him up. Don't let him drown. Go get him if they are not going to get him, over."

"Radio Boston, this is Cutter *Vigilant*. Roger on that."

Eustis was hoping that if he did have to give Kudirka back, he would escape en route and there would be no question who would pick him up first. He indicated that to Admiral Ellis. "Inasmuch as Russian ship will be at anchor and we'll be underway, anticipate that it will probably be reasonable for us to recover man from water, over."

Ellis again cautioned. "Make sure you don't preempt them in taking that action." The Admiral simply wanted the Soviets to have Kudirka back. He could not countenance desertion.

"Radio Boston, this is *Vigilant.* Roger on that. We'll be underway directly and we'll keep you advised of situation as it progresses. Over."

"This is Boston. Roger. Good luck. Out." Ellis had rarely used the term "Good luck" to a commanding officer, but he used it then.

The conversation between Admiral Ellis and Commander Eustis, conducted over a regular marine frequency, was monitored by some people in New Bedford who regularly listened, because their husbands and fathers were fishermen. It was monitored by a New Bedford broadcaster. And it was monitored by radiomen aboard the *Sovetskaya Litva.*

The phone patch with the *Vigilant* was terminated, but Admiral Ellis and Lieutenant Ryan were still connected.

"Ryan?" Ellis asked. The tapes were still recording their voices.

"Yes, sir, Admiral."

"If you hear anything more of this—well, let me know. You had better get in touch with Captain Brown and tell him about this conversation."

"Yes, sir. I'll keep trying and when I reach him, I'll brief him on it."

"Yeah, he'll be home in a while."

"Yes, sir."

"But this, uh, could get a little hairy," Ellis speculated. "I don't know."

"Yes, sir. It sounds like it."

"The problem was that they should never have let him on board in the first place," the Admiral declared.

"Uh huh," Ryan replied noncommittally.

"That would have been difficult to do," Ellis reasoned, then added, "So, let me know what goes on anyway."

"Yes, sir, will do."

"Okay."

"Goodnight."

Aboard the *Vigilant* John Burt learned of the defection from a crewman. He did not give it much thought at the time, except that he had told his wife he would be home at six and now would be a little late.

When Robert Brieze noticed that three Soviets were refusing to leave the ship, he went to the wheelhouse to see what was happening. It was crowded with officers. Pakos and the two fisheries officials had also come up. Brieze asked Obolensky what was going on.

"A sailor from the Russian ship is seeking political asylum," Obolensky replied. "Commander Eustis has been talking with him."

Brieze was not at all surprised that someone would want to defect. He suspected some others might take the man's cue and try to leap across as well.

Gradually, all the civilians and several officers gravitated to the Captain's Cabin. Howard Nickerson found out what happened when he walked in. He would speak little of that night and say he was not a witness to the incident. He would say he felt helpless and without influence: "The worst thing is being a civilian in a military situation."

As the men talked in the Captain's Cabin, in walked Ivan Burkal, the man in the gray sweater, and their interpreter. They looked sullen and said nothing. All three sat down on a couch along the starboard wall, obviously planning to stay. Pakos, Gordon, and Obolensky, who had been standing, sat down in chairs opposite them. No one spoke as the men stared at each other from opposite sides of the cabin. The cabin looked like a comfortably appointed motel room, with bright wall-to-wall carpeting, a couch, chairs, lamps, and colors that contrasted sharply with the mood of the men, turned apprehensive by the presence of the Soviets.

They sat there in silence.

Obolensky finally hurried out to look for Commander Eustis and was soon followed by Lt. Commander Pakos.

The Executive Officer came into the Communications Room just as Eustis was finishing his phone patch with Admiral Ellis.

He recapped for Pakos what Admiral Ellis had said. Neither Eustis nor Pakos was pleased with the order, and neither had to tell the other how they felt. They both knew instinctively that returning Kudirka was not the thing to do.

"The Soviets are in your cabin now, Captain, but none of them is saying anything."

"Set mooring stations, Paul. I'm going back to talk to the defector and see what we can do about this."

He walked to the Watchstander's Head with Lieutenant Lundberg, who continued on down another flight of the stairway and onto the boat deck to supervise the unmooring.

Commander Eustis hesitated a moment outside the door to the head, wondering what he would tell Kudirka.

As "mooring stations" was piped over the loudspeakers, Lieutenant Lundberg, standing by the hatchway near the launch, noticed several people on the *Sovetskaya Litva* pointing animatedly to the bow of the *Vigilant.* "They must have seen him jump," he thought and gazed at the area where they were pointing. The fourteen-foot leap seemed incredible to him. He had even speculated that Kudirka may not have reached the rail, but grabbed the painter line* and hauled himself aboard. Looking at the motions of the Soviets, he was certain Kudirka had jumped right onto the rail. He would recall: "It was a fantastic leap. I don't think I could have jumped a distance like that." The leap from the rail of the *Sovetskaya Litva* to the bow of the *Vigilant* was actually an upward jump and required energy born only of desperation.

*Painter line—a line hanging from the bow of a boat used for towing or making fast.

Lundberg stood a while longer gazing at the *Sovetskaya Litva,* now fully lit. Her lights sparkled in the darkness. The *Vigilant,* by contrast, was dark. Only her anchor lights were on and the passageways glowed a dull red from night lights along the aircastle deck. A chilly, fifteen-knot wind blew across the deck, nudging his hands into his pockets and his shoulders upward to protect his neck from the cold. Lundberg waited for the unmooring, but nothing happened. The details were on station, but no one relayed orders to either unmoor or secure from stations. He stood a few more minutes watching the people on the other ship talking and still pointing. Then he went back inside to the vicinity of the Watchstander's Head.

Meanwhile, the radioman was still trying without success to get Boston to roger for the 2:23 P.M. message. Starting at 5:29 P.M. the teletype in the cutter's Communications Room cleared another weather report, a routine message about the fishing delegation, and a message about the *Vigilant*'s starboard launch which had been left in Portland, Maine, for repairs. After some more routine traffic from Boston, the radioman tried again, but this time experienced some more technical difficulties with the transmitter. It would be another forty-five minutes (6:38 P.M.) before the District would finally roger for the 2:23 P.M. message from the *Vigilant.*

By 5:30 P.M. the Captain's Cabin was crowded; some more officers had come in and were mingling with the delegation. Burkal and the man in the gray sweater were still on the couch along the wall. But their interpreter had gone to the port side and sat down next to Burt. He seemed unperturbed and uninvolved.

Someone had turned on a television set, and highlights of a football game flashed on the screen. No one was really paying attention and someone soon turned it off. The man in the gray sweater and Burkal were conferring in whispers, while the Americans spoke to each other with subdued voices.

Burt and the Soviet interpreter had casually struck up a conversation. "I am a teacher," the interpreter said in a pronounced accent.

"Oh yeah?" Burt replied.

"I am a fleet teacher. I go from boat to boat and give lessons." Genrikas Baltrunas, like Kudirka, was a Lithuanian. He told Burt a little about his professional background, but nothing personal. Brieze joined in. He was naturally curious about the man who came from a country bordering his native Latvia. None of the three mentioned the defection and the conversation soon tapered off.

Some minutes later, Burt turned to Brieze and muttered gruffly, "What's goin' on here? When are we gonna get home?"

"I don't know." Brieze was beginning to worry. He had told his family he would be home by seven. They now would be late as it was.

"We should just take off, put these guys back and take the defector home," Burt declared.

Brieze concurred.

Burkal and the man in the gray sweater were still conferring. Obolensky overheard them, but he could not understand the language. Burkal was Russian, and all day long the Soviets had spoken in that language. But now these two were conferring in Lithuanian and Obolensky knew it was because they did not want him to know what they were saying.

They were planning something, or rather, as was apparent to everyone there, the man in the gray sweater—the commissar— was planning something.

After nodding agreement to something, Burkal got up and approached Obolensky, who was flanked by Gordon and Lieutenant Morehouse.

He stood in front of the U.S. interpreter and said somberly, "One of our sailors is drunk and aboard your ship. He is probably talking with some Americans. Please conduct a search and see that his is returned."

Obolensky translated the remark to the others. Lieutenant Morehouse then hurried out of the cabin to look for Commander Eustis. The other Americans in the cabin took what Burkal said a little more cynically and brushed it off.

Outside the cabin a sailor told the lieutenant from Washington that the Captain was with the defector, so Morehouse went to the wheelhouse where he saw Lt. Commander Pakos. He told him what the Acting Fleet Commander had just requested in the cabin.

"Should I interrupt and tell the Captain," Morehouse asked.

"No. You'd better wait until he comes out," Pakos suggested. Pakos did not want him to disturb the Captain with such an absurd request. He had seen the defector throughout the day, was face to face with him less than an hour earlier, and knew Burkal's statement was a lie.

CHAPTER

14

Just when everything seemed perfect, Commander Eustis was confronted with a major dilemma. He was surprised by Admiral Ellis's order to return the defector and did not feel it was right. As he hesitated in front of the door to the head, he told himself the order was not unequivocal. He would still bring the defector in to New Bedford.

Seaman Fowlie moved from the door and Eustis opened it. The Captain and the defector looked at each other in a silence that made each a little self-conscious. Then Kudirka, his body still quivering with excitement, thanked him again for his being saved. Eustis, a little embarrassed by Kudirka's emotionalism, knew he could not return the defector.

He asked Kudirka who he was and what position he held aboard the Soviet ship.[1]

The ensuing conversation took a half hour, and Eustis would say long afterward that he remembered few details, although the image of Kudirka would remain indelible in the Captain's mind for a long, long time. The pain and humiliation of the memory—the order which challenged the Captain's moral upbringing—and the passage of time would make up the veil that would obscure the moments he and Kudirka spent together.

Simas Kudirka told Eustis his name and that he was a radio operator aboard the Soviet vessel. He said he was from Lithuania. Reaching into his shirt pocket, he pulled out a small bundle of papers and a notebook about the size of a palm. He sorted through them—those possessions that documented his existence—and gave Commander Eustis a booklet containing a number of papers. The Captain browsed through them, but could not recognize the Cyrillic notations. He came upon a photograph. It was a headshot of Kudirka, obviously taken some years earlier. Kudirka now had a receding hairline, he looked more haggard, his face much thinner, but still Eustis thought he must be in his mid-thirties.

The defector sorted through some more of the papers until he came upon another photograph, a headshot of a woman in her early thirties. She was pretty, with short hair, and looked demure. Her lips were upturned in the beginnings of a smile. Kudirka told him it was his wife and added that he had two children.

Eustis was awed by Kudirka. He knew so little of him, yet felt a sympathy and compassion towards him. A devoted husband and family man with two children himself, Eustis remembered thinking: "How could a man leave his family and his whole life so completely as he would have to do? . . . I was very impressed with him, that he had made a decision to do something like this, well knowing what the impact on his family would be."

The Captain of the *Vigilant* leafed through some more of Kudirka's papers, unable to recognize any of them. Handing him back the papers, Eustis said, "They know you're aboard our ship. Three of your people are still aboard in my cabin."

Kudirka's jubilation evaporated and a stern look molded his face. "No give me back! No give me back! They kill me! They kill me!" he repeated as he drew his finger across his throat. "They kill me! They kill me! My life no good over there!" Kudirka exclaimed.

Exasperated, Eustis admitted he did not know what he was going to do. He explained to Kudirka Admiral Ellis's order but

added that if he jumped overboard there would be a launch
standing by to grab him.

"I will jump! I will jump!" Kudirka said excitedly, using the
new word he learned. "You will save me, yes?"

Yes, Eustis would save him. He told Kudirka a launch would
be waiting.

Eustis would later hedge on answering whether he in fact
invited Kudirka to jump into the water so he could bypass his
orders. Pulling the man from the water had taken on the markings of a fetish, and, somehow, for all the officers involved in
the case, a wet defector was different from a dry defector. Eustis
would never say he told Kudirka to jump overboard because "it
would jeopardize people who are still around [in the service],
but I'm sure this is the way people felt." Actually, the tactic
could jeopardize no one but Eustis himself as Commanding
Officer. However, he was reluctant to discuss the subject, because he also did not want to reveal officers who supported him
as condoners of insubordination. Since the subject was later
broached in testimony before the Board of Investigation, and
Eustis cannot be damaged by the case any more than he already
has been, there is no reason not to mention that subject here,
because, in a moral sense, it is to his advantage. Gordon, Obolensky, Brieze, and Kudirka himself, in a subsequent conversation with Obolensky, confirmed that Eustis told the defector to
jump overboard so he could be grabbed by the launch.

The Captain circumspectly said as much in an interview
some months after the incident.

After he told Kudirka about the launch, Eustis ordered
someone to get him a life jacket and instructed Lieutenant
Lundberg to call the Gay Head Coast Guard Station for a
forty-four-foot patrol boat. The Captain was not waiting for the
permission from the District that he had asked for in his 2:23
P.M. message—the message the District had not yet received.

When Kudirka put the vest on, he looked even more like a
man in trouble. Huddled in the dim toilet, he told the Captain

some more about himself. Both had some things in common, superficial things that under the circumstances cemented their short, ill-fated relationship. They were both about the same age —Eustis thirty-seven, Kudirka forty-one, but appearing much younger, each had two children, and both came from seafaring families. They were both Christians, yet their upbringings were alien, and their meeting under such dramatic circumstances attested to it.

Eustis would reminisce: "He really spent most of his time saying how glad he was to be here. I don't recall him talking about whether he had been politically suppressed or had problems of a political nature, although from his concern for himself it was obvious that he had these problems."

During that half hour Eustis was convinced the defector's intentions were genuine and his move was not impulsive. This realization put mounting pressure on the Captain as he approached the hour of the gravest decision of his life.

Shortly after six, Eustis was called to the radio. Lieutenant Ryan of RCC had initiated a phone patch with the *Vigilant.*

En route Eustis ran into Lieutenant Morehouse, who told him the Soviets claimed one of their sailors was drunk aboard the *Vigilant* and they wanted him back. Eustis ignored the report and went to the transmitter in the Communications Room.

"Cutter *Vigilant,* Radio Boston," the operator said. His voice was chopped by static.

"Radio Boston, this is Cutter *Vigilant.* You are broken, but readable, over."

CHAPTER

15

At 6 P.M. Captain Brown came up the gravel walk of his home. It was a modest-looking, navy-gray ranch house nestled in a clump of trees overlooking the ocean off Hesperus Drive in Gloucester. To the east was a large tract of land on which sat a stone castle—The Hammond Museum, a huge storehouse of medieval history and reflection of the age of knighthood and personal honor.

Permeating his home was Brown's love for the sea and the service. "Welcome aboard," proclaimed a wooden placard hanging near a breezeway to the left of the front entrance. Inside, large picture windows afforded a spectacular view of the rocky shore and the sea beyond. The bright furniture and thick cream and green carpets were well appointed and gave one a feeling of sumptuousness. The time was pealed by soft ship's bells which stroked six as he came in. Everywhere there was attention to detail and good taste.

"Halcyon" Brown called his home. The word was displayed on a wooden plaque over the front door. It meant peace, quietude, a happy interlude.

A downstairs den with a sign "Captain's Quarters" on the door was Brown's retreat. It, too, had the flavor of the sea and appropriately so. His father had started the family tradition of Coast Guard service and a full-size painting of him in dress whites graced a wall of the den. A lamp on a small table near the door shone on a color photograph of Captain Brown commissioning his own son into the Coast Guard.

Brown had graduated from the Coast Guard Academy in 1942. After a two-year tour at sea, he began flight training and became an aviator. He was assigned to an air station in Salem, Massachusetts, where he served until 1946. Then a lieutenant, Brown was a member of the International Ice Patrol operating out of Newfoundland from 1946 to 1947. Many times he faced life and death situations in search and rescue operations. He was awarded an Air Medal for "meritorious achievement" in rescuing eighteen survivors of a Belgian airliner crash. For that the Belgian government also designated him a Knight of the Order of Leopold.

From 1947 to 1952 Brown had served as an aviator in East Coast and Great Lakes air stations and was, during that time, promoted to Lieutenant Commander.

After years of flying, the inevitable attrition of older age and necessity to make room for younger blood nudged him into Category III—a grounded administrator. His first staff position was Chief of Search and Rescue Operations of the Ninth District in Cleveland, Ohio. Brown then went on to a succession of positions in operational and staff capacities. He earned the rank of Captain in 1964, served as Commanding Officer of Group Boston starting in 1966, later became Chief of Operations of the First District, and in June, 1970—just five months earlier—was named Chief of Staff under Admiral Ellis.

Now, as Acting Commander, and a minute away from a telephone call that would enmesh him in the greatest crisis of his career, he walked into his home.

His wife, Anne, a slim, dark-haired woman, was waiting with news. She knew from years of experience that a call home from RCC was important. When she told him Lieutenant Ryan had called, he knew instantly what it concerned. Without taking off his coat, he hurried to the telephone and called RCC.

Halcyon was about to end.

Lieutenant Ryan answered the telephone and as he spoke with Brown, tape recorders in RCC recorded their conversation.

"Okay," Ryan said. "At the time the man was on board the *Vigilant* and the Russians were getting ready to cast off."

He relayed the fact that Eustis said there were no Russians aboard the *Vigilant,* then repeated it to make sure it registered. "There was nobody on deck and they were ready to cast off. The Russians appeared to know that the man was on board, but they had not expressed any desire to recover him. The Admiral told him to make sure the Russians knew the guy was aboard and to give him back if the Russians wanted him back."

"Yes," Brown said.

"And then if he did go back, to cast off. If the man jumped overboard and tried to get ashore to be sure to give the Russians a chance to rescue the man. If the Russians did not rescue the man, then we would rescue the man."

"Yes," Brown interjected again.

"That's the way it stood, and the Admiral wanted to make sure you knew about it."

"How did the guy get on the *Vigilant?*"

"I don't know, sir."

"You don't know?"

"No, he just said the man, the CO said the man was on board. So that's the latest thing."

Ryan continued that he received a call from the Woods Hole Coast Guard Station on Cape Cod asking for an explanation about the *Vigilant*'s request for a patrol boat from Gay Head. "I don't know . . . I don't know if the man is still aboard and that's why the *Vigilant* is requesting a rendezvous, or if the *Vigilant* is requesting a forty-four footer out there in case the guy jumps overboard after the *Vigilant* leaves, or what the story is."

"I tell you," Brown replied. "Are things still moving in the same direction?"

"Yes, sir."

"Okay, well, look. I think it might be preferred to keep that fellow on board the *Vigilant* and tell the *Vigilant* to proceed to New Bedford." Brown here was still inclined toward following the staff's advice, which he, as Acting District Commander could legally do, regardless of Admiral Ellis's instructions to Commander Eustis.

He asked whether Ryan had notified Flag Plot at Headquarters.

"No, sir."

"Okay, notify Flag Plot that the *Vigilant* has the Russian aboard."

"Should I call the *Vigilant* first and see if the guy is still aboard?"

"Yes," Brown replied.

"Fine. Also, we put the *Decisive* on Bravo Zero. Did we ever take her off?" Ryan reminded. The *Decisive* had been waiting for an emergency assignment all afternoon.

"Take her off Bravo Zero now, Ken."

"All right, sir. I'll get a hold of . . . I'll set up a phone patch and get the latest information."

Captain Brown cautioned the RCC Controller to keep the defection secret and directed him to contact U.S. Immigration authorities at Boston's Logan Airport. "Get a hold of the supervisor and make sure you know what his name is. And tell him for the time being, that this information is to be held closed. In other words . . ."

"Uh huh," Lieutenant Ryan interjected.

Brown again cautioned him that he was not to say much over the phone. "While you're doing that," he continued, "I think Moller can . . . I don't know, do all these things that got to be done." He was referring to Radarman Moller, the Assistant Controller, suggesting the duty officer begin taking procedural steps to inform appropriate officers in the District and in Headquarters. "I don't know who is going to hold the press on this thing."

"Uh huh," Ryan interjected again. "Well, I think we better find . . . the first thing we ought to find out is, if the man stayed aboard."

"Yeah," Brown concurred.

"And then work from there and notify Flag Plot and see how they want to handle it," Lieutenant Ryan suggested.

He was taking his cue from Brown. Although Ryan had heard Admiral Ellis order Commander Eustis to return the defector, it hinged upon whether the Soviets would want him back. And he heard Eustis say he might be coming in with the defector. So Captain Brown's statement that the defector should be brought to New Bedford was not contradictory to Ryan, and he was suggesting the necessary routine procedures to be followed.

For his part, Brown was too preoccupied to tell Lieutenant Ryan that the case should be in the hands of the State Department entirely. He was considering new factors. "And maybe we can get them to release some plain language type of thing," Brown said, indicating a news release could come from Washington.

Brown asked Ryan to contact Lt. (jg) Graham Chynoweth, Public Information Officer of the First District, and have him stand by. "It might be desirable for him to go to New Bedford, but, uh, this is something to kind of hold on to for the time being."

"Uh huh," Ryan concurred. "All right, I'll get a hold of Chynoweth and tell him to stand by until something definite comes in."

"I will be here," Brown said.

"All right, sir. I will get in touch with you as soon as I can get everything on it, and I'll start in on it."

"Okay."

"All right, sir. Good night."

Twenty minutes later Lieutenant Ryan completed a phone patch with the *Vigilant*. It was then that Commander Eustis had interrupted his talk with Kudirka to come to the transmitter.

Eustis told Ryan that Kudirka was still on board and feared he would be killed if returned. "His indications are that, uh, regardless of what we do, that, uh, he will go over the side as soon as we depart this area and, uh, hope for the best, uh, over."

Static chopped the airwaves, forcing numerous pauses punctuated by "uhs."

"Uh, this is Boston Radio. Do you wish to talk to Captain Brown, over?"

"Uh, Boston Rescue, this is *Vigilant.* Uh, roger. I would appreciate any, uh, assistance or, uh, information that the, uh, Chief of Staff might provide at this time, uh, over."

Eustis here was referring to Brown as Chief of Staff and not Acting District Commander. He was in effect ignoring instructions received from Admiral Ellis and was searching for something more favorable from Captain Brown.

"This is Boston RCC, roger. Wait one and I will get him on the conference call. I'll get back to you, over."

Some minutes later the connection with Captain Brown was complete.

"Ralph, uh, this is Captain Brown." It was the first contact Captain Brown and Commander Eustis had had all day.

"Captain, uh, the present situation is that I, uh, have presently on board one Russian defector, uh, the Communications Officer on board, uh, plus three of his, uh, superiors that are down in the Cabin."

This surprised Brown. He thought at first there were four defectors, but as he listened he realized what Eustis was saying.

"Uh, defector indicates his intentions are regardless of what we do tonight, uh, he's going over the side if he has the chance when we depart here."

He continued, "I have, uh, talked considerably with the individual within the last half hour. I believe he is sincere in his, uh, intentions to defect to this country. The political situation,

I believe, is, uh, tense at this time. Today's affair went, uh, pretty well until this situation arose. Uh, I would recommend —uh, rather, I am looking for instructions."

Eustis already had instructions from Admiral Ellis, but was acting as if they did not exist.

Before Brown could even respond, Eustis suggested they keep the defector and escort the Soviet ship back into international waters.

At that point a patrol aircraft looking for landing instructions cut into the frequency.

"Yes, uh, Ralph, I didn't get but very little of that. You were broken up plus, uh, the beeper is interfering. Now, exactly how many people do you have aboard?"

Eustis repeated the situation to Captain Brown, who acknowledged that he understood. "Now, are the four or five officers that are aboard—are they aboard at our invitation?"

"The four to five officers that are aboard are on board at our invitation," Eustis responded. "I say again. They are on board at our invitation."

Static kept interfering and Brown kept asking for clarification. Commander Eustis again repeated the situation, that he had a defector aboard plus several Soviet officers.

"Are they trying to convince him to go aboard the Russian ship?"

"Boston Rescue, this is *Vigilant*. The Russian officers have had no communications with the defector since he has arrived aboard the *Vigilant*." He told Brown that he himself was the only man who had talked with Kudirka.

"Uh, roger that Captain, uh, I understand and, uh, I also understand that you are still alongside of the *Kaliningrad*." Brown was not yet aware the ship was actually the *Sovetskaya Litva*.

"Boston Rescue, this is *Vigilant*. Uh, roger your last, uh, roger your last, over."

Captain Brown kept pressing for clarification. He asked

again whether the Soviet officers were invited aboard. Were they aware of the defection?

Commander Eustis replied that the officers did know Kudirka was aboard, but emphasized they only indicated so "informally."

Brown was quickly digesting all the information. His only fear, as had been throughout the day, was how the Soviets would react to the situation. He wondered if he had all the information. "Uh, roger on that. Um, stand by please. *Vigilant,* um, I have no further . . ." he thought a moment, then, "Oh, one more question, uh . . ."

The patrol aircraft again cut into the frequency, asking for landing instructions.

Brown was still talking. "*Vigilant,* uh, have the Russian officers requested the return of the individual, have they requested his return at all? Over." He heard no reply.

The Boston Radio operator cut in, saying he had not switched Brown into the circuit. Brown repeated the question.

"Boston Rescue, this is *Vigilant.* Uh, on your last, Soviet officers have, uh, informed via my Executive Officer that individual be returned to Soviet vessel. They have not requested his return by name or position, uh, over."

Brown asked how long Eustis expected the Soviet officers to remain on board and Eustis replied they were waiting for a decision.

"Uh, it appears to me," Eustis declared, "that the political situation is such, uh, that we should return all Soviet officers, uh, to their vessel and apprise them that we will stand by with, uh, possible political refugee aboard until further advised, uh, over." Eustis was anxious to get the Soviets off his ship.

But Brown was worried about what the Soviets would do. "Um, do you think that they would leave the *Vigilant,* uh, at your request and with the defector still aboard?" He repeated it: "Do you think that they would, uh, leave the *Vigilant* and, uh, still leave the defector aboard? Over." The consideration was incredible, since the Soviet vessel as well as the *Vigilant* were in territorial waters and under the jurisdiction of the United States.

Eustis reminded Brown of that. "Uh, Boston Rescue, this is Cutter *Vigilant*, uh, believe that they, uh, probably would depart *Vigilant* at this time, uh, if directed to do so, but, uh, would be very unhappy about it. They are presently within U.S. territorial seas and we have, uh, full jurisdiction of the situation, over."

"Roger on that," Brown replied. "This is a situation which is going to have to be resolved by State Department. Uh, I would suggest that you ask the officers to return to their own ship, ask the officers to return to their own ship and remain in your present position, over."

Captain Brown's stance here was unequivocal; he stated flatly that the decision on Kudirka was to be made by Washington.

Pleased, Eustis rogered the statement and repeated his instructions. "I should, uh, tell officers to return to their own ship and stand by awaiting further instructions from U.S. State Department, uh, over."

"That is Charlie. That is Charlie," Brown declared, affirming what Eustis said. "Do you have anything further for me?"

There was nothing more. Eustis would stand by for further instructions. From here on the Captain of the *Vigilant* had every reason to believe that all subsequent instructions would be with the approval or direction of the State Department.

But from here on Captain Brown would unwittingly befuddle his own plans.

"Tell Commander Eustis that I'll go ahead and call the Admiral and advise him of the situation," Brown told Lieutenant Ryan over the phone when Eustis had signed off the phone patch.

"All right, sir. Do you want me to call Flag Plot on this or, uh . . ."

"No. Hold on a minute. I'll get back to you shortly."

It was a simple phrase mentioned in passing: *"No. Hold on a minute. I'll get back to you shortly,"* but in saying it, Brown broke the critical relay net between the RCC Controller in Boston and Flag Plot at Headquarters. Had Brown not said it, Lieutenant Ryan would have routinely called Flag Plot and, even though he would not know it, set in motion the process for getting further advice from the State Department. But Brown told the lieutenant to wait. He wanted first to check with Admiral Ellis. He did not want to go over the Admiral's head without his knowledge.

Everything now rested on Captain Brown's shoulders. He knew he was trapped between two contradictory positions: he knew the decision was up to the State Department and he knew that Admiral Ellis wanted the defector returned. He would either have to convince Ellis to change his mind, the possibility of which he realized was unlikely; ignore Ellis's instructions; or ignore what Headquarters had said. He was suddenly in a bind and felt inextricably caught. As he put the telephone down an uneasy feeling came over him—a feeling that his career was at an end.[1]

CHAPTER

16

Captain Brown began wondering how he was going to solve his problem as he took off his coat. He had had it on since he came home and was beginning to feel hot. His wife took it to a closet while he slowly picked up the telephone again to dial Admiral Ellis's home number.[1] He would have to convince him to keep the defector.

Ellis, who during his post-operative convalescence was limited to two trips up and down stairs daily, had come downstairs for dinner. He was in the midst of a meal when the telephone rang. Brown was familiar with his Admiral's habits and knew Ellis would be eating when he called shortly after 6:30 P.M.

"I'm sorry for interrupting your dinner, Admiral," Brown said. "Lieutenant Ryan told me you were in contact with Commander Eustis, and I went to him for an updating."

"My God!" Ellis exploded. "Is Eustis still alongside?" He had imagined a very simple, civil, routine transfer.

"Yes, sir. He's still alongside." He was not talking on a friend-to-friend basis anymore, having been cowed by Ellis's first reaction. "He still has the Russian officers in his cabin, but they haven't indicated their intentions or desires. They're like mummies."

"I told Eustis to return the guy if they made a request for him. Did he ask if they wanted him back?"

"I don't know, Admiral."

"Did you get anything from the Commandant?"

"No, sir." Brown told him that the only instructions he received from Headquarters were to follow traditional search and rescue procedures if the man was in the water. "I told Commander Eustis to keep the defector in seclusion, to invite the Russian officers to leave the ship, and to stay alongside the Russian vessel to give us time to get further advice from the Commandant."

Ellis squelched the idea with a facetious, "If you haven't gotten anything out of Washington by now, you're never going to get anything out of Washington."

This phrase stuck in Brown's mind and he had no argument, because he felt Ellis was right. What had Washington told him up to now? Nothing—or so he thought. Brown's military mind worked in a very ordered fashion. He had been exposed to military discipline and routine almost all his life. The supreme rule was deeply embedded in his mind: one follows one's orders —regardless of what they are. Duty was everything, and Brown was keenly aware of this. Admiral Ellis was giving instructions, specific instructions, whereas Admiral Hammond in Washington had not.

"Go back to Eustis and tell him if they don't know the man is aboard to make sure they do know he is aboard, and further tell them if they want the man returned to their ship they're going to have to make a request for him. And if they don't want him back aboard, they can take him and put him ashore themselves."

"I'll have to go back to Eustis," Brown replied. That ended the conversation. He would no longer pursue advice from Washington. Brown would explain to the Board of Investigation: "I assumed these last instructions were given in lieu of requesting additional advice from the Commandant [Headquarters]."

The only other connection to Washington, the RCC–Flag

Plot–State Department communications link, he had unwittingly destroyed some minutes earlier by telling Lieutenant Ryan, the RCC Controller, to "hold on a minute."

Imbued with the sense of unwavering respect for his superiors and to duty that for thirty years had nurtured his career, Captain Brown dialed RCC for another phone patch with the *Vigilant* so he could relay Admiral Ellis's instructions. His instincts, however, still called out for compassion towards the defector. These conflicting emotions made Brown visibly disconsolate as he sat at the edge of his couch by his telephone. He looked silently at his wife standing nearby.

Aboard the *Vigilant* Captain Brown's call had evoked relief and gratitude in Commander Eustis. He hurried from the Communications Room to the Watchstander's Head. "I'm still waiting for instructions from my superiors," he said innocently as he stuck his head in the doorway, but elicited fearful concern from Kudirka.

"No give me back! No give me back!" the defector replied in a warning tone.

Eustis reassured him, then went to the wheelhouse to tell his Executive Officer what Brown had said. They were both pleased that the State Department would decide the issue.

"I'm going down to get the Russians off," Eustis told him and descended the stairway.

Pakos stayed awhile in the wheelhouse, then also went below. He walked into the Officers' Wardroom where several officers were gathered, discussing the situation. He sat down by Lt.(jg) Lawrence Hale.

"I don't think we're going to return him," he said. "The Captain doesn't want to give him back."

Lieutenant Hale seemed pleased. Rumors had spread among the crew after the phone patch with Admiral Ellis that the defector would have to be returned; now things began to look brighter.

Pakos continued, "If they tell me to take over and obey because Commander Eustis won't, I'll also refuse."

Inside the Captain's Cabin, forward of the Officers' Wardroom, Alexis Obolensky and William Gordon had been discussing the situation with the other civilians. There was no question in any of their minds that Kudirka should be kept. The case to them was simple: the Soviets were in U.S. territorial waters and the Americans had complete control of the situation. A man's political rights were at stake. Kudirka should be handed over to the State Department, which, they all knew, was routine in defection cases.

Ivan Burkal and the other two Soviets sensed this also. Obolensky would say long afterward that he exchanged some words with Burkal (he did not remember specifics) and came away with the feeling that the Soviets felt precarious and would have left the ship if ordered to do so. The other Americans echoed this idea. They all sensed that the Soviets would have left the *Vigilant* at that point if ordered off.

While the Americans huddled, the man in the gray sweater was piped back aboard his ship, moments before Commander Eustis walked in after his first phone patch with Captain Brown. Some of the others were slightly puzzled by the commissar's movements, but Brieze immediately deduced that the man in the gray sweater was going back to confer with someone. Brieze, with his innate suspicion of the Soviets, believed they were monitoring the phone patches and taking their cues from them. As it turned out, he was right.

When Commander Eustis walked in, all eyes turned towards him. Here was the man who had the fate of Kudirka in his hands—the Captain of the *Vigilant.* He walked up to Baltrunas, who was on the couch next to Burt and Brieze. "I can do one of two things. I can either give you the defector, or I can order you off my ship and take the defector back to New Bedford," he said matter-of-factly. Burt and Brieze listened silently, hoping the Soviets would be ordered off.

Baltrunas rose, went across the cabin to Burkal and repeated

what Eustis had said. The Captain continued to both of them,
"If he wants to return to his ship, he can go. Otherwise, you
will have to leave this ship, while we get orders from our State
Department."

This no doubt brightened Burkal's prospects. The Captain
was accommodating him by revealing his options. If, as Obolensky had sensed in talking with him, Burkal felt precarious,
he now stiffened, because things all of a sudden appeared to be
negotiable.

Feeling on firmer ground, Burkal refused to leave and asked
to see Kudirka, but Eustis would not let him.

"They can't give him back," Brieze muttered to no one in
particular as he listened to the exchange. He looked out of place
with his work clothes and cap, commenting on fateful negotiations between two uniformed officers.

Gordon and Obolensky were restless and talked between
themselves, while Eustis spoke to Burkal. Obolensky brushed
the back of his head with his hand, as was typical of him when
he was in deep thought. Gordon looked unperturbed, but was
worried.

"Could we speak to you alone?" Gordon asked Eustis, and
the Captain immediately agreed. He seemed eager for opinions.
The two civilian fisheries officials walked out with him and went
into an adjoining stateroom where Gordon and Obolensky insisted the matter was not open for discussion and should be
handled strictly by the State Department.

Commander Eustis reassured them that his superiors were
getting in touch with the State Department. Brown had told
him as much just minutes earlier. Gordon and Obolensky urged
Eustis to speak again to his superiors, tell them the defector
adamantly refused to return, and insist that asylum be granted.
They told him an issue of human rights was at stake and had
to be considered. None of the men remembered details of their
conversation, but Gordon would recall: "Obolensky and I were
not satisfied personally that the State Department had been

adequately appraised of the situation . . . being aware of other incidents, we could philosophize that the *Vigilant* was U.S. territory regardless of where it was, and that anyone aboard it should be treated either as a U.S. citizen or as a defector would as if on shore . . . Technically it [the *Sovetskaya Litva*], too, was on U.S. soil and could be ordered to leave or be seized . . . This was discussed among ourselves."

Commander Eustis wholeheartedly agreed and assured Gordon and Obolensky that his superiors were that very moment getting advice from the State Department.

But, while the essence of Captain Brown's first telephone patch was spreading optimism throughout the cutter, Brown had again requested a connection, this time to relay what Admiral Ellis had just told him. The tapes at RCC again recorded the conversation.

"Radio Boston, this is Cutter *Vigilant.* Roger," the radioman said. "The Executive Officer is on the bridge. The Captain is in conference with the Russians, over."

Lieutenant Ryan, who was monitoring the call, asked Captain Brown with whom he wished to speak.

"I'll talk to Commander Eustis, I guess," he said resignedly.

"*Vigilant,* Boston," the operator relayed to the ship. "They'd like to talk to Commander Eustis."

Lt. Commander Pakos had come to the radio. "Boston Radio, this is Cutter *Vigilant.* Roger. At the present time Commander Eustis is, uh, trying to explain to the Russian officers that, uh, we are going to stand by and await a decision from the State Department and are trying to encourage them to return to the Russian ship. However, if this is really priority traffic, I'll try and break him loose."

"Uh, *Vigilant?* Am I talking to Commander Pakos?"

"Yes, sir, you are. This is Commander Pakos."

"The situation is this," Brown started, "and I understand in talking with the District Commander that instructions to Commander Eustis were to ask the Russians if they wanted the defector to return aboard. Was this question ever put to them point blank to your knowledge? Over."

"This is *Vigilant.* I haven't any specific knowledge on that, Captain."

"I'm going to have to talk with Commander Eustis."

Pakos started to put down the microphone, then in an afterthought continued. "Uh, Captain Brown. Maybe I can shorten some of the traffic here. If the question is posed or was posed, uh, and the answer is in the affirmative, do you want me to pass on any action for Commander Eustis or, uh, do you still want to speak with him? Over."

"If their reply is in the affirmative, then the man is to be returned to the Russian vessel, over."

"This is *Vigilant.* Roger. Uh, I understand that, Captain, and I'll pass that along to Captain Eustis and I'll advise you within two or three minutes on this subject, Captain."

Pakos put down the microphone and left to look for Commander Eustis. He was perturbed by the order.

Pakos found Eustis conferring with Gordon and Obolensky in the stateroom adjoining the Captain's Cabin. He told him Captain Brown was on a phone patch. "He said if the Soviets ask for the defector he is to be returned."

Gordon and Obolensky looked at Eustis, their deepest suspicions confirmed.

Meanwhile, Captain Brown was still on the line with the *Vigilant.* "Uh, are we open at both ends at the moment?"

"No, sir, we're not," the operator replied. "Do you want me to hold this phone patch active or hang up and have them call you back?"

"No. Hold the phone patch active for the moment." Brown was waiting for Commander Eustis to come to the microphone.

"Just disconnect the transmitter," Lieutenant Ryan interjected as he listened in.

"Ken? Can you talk to me now?" Brown asked.

"Yes, sir."

Although Brown still had deep misgivings about Admiral Ellis's instructions, he had not revealed them to either Commander Eustis or Lt. Commander Pakos, because it would have undermined the instructions he felt duty-bound to give. But he did speak more openly to the RCC Controller, revealing to Lieutenant Ryan some of his apprehension over the decision.

"Now," Brown said, "did you understand Commander Eustis to say that if this fellow was to be returned to the Russians' vessel, he would go over the side at this first opportunity?"

"Yes, sir," Ryan replied. "The way it sounded he said the man was in fear of his life and he said he would go over the side even if, uh, even if he received no help from the *Vigilant*."

"Okay. I'm going back to the Admiral with that piece of information." Brown still hoped he could persuade Ellis to reconsider his decision.

"Aye, sir. And you're going to call me back in four or five?"

"Yes. I will be back just as fast as I can."

"All right, sir," Ryan replied and hung up.

Again Brown hurriedly dialed the home of Admiral Ellis, who was still eating dinner. When the Admiral answered, Brown told him what he hoped would be a shocking enough fact to change Ellis's mind. "When I spoke with Commander Eustis he said the man stated his life would be in danger if he was returned."

"Brown! They are not barbarians!" Ellis retorted in exasperation. "We have no reason to believe that this would actually happen! Get the guy back aboard!"

With a long, resigned, drawn-out sigh and in a breaking voice, Brown said, "Yes—sir," and put down the telephone.

While the case seemed destined to be decided on a parochial level—both in reasoning and procedure—a chance for widespread dissemination of the news and accompanying public scrutiny occurred about that same time in New Bedford, home port of the *Vigilant.*

Newsman Bob Couto had hurried to work shortly before 6 P.M. to a single-story, brick, waterfront building that housed the facilities of radio station WBSM. The building, just east of a steel bridge that seperated New Bedford from adjacent Fairhaven, was next to a harbor channel, and its southern windows faced the hurricane dike that enclosed the harbor far beyond the bridge.

The panorama included State Pier, where the *Vigilant* had her berth. At the pier that evening was the high endurance cutter *Escanaba,* which shared a dock with the *Vigilant.* But the *Escanaba* was only a massive shadow in the dark, and the view from the radio building at night was one only of night lights in the city and moving headlights along the bridge.

Couto, in his late twenties and a veteran broadcaster, exuded confidence and took pride in his work. His tenacity in pursuing news of the *Vigilant* incident during the coming weeks and his success in getting details that would be quoted by major newspapers would win for him a United Press International broadcasters' award and a Story of the Year Award.

When he arrived in the newsroom, Couto looked over some items coming over the UPI broadcast wire. He was casually dressed for his night stint and perused the copy through horn-rimmed glasses that gave him a studious air. That night he was onto something unique. Looking at the routine copy, he kept pondering on what he had heard earlier. A "high-placed confidential source" had told him that someone would defect to the *Vigilant.* He learned this in mid-afternoon before Kudirka actually defected. Couto would adamantly refuse to reveal his source, but would assure that it "was a source of information as good as being on board the ship."[2]

Couto had received his tip about 3 P.M., about one half hour after the staff conference in Captain Brown's office. Who could have given Couto this information? Could it have been an officer in the First District? One of the officers in the staff meeting? Someone who wanted to make sure the defection was made public before a rash decision was made? Commander Eustis also speculated some months afterward that someone in the First District had leaked information to Couto—information that had been marked "Secret." The mystery is too tantalizing and unfortunately remains a mystery.

Even though the defection was classified, that designation was becoming superfluous as the day progressed, especially after Boston and the *Vigilant* used regular, publicly accessible frequencies for their telephone patches. Sure enough, soon after Admiral Ellis's 5:15 P.M. instructions to Commander Eustis, Couto had received a telephone tip at his home from a woman who monitored the marine frequency. Her call was soon followed by another one from someone else.

Admiral Ellis had at that time directed Commander Eustis to return the defector, but none of Couto's callers alluded to that fact. They apparently failed to attach to it any particular significance, since the defection itself was a big enough item.

When Couto arrived at work, he knew definitely that there was a defector aboard the *Vigilant,* and he was determined to pursue the story.

Shortly before 7 P.M., just after Captain Brown's call to Admiral Ellis, Couto called RCC in Boston. Navigation news was part of his regular beat, and he was a familiar caller. Radarman Moller, the Assistant Controller, answered the telephone. Regular beeps on the line indicated their voices were being captured on tape. Couto identified himself and asked if there was any news involving local vessels. He wanted to see if the information about the defection would be volunteered.

"Everything's quiet," Moller replied.

"Do you know where the *Vigilant* is?" Couto asked.

Moller hesitated. He had already been briefed to keep the case quiet. He turned to Lieutenant Ryan sitting near him at the horseshoe-shaped table and told him a New Bedford radio station wanted to know where the *Vigilant* was.

"Tell them she's on OS [Offshore] Patrol," Ryan said, "but don't give them any geographical locations." Moller repeated that to Couto.

"Where is that?" Couto persisted.

Moller again turned to Ryan. "He wants to know where that is, sir."

"Tell them it stretches all the way from Maine to the Banks."

When Moller repeated that, Couto knew he was being given the run-around. But it confirmed his knowledge that something was going on. He asked for the *Vigilant*'s call signs so he could reach the ship himself, but Moller told him the marine operator would not call a military ship for him.

He then tried a different approach. "What other Coast Guard vessels are in port?"

"The *Escanaba*," Moller replied. "Why do you want to know?"

"We understand there's a defector aboard the *Vigilant* and we want to talk with someone aboard the ship."

"I don't know anything about it. I have no idea what you're talking about," Moller declared.

Couto thanked him and hung up. He had not learned anything new, but he already had enough information for a story.

WBSM was a client of UPI, and Couto was a stringer for the wire service. He called the Boston bureau fifteen minutes later and reported the defection. UPI had heard nothing, but would check it out. Wire services were notoriously undermanned and overworked, and not all stories could possibly be checked. The intention may have been there, but Couto's tip was not followed up that night.

Snow-haired veteran reporter Bill Brennan, who specialized in navigation news for WBSM, had also monitored the early phone patches and he had immediately called the station. Couto was already working on the story and Brennan's call only confirmed its veracity for his colleague.

During the station's 8 P.M. news broadcast Couto would lead with the following story:

WBSM News has exclusively learned that a Russian seaman has defected aboard the Coast Guard Cutter *Vigilant* of New Bedford. The *Vigilant* was tied alongside the Soviet trawler at the fishing grounds while talks between three representatives of the New Bedford Seafood Producers Association and the Soviets were being conducted. Further developments as they are received.

Couto did not know at the time that more than three representatives were involved in the talks and not all of them were of the Seafood Producers Association. And neither he nor anyone else was aware at the time that Simas Kudirka was not a Russian—a crucial, but little-known technicality.[3] Couto did not report that Admiral Ellis and Captain Brown were ordering Commander Eustis to return the defector, because he did not have enough facts to state that unequivocally. Captain Brown himself, in his first phone patch, had left the issue open.

Meanwhile, aboard the *Vigilant,* Lt. Commander Pakos had walked in on Eustis, Gordon, and Obolensky with different news from Captain Brown.

CHAPTER

17

"Why should we have to return him, Paul?" Commander Eustis asked his Executive Officer. "Captain Brown just said that State Department was going to decide that."

"That's what he passed on to me, Captain. If they make a request, we have to give him back." Pakos told him Brown was on a phone patch waiting for him.

Eustis hurried to the transmitter in the company of his Executive Officer and the two civilians. He picked up the microphone and acknowledged his presence.

"Did you get my last message that I passed to Commander Pakos?" Brown's voice crackled over the receiver. The reels of tape at RCC in Boston again picked up their conversation.

"Captain, roger on that," Eustis replied. He told Brown that the Soviets had not formally requested Kudirka's return. "The situation, uh, appears to be at the state now that, uh, we have, uh, individual rights at stake possibly." Trying to lead him to a different decision, Eustis pressed on. "If we direct Soviet officers to return aboard their vessel, uh, I believe they will do so, uh, at this time, leaving further situation with, uh, Soviet defector aboard. Uh, believe if we direct them to return aboard vessel with, uh, subject in company, believe his life is probably in jeopardy, uh, over."

"I roger that," Brown answered. "Uh, you are directed to get a positive answer from the master of the vessel whether he wants individual returned aboard, over."

Commander Eustis replied he would contact the master of the vessel and see what he wanted.

"I understand that," Brown said. "That's a roger and if his response is in the affirmative, if his response is in the affirmative, the individual will be returned to the vessel, over."

Eustis acknowledged, but would not give up. "We have a State Department and Fisheries officer from Washington, uh, standing by here at this time. Uh, I will put him on the phone here, uh, and give his informed opinion to you at this time, Captain, over." Eustis was under the mistaken impression that Obolensky was from the State Department.

"Uh, *Vigilant,* this is Boston. Uh, again, the Fisheries agent has no responsibility in this matter whatsoever, over."

But Eustis still was not giving up. He told Brown he would find out if the Soviets wanted Kudirka back, and if they did, he would direct him to return. He added, however, that he ex- pected Kudirka to escape and be picked up by the cutter or by the forty-four-foot patrol boat that was already cruising near the anchorage, but out of sight. Eustis was revealing to Brown the setup he had himself contrived in order to sidestep his orders, but Brown instantly recognized it.

"Roger, Roger," Brown cried. "I understand what you are saying. Uh, you are ordered to take all necessary precautions, take all necessary precautions to preclude any type of incident occurring from your vessel, over."

Eustis rogered Brown's statement. "Uh, will take all precau- tions necessary to, uh, preclude incident from *Vigilant,* uh, however" —he stuck in—"anticipate that if man goes in the water, we should make attempts to pick him up from the water and that we may be logical agency to stand by and pick man up from water, over."

Eustis was still cautioning Brown that Kudirka would some- how be falling into the water.

"This is Boston," Brown retorted. "I think you misinterpret what your last order was. You are to take all precautions to prevent the incident from occurring. Do you understand? All precautions to prevent the incident from occurring, over."

Brown wanted to make sure Eustis did not let Kudirka go into the water, but Eustis understood it to mean he should not be saved if he went into the water. Eustis told Brown, "If, uh, man goes in water we will, uh, make no attempt to recover until such time as, uh, Soviet vessel has made all reasonable attempts to recover the individual, over."

Now Brown started splitting hairs. "Uh, I will clarify a little further, I will clarify. Once the individual is returned to his parent vessel, assuming that the command desires him back aboard, once the individual is aboard the foreign vessel, at that point your most direct responsibility has been, uh, completed. Any incident occurring after that must be done within your own discretion and our basic Coast Guard mission of search and rescue, over."

Captain Brown was outlining the Coast Guard's role of search and rescue so literally as to make it ludicrous. If Kudirka escaped from the Soviets after he was returned, the cutter could "search" for and "rescue" him. To duplicate the situation that already existed, Eustis was to risk Kudirka's life all over again just to satisfy an inane stipulation—that of a "man in the water." That stipulation arose quite by accident earlier in the afternoon when Boston could elicit no specific instructions from Headquarters. Since the question of what to do about a "man in the water" was the most specific point bandied around in telephone calls between Boston and Headquarters and the State Department, it somehow grew into a determining factor. What to do with Kudirka had remained unsolved, but the phrase "man in the water" stuck and became a controlling factor for action. It was a molehill that became a mountain. Actually, Captain Brown's original concern had been only over Soviet reaction to the defection. The Soviets had, in fact, not reacted at all, but the stipulation "man in the water" was already deeply embedded in the minds of officers trained to follow orders unquestioningly.

Brown would say months later: ". . . If he gets aboard the other ship and then goes in the water, if he gets away from them, that's not our problem. Then we've got a whole new ballgame." He would never explain why it was the Coast Guard's problem when Kudirka first escaped, but suddenly would not be the Coast Guard's problem if he escaped again.

Eustis was repeating Brown's order, as his voice rose and faded over the airwaves. "Uh, roger on that. Will direct, uh, Soviet officers to, uh, return to their vessel and subject individual to return to his vessel. Any incident that recurs after he returns to his vessel"—Eustis again stuck in a qualifier—"or attempts to return to his vessel, we will comply with, uh, normal search and rescue procedures and recover individual as necessary." Commander Eustis was still trying to tell Brown he would rescue the defector even before he was in Soviet hands, because he knew once the Soviets had Kudirka, they would make sure he would not escape again.

"*Vigilant,* this is Boston again. Uh, we will do it this way. There must be a formal request, there must be a specific request by the master of the Russian vessel that the individual be returned, that the individual be returned. That is point number one. Point number two: if the master specifically requests that the individual be returned to his ship, you will return him. The individual will be returned and placed in the custody of the master of the Russian ship. At this point, at this point you may break contact with the Russian vessel and continue your surveillance and routine patrol."

Captain Brown emphasized again: "You will assure that no incident occurs during the transfer of the individual from your vessel to the Russian vessel. Do you understand?"

"Roger your last," Eustis replied through his microphone. Gordon and Obolensky and Lt. Commander Pakos saw that in

spite of rogering his instructions, Eustis was still trying to
maneuver around them. "We will discuss that with the Soviet
master, uh, directing him and his personnel to return to their
unit. We will, uh, attempt to have, uh, subject individual, uh,
return to his unit and then depart Soviet vessel and escort them
outside of territorial seas."

Commander Eustis would direct the Soviets to return to their
ship and only then attempt to have Kudirka go back. This was
different from Brown's orders, and Brown sensed it.

He reiterated the need for a formal request from the Soviets.

Eustis was getting garble over his receiver. Brown again
insisted on the need for a request. "He is not to be returned as
a matter of course. He is to be returned only if the master of
the vessel has specifically directed his return. Do you understand? Over."

Eustis was still getting garble and did not understand. But
the Soviets monitoring the conversation aboard the *Sovetskaya
Litva* did understand.

Lt. Commander Pakos, who had been listening on a second
receiver, then cut in. "Uh, Captain Brown, this is Lt. Commander Pakos here. I'm reading you on my receiver. The Captain is getting a lot of garbles. I understand the message and,
uh, just discussed it with him. Stand by, he is right here."

"Boston Rescue, uh, this is Cutter *Vigilant,* uh, roger your
last," Eustis said through another microphone. "Uh, this is
Cutter *Vigilant* standing by this frequency, over." He was getting a little restless, because he had gained little headway with
Brown.

"Roger, this is Boston. All right, you understand my last
transmission. The individual is not to be returned until the
master specifically requests his return. Point number two: if the
master has requested his return, you will assure yourself . . ."

Eustis cut in without waiting for Brown to finish. "Boston
Rescue, this is Cutter *Vigilant.* I'm, uh, standing by this frequency at this time, uh, going to discuss matters further with,

uh, the Soviet skipper and directing him to return to his vessel at this time. I roger your last, over."

"This is Boston. This is Boston. Roger on that," Brown replied. "Ken—"

"Radio Boston, disconnect transmitter," Lieutenant Ryan interjected.

Captain Brown was worried. He was certain Eustis did not really understand what he was saying. He repeated his misgivings to Lieutenant Ryan.

"It sounded to me like he understood what you said," Ryan replied.

"You mean at the end?"

"Yes, sir. But it sounded like he had something else going and that's why he said that he, uh, would call you back." Actually, Eustis had not said he would call back.

"Yes, I understand that, too," Brown said. "But up until that time, uh, I still have the impression that we'll go ahead and turn this fellow over to them and they can all go back together."

Ryan reminded him that Eustis must have heard the part about the need for a request.

"That is correct," Brown replied.

"It sounded like that was what he rogered for."

Captain Brown was still uncertain and asked Ryan if he understood Eustis to say that he was ordering all the Soviets back, including Kudirka.

"Uh, I don't, uh, I didn't quite know about him going back. I know he said something about telling the officers to return."

"That's right," Brown concurred.

"But I don't, uh, I didn't quite understand why he was doing that," Ryan countered.

"Because I told him to do this," Brown said, referring to his earlier phone patch.

"Right, right. You told him to do that, but why should he . . . I don't understand why he was saying that when you were saying, you know, uh, the Russians . . . the skipper had to request his return."

Ryan here had caught the gist of Eustis's statement. The Captain was intending to direct the Soviets off the *Vigilant* without asking them for a request, thus very technically still following orders while saving Kudirka.

Brown did not catch the nuance and replied, "I want to make very positive and very certain that they do want this fellow to return."

"Right."

"We are not going to give him over, period, without even so much as a request."

"Uh huh."

"And I think he kind of missed that originally."

"I think I have secure contact," Ryan said. "Do you want me to try and get this in writing to him in just a note type of thing?"

"Like what?"

"Just what you said, your three points, sir."

"Do you want to make some notes, Ken? Are you going to rap this out on Orestes?"*

"Yes, sir. Just, uh, a note from Captain Brown to Captain Eustis."

"Rap it out."

"Right, sir, and I'll get back to you." Ryan hung up and went next door to the Communications Center to send the message.

Meanwhile, Captain Brown sat hunched over on his couch, disconsolate. Putting down the telephone, he looked up at his wife, who had been listening, and said bitterly: "I spent all my life saving people and I finally have to give an order—and I think it's for a man to be killed."

At RCC, Lieutenant Ryan found the machinery still malfunctioning. He decided to call the *Vigilant* directly and initiated another phone patch.

*Orestes was the on-line crypto.

Commander Eustis wearily returned to the transmitter. "Radio Boston, this is Commander Eustis here. Uh, over."

"Yes, sir, Captain. This is the RCC. Ah, I tried to get you by another means, but apparently we've lost comms. Captain Brown is concerned about the, uh, interpretation in his last instructions. He wanted me to clarify to you that the number one point to follow, the number one thing on the agenda is that the skipper of the Russian boat must request the man's return prior to your returning him. That is what this all hinges on. The skipper must specifically request the man's return, over."

Eustis again acknowledged his instructions. Now he knew he could no longer maneuver around the orders. They had been reiterated too specifically. "Uh, roger on that. Uh, I'm departing bridge at this time, uh, to discuss the matter further with the, uh, Soviet officers. Will advise you further of any, uh, further developments, over."

He felt drained as he put down the microphone.

Lieutenant Ryan again dialed Captain Brown's number and told him Eustis understood the orders.

"He does?"

"Yeah."

"What a lousy job," Brown said with disgust.

"And he's caught right in the middle," Ryan added.

"No he isn't."

"Well, you are maybe, I don't know."

"You bet your ever-lovin' bippy."

"Yeah."

"Hey, uh, do you know how to knit?" Brown asked facetiously.

"Knit?"

"Yes."

"No, sir."

Brown spelled it. "K-N-I-T."

"No, sir."

"Maybe I oughta take that up."

Ryan was a little puzzled. "What I meant . . ."

"I got my thirty in anyway," Brown went on, referring to his years of service. He knew something was going to happen to him as a result of this case.

Lieutenant Ryan interrupted his thoughts and mentioned the call from Bob Couto of WBSM.

"About what?" Captain Brown asked.

"This New Bedford radio station."

"Yeah."

Ryan detailed Couto's call.

"All these New Bedford people are aboard, too," Brown said. He knew it would be impossible to keep the case a secret.

Brown again switched his thoughts, this time to Commander Eustis. "I know exactly what he's trying to say."

"Yes, he's . . ." Ryan started.

"I know exactly what he's trying to say. But this is one of those cases I cannot permit him to rationalize."

Lieutenant Ryan understood the dilemma. "And you can't say, 'Okay, if the man does jump you can save him,' because you're not supposed to say that either."

"No."

"No."

"Well, it's a lousy position to be in," Brown declared. "I would have done it differently, I think."

Captain Brown still had time to rectify the situation, but neither his compassion for Kudirka's plight, nor his inner criticism of the decision itself was strong enough to sustain at least an argument against Admiral Ellis's unflinching opinion, to which Brown now felt completely subordinate.

CHAPTER

18

The men standing around the transmitter saw how crestfallen Commander Eustis looked after his talk with Captain Brown. He put the microphone back on its hook and told Obolensky what the interpreter had already heard over the receiver.

"This is a Coast Guard matter. I've been informed by my superiors in Boston that you're not to get involved in this."

Gordon and Obolensky knew it was not a Coast Guard matter at all, but a matter for the U.S. State Department. They now reiterated to him the political implications involved in the case and that the State Department must be made aware of what was happening.

Eustis replied that his superiors had consulted Washington, although the civilians noticed that he did not seem convinced of that himself. "I have to follow my orders," he said. He then left the Communications Room and the vicinity of the Watchstander's Head where Kudirka was closeted. The proximity of the defector's refuge and the thoughts going through Eustis's mind were giving him pangs of conscience. He moved away from there and went to the wheelhouse, followed by the two civilians and Lt. Commander Pakos, repeating on the way that he was an officer and had to follow orders.

Lieutenant Lundberg was standing forward at the conn. He did not see the group come in, but heard them talking. When he heard Eustis repeat his orders, he once again envisioned the stories told him by his Latvian neighbors. "Oh, my God! They're giving him back to the same fate!" he thought. Lundberg continued scanning outside to see if the forty-four-foot patrol boat was cruising around as instructed. He kept peering into the darkness, unsettled by what he had heard and figuring the patrol boat was cruising around in vain.

The Captain, however, was in no hurry to carry out his orders and lingered in the wheelhouse. Lt. Commander Pakos also had deep misgivings about the order, but supported his Captain's every move. All the men in the wheelhouse were unanimous in their opinion that Kudirka should not be returned, but Eustis kept bringing up his obligation to follow orders. Pakos would say in an official statement written after the incident that "things continued in limbo."

Having been in the government bureaucracy long enough to know it thoroughly, William Gordon was not satisfied that all avenues had been explored. He strongly suspected that this type of order could only have been engendered in some low-level office. "Let me call some people I know in Washington," he asked Eustis. "We should try to reach State through our own channels so we can have the assurance that this guy's life might not be jeopardized by returning him."

Commander Eustis immediately agreed, but told Gordon he would first try to persuade the Soviets to leave the ship without Kudirka. They filed down the stairs with Eustis leading the way. His ultimate responsibility was visibly symbolized on the back of his foul-weather jacket with two simple letters—CO. Looking at the letters on his back, Gordon knew that he and the other civilians were alien to the situation in which Eustis had become enmeshed. Yet, as he and Obolensky followed him, they sensed he needed their moral support and still valued their advice.

They walked into the cabin to find that the man in the gray sweater had returned from the *Sovetskaya Litva* and was intently saying something to Burkal. He was speaking purposefully in Lithuanian, so Obolensky or anyone they suspected of knowing Russian would not understand.

Standing by the door, Eustis waited for the two to finish talking. His tensed muscles and agitated fingers showed he was trying to control a seething discontent. Then, in an emotional, but controlled tone he told Burkal: "I have orders to return him." His voice was on the verge of breaking up as he spoke. "As an officer and a seaman I have to take orders from a higher source." He explained that he found the order distasteful and asked Burkal as a fellow-officer to understand the situation. "Please leave this ship and let the issue be resolved on a diplomatic level."

The man in the gray sweater started saying something to Burkal as Obolensky translated. At the same time Robert Brieze leaped up from his seat. "Captain! You cannot do this! Lithuania is next to Latvia where I come from! The Russians occupied the country!" His accent was even more pronounced as he blurted his appeals. "Lithuania still has a legation in Washington! I escaped from the Russians myself in 1944! I know how they treat defectors! You cannot do this! He will lose his life or be exiled to Siberia!"

"Bob, I'm sorry, I can't help you. I have my orders," Eustis said dejectedly.

In the midst of this exchange, Burkal again refused to leave the ship as he had done on the flight deck and earlier in the cabin.

Trembling with excitement, Brieze sat down to be comforted by Burt and Nickerson. Kudirka's plight was resurrecting his own nightmarish past.

Eustis realized what Brieze was saying and it pained him all the more. He did not speak, trying to maintain his composure. Burkal was again asking to see Kudirka. After several more moments Commander Eustis replied he could not. He realized it was time to speak to the man himself. Asking Obolensky to

accompany him, he left for the Watchstander's Head. It would
be easier to break the bad news in the company of the interpreter.

Another seaman was guarding the door when the two walked
up. Wordlessly he stepped aside, and the Captain opened the
door. Kudirka stood apprehensively watching Eustis and Obolensky as they both crowded into the facility. They knew by his
look that he suspected something was wrong.

"No send me back! No send me back!" Kudirka warned.

Eustis told Obolensky what to tell him and Obolensky said
in Russian, "Asylum has been refused for you, and the Captain
of the U.S. vessel is under orders from his superiors to return
you to your ship."[1]

Without betraying any panic or visible reaction, Kudirka
replied, also in Russian, "I will not go back under any circumstances. I would rather jump overboard and drown or die from
exposure in the cold water."

Eustis said nothing after he heard the translation. He already
knew that.

Kudirka continued, his voice emotional, but under control,
"The U.S. Captain told me that a small boat will be waiting if
I jump overboard. I will be rescued." He repeated that he would
jump, even if the odds were against survival. He had nothing
to lose.

Obolensky noticed that Kudirka was "almost at a breaking
point, but as controlled as any person could be in such circumstances." He turned from the defector and repeated Kudirka's
statement to Commander Eustis.

Eustis motioned Obolensky out of the head. "Let's go back.
I'll have to speak to the Soviets again." He knew then he would
not order Kudirka off his ship. Maybe letting him jump overboard was the only solution. Having seen the apprehension
deep in Kudirka's eyes, Eustis believed more than ever that his
life would definitely be in jeopardy if he was returned.

CHAPTER

19

"They cannot do this! Someone should call the State Department!" Brieze was pleading to John Burt when Commander Eustis and Obolensky came back into the cabin. They walked over to Burkal, who was standing near the couch at the starboard bulkhead, and before Eustis could say anything, the Acting Fleet Commander repeated his request to see Kudirka. Eustis again refused.

Through Obolensky he asked instead, "Would you go back to your vessel without the defector while we try to convince him to return on his own?" Lt. Commander Pakos was standing nearby listening. Eustis could tell by the look on his face that Pakos supported his actions and, more important, knew that he sympathized just as deeply with the defector's dilemma.

"*Nyet!*" Burkal replied adamantly to his question. To Obolensky Burkal's actions did not seem characteristic of the man he had known for those three days at the University of Rhode Island seminar. He noticed that Burkal was totally under the thumb of the man in the gray sweater, as did everyone else.

It was at this point that the man in the gray sweater once more left the cabin to go to his own ship. Everyone watched him, knowing that any Soviet move would be made through him. Most probably the commissar had not expected Eustis's intransigence, because he had no doubt learned from his radiomen on his last trip to the *Sovetskaya Litva* what Admiral Ellis and Captain Brown had told Eustis during their phone patches. He would have to somehow force the Captain's hand and left the *Vigilant,* this time to arrange something from which Eustis could not back away.

Gordon reminded the Captain that he had made a request for a telephone call and asked to speak to him in private again. Eustis, Gordon, and Obolensky went to the adjoining state-room. The Captain was upset and worried. He told the two civilians he was very concerned for Kudirka's life. "It's like committing murder to return him."

"Let me call those people I know," Gordon asked.

"Okay, call them." Eustis was obviously still willing at this point to get some outside influence into the decision-making process.

They went back to the Captain's Cabin, where Eustis told his Executive Officer that Gordon would make a phone patch with associates in Washington. Pakos agreed without additional comment. He was giving Eustis full moral support in his actions.

The time by then was shortly after 8 P.M.

Suddenly, the man in the gray sweater was back in the cabin. He was taking short, rapid breaths from hurrying and seemed smug. Stepping up to Eustis, he arrogantly stuck out his hand and gave him a piece of paper. Eustis looked at a note with Cyrillic typing. He could not read the script, but knew instantly what it was.

He handed the note to Obolensky who read aloud the following written in capital letters:

LITHUANIAN FISHERIES ADMINISTRATION
KLAIPEDA BASE OF THE REFRIGERATOR
FLEET
MOTHER SHIP SOVETSKAYA LITVA

Rear Admiral William B. Ellis, USCG, Commander of the First Coast Guard District, Boston, Massachusetts.

Captain Fletcher W. Brown, Jr., USCG, Chief of Staff of the First Coast Guard District.

Commander Ralph W. Eustis, USCG, Captain of the cutter *Vigilant,* reads a statement to the press two days after the incident. He had been ordered back to New Bedford from routine patrol to explain the bizarre happenings aboard his ship.

—*Romas Slezas*

Lieutenant Commander Paul E. Pakos, USCG, Executive Officer of the cutter *Vigilant,* ponders the incident four months after it occurred. It would take him a long time to divine the extent of his responsibility in it.

Rear Admiral Robert E. Hammond, USCG, Chief of the Office of Operations at Coast Guard Headquarters in Washington, D.C. (above left)

Captain Wallace C. Dahlgren, USCG, Chief of the Intelligence Division in the Office of Operations. (above right)

Edward L. Killham, Officer in Charge of the Bilateral Section of the Office of Soviet Union Affairs in the U.S. Department of State. (bottom)

The Coast Guard cutter *Vigilant* (**WMEC–617**), a 210-foot medium endurance cutter based in New Bedford, Massachusetts.

The *Sovetskaya Litva* [*Soviet Lithuania*] (M–26402), a 509-foot refrigerated factory trawler of the Soviet Union that operates along the East Coast of the United States.

The tire rig used to lift delegates from the *Vigilant* to the *Sovetskaya Litva*. On it are Commander Eustis *(center)*; Lieutenant Leo Morehouse, USCG, an observer from Coast Guard Headquarters; and Howard Nickerson, a civilian delegate.

To the right of the tire rig, Ivan Burkal, the Acting Soviet Fleet Commander *(second from left)* is greeting Alexis Obolensky *(partially visible)*, the U.S. interpreter. Left of the rig is John Burt, a civilian delegate, and next to him is Robert Brieze, another civilian delegate.

—Official U.S. Coast Guard Photo

The *Sovetskaya Litva* as seen from the *Vigilant*.

Simas Kudirka and his wife, Genele. Kudirka's picture is an identification photo, probably taken several years before the incident. Both pictures were among articles he left with the Americans.

A seaman looks from the *Vigilant*'s bridge toward
Kudirka who is leaning over the rail of the *Sovetskaya Litva* studying the bow area of the cutter.

—*Romas Slezas*

Flight deck and bridge area of the *Vigilant* where much of the incident occurred. On the left is the launch used to transport Kudirka. He was tied by the Soviets to the davit supporting it. The open hatch on the right is the helicopter handling shack inside of which Kudirka was wrapped by the Soviets in a blanket after having been beaten senseless. Talking with the author on the signal bridge is Lieutenant Douglas Lundberg, USCG, Operations Officer of the *Vigilant*. Lundberg was the first to speak with Kudirka that day. He was standing on the bridge wing near the signal light at the top left of the photo.

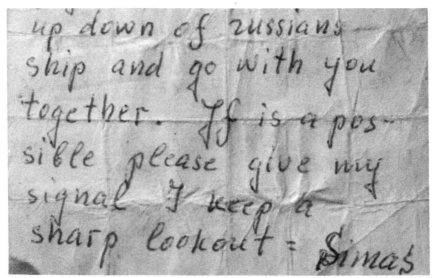

Side one of the message written by Simas Kudirka. He hid it in a pack of cigarettes which he tossed to Lieutenant Lundberg.

Lieutenant Lundberg cautiously talking with the author. It was the first contact with men of the *Vigilant*. The ship had just come in from a routine patrol without her captain, Commander Ralph W. Eustis, who had been suspended from duty, pending the outcome of a Coast Guard investigation.

Ivan Burkal (third from left), the major Russian figure in the incident, visits New Bedford, Mass., together with several comrades eight months prior to the incident. Standing from left by the Whaleman's Statue are: Howard Nickerson, Executive Director of the New Bedford Seafood Dealers Association, who was aboard the *Vigilant* that fateful day, and Russell T. Norris, Regional Director of the National Marine Fisheries Service. The Soviets are: Viktor A. Zakharov, Commander of the North Atlantic Fishing Fleet; Burkal, the Assistant Commander; Ivan Moskuyn and Lev Fominykh, two assistants.

Visibly disturbed (l. to r.), Robert Brieze, Howard Nickerson, and John Burt meet at the New Bedford Fishermen's Union Hall the day after the incident. All three witnessed what happened aboard the *Vigilant* the night before.

—Romas Slezas

Lieutenant Lundberg points toward the flight deck where the Soviets came aboard. In the background is the passageway leading to the Captain's Cabin where Robert Brieze reported Kudirka was bloodied by the Soviets while trying to reach safety in the cabin.

—Romas Slezas

The Watchstander's Head where Simas Kudirka spent his entire six and a half hours of freedom.

—Romas Slezas

The Captain's Cabin where most of the negotiations for Kudirka occurred. This is the view he saw when he opened the door seeking help while trying to evade the Soviets who had come for him. The cabin at the time was filled with officers and civilians.

—*Jonas Garla*

Members of the Lithuanian Student Association of North America march from their convention site to the Federal Building of Cleveland, Ohio. This demonstration sparked widespread publicity for the incident.

'...AFTER ALL, WHAT'S A LITHUANIAN DEFECTOR BETWEEN FRIENDS?'

—*Pat Oliphant*

Several of the political cartoons
that appeared in the national press
after the incident.

—*Szep, in* The Boston Globe

—*Hy Rosen*

"HONORED—Soviet 'BOOT AWARD,'
naming him Humanitarian of the Year, is
presented in Boston ceremony to Adm.
W. B. Ellis, commandant, 1st Coast
Guard District. Representing the USSR
is Col. Vladimir K. Blockoff, winner of
last year's award for his dramatic rescue
of Czech people from the scurrilous
Dubcek."

A random selection of newspaper articles and editorials that appeared in the national press as a result of the *Vigilant* incident.

—*Anthony Kalvaitis*

NOVEMBER 23, 1970

TO THE LEADERS OF THE U.S.
DELEGATION OF FISHERY
REPRESENTATIVES
TO THE CAPTAIN OF COAST GUARD
CUTTER "VIGILANT"

DURING OUR MEETING ON NOVEMBER 23, 1970,
THE RADIO OPERATOR KUDIRKA PENE-
TRATED INTO MY STATEROOM, FORCED THE
SAFE, TOOK MONEY FROM THE SAFE IN THE
AMOUNT OF 3,000 RUBLES, JUMPED OVER THE
FENDER, AND HID ON YOUR VESSEL. REQUEST
YOU CONDUCT A SEARCH AND RETURN HIM
TO MY VESSEL. I LODGE A MARITIME PROTEST
IN THIS MATTER.

CAPTAIN OF MOTHER SHIP
SOVETSKAYA LITVA
/s/ POPOV

No sooner had Obolensky finished translating when Brieze was again on his feet shouting, "They always accuse someone of being a criminal who is seeking freedom! It's a lie!"

One of the men, he did not remember who, warned him to sit down and not interfere. It was a Coast Guard matter.

The man in the gray sweater asked that Eustis endorse the note. Eustis wordlessly, slowly, took the paper from Obolensky, walked several steps to his desk, took a pen, and leaning over the paper, wrote that he understood what the note said and signed it.

Without a question or search of Kudirka, he accepted it as fulfillment of the stipulation for a "formal request." Here now was a new issue with legal implications, but none of the officers thought to consider it. It would be John Burt, the gruff, self-educated union representative who would raise the issue later, only to have it fall on deaf ears. To Eustis it was simply a formal request which he had been instructed to get, but never did. The Soviets, having heard the stipulation over their radio, obliged him without his having to ask. The contents to Eustis were immaterial and he never realized that the accusation of theft opened new possibilities to keep Kudirka, namely, investigating the charge.[1] He would learn that only in hindsight long after the fateful night. Even Admiral Ellis, whose very brief conversations with Captain Brown sparked the entire incident, would say of the note: "That smelled to me right away."

Commander Eustis had signed the note still thinking of another possibility to save Kudirka. It would be a final effort. He told Gordon to make his call to his contacts. Asking Lt. Commander Pakos and Obolensky to accompany them, Eustis led the way to the bridge.

"I'd like to call Russel Norris in Gloucester," Gordon said when they were all standing around the transmitter. Norris was Gordon's colleague and Regional Director of NMFS.

The phone patch was completed, but Norris was not at home.

Gordon then asked to call Carl Depiero, an administrative officer in NMFS. Depiero was home that night, but technical difficulties in the hookup precluded completion of the call.

Next he asked for another phone patch with Washington, this time the home of Dennis Moore who was Assistant Chief for International Affairs in the Commerce Department. Moore was Obolensky's supervisor and had a number of contacts in the State Department.

Moore was not at home.

Totally frustrated, Gordon turned to Eustis and, having exhausted all the reasonable arguments he could muster, simply asked Eustis if he really believed the order was legal. Commander Eustis did not reply directly. He was still agonizing over that question himself.

"The usual practice in defector cases is to take the person into custody," Obolensky reminded again. He was irritated, impatient. He was wondering how such a clear issue could be mishandled.[2] Both civilians reiterated that the State Department may not have been involved in the decision, because Eustis's order was unusual.

"Are you sure the decision was not made solely by the Coast Guard?" he asked.

Eustis had to concede that perhaps Obolensky was right, perhaps the State Department had not been informed. But he was not sure what strength he could put into the interpreter's statements. What weight did they carry compared to his own orders? He would explain much later: "My first reaction to some of his comments was . . . He's worked with the State Department. He knows what their policies are, but he's not an adviser. He's nothing but an interpreter—by title anyway—and where does he really fit into the picture? . . . I felt he had information and talent we needed that day." Still, Eustis could not bring himself to disobey an order on the basis of what Obolensky and Gordon argued. He totally agreed with them; he felt the Coast Guard policy was wrong. But could he disobey Captain Brown and Admiral Ellis and then explain his actions by claiming he listened to the advice of two civilians?

Since Eustis seemed willing to discuss the issue with Gordon and Obolensky and since they were speaking of moral and philosophical implications, Lt. Commander Pakos now entered the picture.[3] Up to that point he had kept a low profile in the case and supported his Captain's beliefs that the man should be kept. Now, however, it was time for action. It was time either to act on their beliefs or squelch them in favor of military discipline. Not wanting to drive a wedge between himself and his Captain at a time when Eustis needed all the moral support he could get, Pakos subtly suggested the alternatives without actually saying which he himself would choose. This way, regardless of what Eustis decided to do, Pakos could and would fully support him without having at any time revealed any cross-purposes. Eustis would say of his Executive Officer: "He was not the kind that would show any sign of discontent with what you decided, particularly in this thing."

"I raised the discussion of the Nuremberg Trials," Pakos told the Board of Investigation. "I questioned if such an order was legal."

"Compare it to My Lai," Gordon added.[4] He was referring to the killing by U.S. troops of more than 100 persons during a combat sweep in South Vietnam. Lieutenant William Calley, a junior army officer, at the time was on trial for murder and would eventually be found guilty, even though he had argued that he followed orders.

Commander Eustis considered the parallels. They rang too true.

The four participants standing around the mute transmitter discussed the issue at length, but their recollections of specifics would be vague. They did remember agreeing that there was a real possibility Kudirka would either be killed or spend the rest of his life in a prison or labor camp if he was returned. Again, they pondered if a decision leading to such consequences was legal.

Eustis told the men he had orders not to let an incident occur, but both Gordon and Obolensky insisted an incident had already occurred. It was now a diplomatic matter and had to be handled by the State Department. Was Eustis really sure the State Department knew about the situation? Gordon and Obolensky were too familiar with the bureaucracy to presume that the State Department knew. Messages often got lost in shuffles from desk to desk. This had to be the case here, too, otherwise Eustis would never have received the order to give Kudirka back to the Soviets.

Slowly Eustis was beginning to turn rigid in his stand. An order was an order, and he began to argue that way more and more.

Gordon and Obolensky went over old facts. "The Soviet ship is in U.S. waters." "You can legally keep the man and order the

Soviets off your ship." "You can seize the whole ship if you want to."

Pakos favored the position that the order was not legal and that Eustis was under no moral compulsion to carry it out. He was not actually saying that outright, but his questions were leading.

"If you decide to disobey the order, you will perhaps be a hero in the eyes of the United States public," Pakos said. "Whereas if you obey the Coast Guard order, you will be true to the Coast Guard, but in the eyes of the U.S. public you will have done something wrong and improper."

Commander Eustis was tormented by the alternatives. It was plain to Pakos and the two civilians that he faced the option of leaving the Coast Guard and a solid career or staying with it and obeying an order he deeply disagreed with. "The impact of all this was a very, very heavy burden on Captain Eustis," Pakos told the board. Gordon and Obolensky sensed that burden, but only Pakos—a fellow-officer—could fully appreciate the dilemma.

Trying to ease his Captain's mind, Pakos offered him unequivocal support. "If you decide not to carry out this order, I and the crew will support you 100 percent."

The Captain thought awhile, then reminded the three that they were looking at only part of the picture—the part that was evident aboard ship. There must be more to the situation. Someone must have a good reason for giving the defector back.

Pakos interjected that that could be true. "What if someone is negotiating for release of prisoners in North Vietnam and we don't do what we are told. Maybe some American prisoners are being given in exchange for him." Eustis grabbed for that rationale. Of course, he thought, that must be the case. Commander Eustis by then was grasping at any straw which held the explanation of the order and he did not think to consider that nations do not exchange prisoners for someone who is not one of their own subjects; Kudirka to the North Vietnamese was nothing.

"I'm the guy in the middle who has to carry out this order," he declared bitterly. His face showed strain and his eyes were brimming with moisture. He was hopelessly searching his mind and conscience for some clue, some answer. He would remember long afterward: "All these things passed through my mind —Nuremberg, My Lai, the question of a legal order—but again, because of my reasons that we didn't know the whole situation, this [returning Kudirka] was all we could do. Our system has to function on all of us having respect for our superiors."

Commander Eustis looked at Pakos, Gordon, and Obolensky. Without any more words, they knew what he would do. His torment announced the decision. Eustis picked up the microphone from its hook on the transmitter, clicked it on, and asked the Boston Radio Station for a phone patch with Captain Brown.

The hookup was completed after some minutes during which Lieutenant Ryan had to ask the operator to break in on a telephone conversation Brown was having.

It was 8:19 P.M. when Captain Brown was on the line to the *Vigilant.*

"*Vigilant,* um, this is Boston," Brown began. "Uh, go ahead."

"Radio Boston, uh, this is Cutter *Vigilant.* Uh, present situation is, uh, I'm still moored alongside Soviet vessel. I have official request in writing for return of alleged defector in writing."

It was the first time Eustis used the word "alleged," which was an obvious reaction to the contents of the note.

"That's it," Gordon said as he turned to Lt. Commander Pakos. "He's declared himself now."

"Uh, our present intentions are, uh, to return defector to the Soviet officers that are aboard *Vigilant,* make him depart vessel in custody of Soviet officers aboard *Vigilant,* to depart Soviet vessel, and escort Soviet vessel out of U.S. territorial seas." Eustis's next few words were destroyed by static.

"*Vigilant,* uh, Captain, I didn't get any of that," Brown's voice crackled over the receiver.

Eustis repeated what he would do.

Lt. Commander Pakos became utterly dejected, because Commander Eustis had indeed "declared himself." Pakos had been ready to refuse the order in support of his Captain, but now knew that support would have to be in obeying the order. Regardless of the action to be taken, he felt honor-bound to his friend and superior officer. Desperately, he hoped something new would occur that would warrant a review of the situation.

Eustis was still talking with Captain Brown.

"Uh, this is Boston. I roger that," Brown was saying. "You still have not answered the question. Has the master of the vessel requested the return of the defector? Over."

"Boston Rescue, this is *Vigilant.* I have formal request in writing at this time from the master of the Soviet vessel for return of defector, over," Eustis replied curtly.

"Roger, roger on your transmission, and, uh, uh, proceed as in accordance with your total message, over."

"Boston Rescue, this is Cutter *Vigilant.* Uh, roger that, uh, am getting underway at this time, uh, over."

This was a fateful statement. It would mislead Boston and Washington into thinking the case was over.

Captain Brown then asked Commander Eustis to advise him when the Soviet ship left territorial waters.

"Boston, unplug," Lieutenant Ryan said. He asked Brown, who was still on the phone, "Do you want me to bring Flag Plot up to date?"

"Uh, yeah," Brown answered. He was wondering what reaction Headquarters would have.

"And tell them a SITREP [Situation Report] will be, uh, forthcoming in the morning, or something like that?" Ryan suggested.

"Uh, yeah," Brown said again.

"All right, sir."

"And if the press calls, uh, there is no comment. We have no information that can be released to the press at this time."

"All right, sir."

Ryan cradled his telephone and in the same motion picked it up again to dial Flag Plot at Coast Guard Headquarters.

CHAPTER

20

The day had passed uneventfully for Lieutenant Wayne Tritbough in Flag Plot at Coast Guard Headquarters. He had logged routine items since 8:00 that morning when he came on duty. RCC Cleveland reported the motor vessel *Vermont* had run aground in the Detroit River and was blocking a channel. Another vessel had lost power between Marshall and Fort Washington. Various personnel were coming in from or going on leave. A seaman in San Juan was believed AWOL, but a call to San Juan confirmed he was on base.

All these items were logged routinely. It was doubly important that they be noted, because a bank of tape recorders in gray, steel cabinets with counter tops were not operating. The recorders were supposed to tape all calls coming in to Flag Plot from the Coast Guard Districts, but they had been out of order for a full year and more. No one had bothered to fix them, and Duty Officers had come to live with the fact.

Everything was in a small, carpeted room on the eighth floor of the DOT Building. The room did not even look like a Flag Plot, but more like a regular office. RCC at Boston, which served a similar function, could immediately be recognized as some kind of coordinating center, whereas Flag Plot looked austere by comparison. Lieutenant Tritbough was sitting behind the low cabinets housing the idle tape recorders. The cabinets doubled as a work table.

At 8:24 a telephone on top of the work counter rang. It was the call Lieutenant Tritbough had been told to expect. Although the tapes at Flag Plot did not work, those at RCC recorded the ensuing conversation.

"Coast Guard Washington, Duty Officer," Tritbough said after he picked up the receiver.

"This is Lieutenant Ryan, RCC Boston. Are you aware of the situation?"

"Right."

"Yeah, okay. The man came over to the *Vigilant,* but he is going back aboard the vessel now, the Russian vessel."

"Okay. How did he come over to the *Vigilant?*"

"Apparently in one of those tour things, you know. They are giving some of the Russians a tour of the ship or something."

"Okay."

Lieutenant Ryan explained the situation. "He came over, a group was invited over and he came over with the group. Then he didn't want to go back. But now, because the skipper of the vessel requested in writing that the man be returned, he is being returned, and shortly the *Vigilant* will get underway, disconnect from the Russian ship and escort it outside of the territorial waters and the contiguous zone."

"Okay. Standby a minute here, please," Tritbough said. He was writing the information on a pad. "He requested the man be returned, correct?"

"Right. Right."

"And they have or are returning him?" Tritbough was surprised at the information. He knew the decision had been made solely at the District level, because he himself was to be the link to the State Department. However, he did not question the validity of the decision.[1]

"They . . . well, we just finished a phone patch with the *Vigilant,* " Ryan continued. "They say that at this time . . . they

. . . when he finished talking they will be returning the man to the Russian vessel in custody of Russian officers, ship's officers. They are aboard. They were apparently . . . they were over for coffee with the Captain when all of this came about."

"Okay. 'Returning man to vessel,' " Lieutenant Tritbough repeated as he jotted down the information.

"In the custody of Russian ship's officers," Lieutenant Ryan added.

"What are the man's feelings in this regard?" Tritbough asked. He had not expected a return.

"He, uh, previously he did not want to return and he stated that he would probably go overboard if he has the chance."

"Okay."

"The *Vigilant* is aware of this and they will be keeping a sharp lookout for him," Ryan offered.

"Okay. Okay," Tritbough repeated several of the salient points to make sure he heard them right and Ryan verified them.

"Chief of Staff here says he'll send a SITREP in the morning," Lieutenant Ryan told him.

"Okay."

"Okay. If nothing else comes up we will . . . this is it. How do you want to handle the press?" he asked Lieutenant Tritbough. "It's leaked out somehow."

"Oh, boy!" Tritbough exclaimed and gave a short laugh. "Have you gotten anything?"

"No, I haven't got anything. All I have got is one call from one radio station in New Bedford. Said, 'Hey, I hear there is a Russian defector out there.' You know."

"Yeah," Tritbough answered.

Lieutenant Ryan told him he denied all knowledge of the incident, but added that someone heard a news report about it anyway. (This was Bob Couto's 8 P.M. broadcast over WBSM.) He asked Tritbough if Washington wanted to handle publicity on the matter.

"Well, I will have to check with people on this, of course,"
the Flag Plot Duty Officer responded.

"Right. Okay. All right. If I do get any calls, I will say 'No
comment' or 'Unable to make comment at this time' or something like that."

"Okay. Unless I advise you otherwise, go ahead with that
plan."

"Right."

"Okay. Thank you. Goodbye."

As soon as he hung up, Lieutenant Tritbough called the
home of Rear Admiral Hammond, feeling he might want to
overrule the decision.

"Sir, I have some information on the case of the *Vigilant,*"
he began when Hammond answered.

Hammond listened as Lieutenant Tritbough relayed everything Lieutenant Ryan had told him.

The Admiral acknowledged the information. He would tell
the Board of Investigation: "I thought what had happened was
that he had come aboard, that the . . . either the ship or the
District had urged him to go back and not cause an incident
between the two vessels on a fisheries conference, and that the
man had either agreed to go back or had been led back. I just
felt that he had gone back really of his own free will. Practically
so."

Admiral Hammond testified he was convinced that, since the
State Department (Killham in the Bilateral Section of the
Soviet Desk) had earlier said they did not want to encourage
a defection, it had somehow relayed word to the First District
to refuse to take Kudirka. Admiral Hammond was content with
Lieutenant Tritbough's information and did not pursue the
matter further, only to regret it later.

The Duty Officer told Hammond he would be calling other
officers with the information and ended the conversation. High-
ranking officers were rarely called, as Lieutenant Tritbough was
to do, but this situation, in the Lieutenant's way of thinking,

was on a par with marine disasters, oil spills, and other crucial matters that required briefings up the line of command.

Tritbough called Admiral Chester R. Bender, Commandant of the Coast Guard; Vice Admiral Thomas R. Sargent, III, the Assistant Commandant; Rear Admiral V. Goehring, Chief of Staff; Captain Donald H. Luzius, Assistant Chief of Operations; and Admiral Roberick Y. Edwards, Chief of the Office of Public and International Affairs.

Tritbough testified to the board that the reactions of all the ranking officers were only "hmmms" and "I sees" as they listened to the information. Admiral Hammond testified that he had asked Tritbough to inform the officers. Tritbough, however, steadfastly maintained that Hammond did not ask him to do anything and that he, Tritbough himself, initiated the calls.[2]

In any case, the officers accepted the information as presented and saw nothing unusual in it—at least not unusual enough to follow up.

When Admiral Bender, the Commandant, received the briefing from Tritbough, he immediately called Admiral Hammond and asked if he had any suggestions. Hammond replied that as far as he could determine, the case was closed. Bender was satisfied and thought nothing more of it.

Captain Brown would recall several months later: "Everybody went back to bed and forgot about it and had no interest in the situation. And that is probably the biggest impression I have from the level of action taken in Washington. Among all the staff officers concerned . . . they didn't care. Ho-hum. Because no one made any checks." Though tinged with the bitter realization that inquiries from Headquarters would have saved his own skin, Brown's view is nevertheless correct.

About twelve minutes after Lieutenant Ryan gave him the fateful information, Lieutenant Tritbough called the Operations Center in the State Department.

State Ops as it was called, was located in the huge complex of buildings making up the U.S. Department of State sprawled along a full city block in downtown Washington. The complex housed an entrenched bureaucracy as old as the Republic where government workers have seen presidents come and go without really being affected by the foreign policy of their administrations. The State Department had a life of its own, as did all huge bureaucracies. It was a giant that no president was ever able really to mold or control during his short terms in office. Many presidents had created their own little "state departments" in the form of special assistants, special advisers on foreign policy, and burgeoning White House staffs. Such little "state departments" were the only defense against the unfathomable department of government where presidential policies and programs could be unwittingly altered, slowed, or just lost in the shuffle from bureau to bureau and from bureaucrat to bureaucrat.

Kevin McGuire, Foreign Service Officer, Class 6, was on duty in the Operations Center that day.[3] His job was similar to that of Lieutenant Ryan in RCC Boston, and Lieutenant Tritbough in Flag Plot. McGuire was the Assistant Watch Officer. With him was the Watch Officer, Robert Rich, who was Deputy Director of the Operations Center.

The telephone rang.

McGuire answered and Lieutenant Tritbough asked him if he was familiar with the case. McGuire did not immediately associate the defection with any information he had. No one had told him anything about the *Vigilant.*

Tritbough then related what he had heard from Lieutenant Ryan. "The man came aboard the *Vigilant,* had requested to stay aboard, and is being returned at the request of his vessel's master in the custody of his fellow-officers. The *Vigilant* will then escort them outside the twelve-mile limit, and they will be looking for the man if he jumps over the side." Tritbough added, "You might want to pass that on to your Soviet Desk."

"Probably," McGuire replied, still trying to recall if he knew anything about the information. "Does this adequately summarize what you are saying, 'The case has been resolved with the return of the man to his vessel'? "

"Yes," Tritbough said.

"Okay. We'll relay it to the appropriate Department Duty Officer."

Lieutenant Tritbough said in testimony that McGuire asked him questions to clarify the information, because at first McGuire seemed unfamiliar with the case. Tritbough claimed he did not remember the State Department Duty Officer using the term "case has been resolved" when he rephrased his, Tritbough's, information. However, judging from the information passed from Boston, it would seem reasonable that McGuire—like the others who were called in Washington—believed the case was over.

During testimony before the Board of Investigation McGuire and Lieutenant Tritbough took issue with the tense of the phrase "case has been resolved" (as opposed to "case is being resolved"). Tritbough insisted he did not recall using the phrase "case has been resolved." The implication is that McGuire should have told appropriate persons that there was still time to act on the case, because it was still in progress. McGuire insisted he was certain Lieutenant Tritbough said "case has been resolved"; the implication being that the State Department was absolved from pursuing the matter further.

Had the tape recorders in Flag Plot at Coast Guard Headquarters been working, there would have been no question about the words used. It just so happened that tape recorders at the Operations Center of the State Department also had been malfunctioning and were removed sometime previously.

When McGuire put his receiver down he was still unsure to what the Coast Guard Duty Officer was referring. State Department Duty Officers often received specific instructions from departments to watch for certain developments or cables. Neither McGuire nor his superior was informed by the Bilateral Section of the Soviet Desk about the *Vigilant* case. A copy of the first message sent by the *Vigilant* to Boston and forwarded to Washington was tacked to a reading board in the State Department's Operations Center. McGuire had scanned the

board and had seen the message, but had forgotten about it. Up
to several hundred cables per day came into the Operations
Center and had to be handled by two officers. It was hard to
remember them all.

McGuire testified he did not associate Lieutenant Tritbough's call with any message, because Tritbough had not mentioned the word "defection" or the nationality of the man.
However, Tritbough had asked that the information be passed
to the Soviet Desk, which should have been a clue to McGuire.

In any event, the information was about the resolution of a
case and could not by any means be interpreted as a search for
guidance. Had someone in the Bilateral Section told the Duty
Officers that the Coast Guard would be contacting them for
guidance, McGuire and Rich might have reacted differently.
Now, they would only pass Tritbough's information routinely
to the appropriate department.

McGuire told Rich, his superior, what Lieutenant Tritbough
had said and asked him if he knew anything about it.

"Yes, we do have a cable on something about this," Rich
replied. He went to the reading board, found the copy of the
Vigilant's first message, and showed it to McGuire, who then
remembered seeing it before. He recalled no instructions relating to the message.

He recalled none, because there had been none.

Before Edward Killham had left his office about 6:30 that
evening—two hours previously—he had briefed Edward Mainland, one of three assistants. Mainland was the Watch Officer
for the Bilateral Section that evening.[4] That is, he would be at
home, but any business coming into the Bilateral Section would
be forwarded to him by the Operations Center. His job that
night was similar to Lieutenant Ryan's and Lieutenant Tritbough's, except that he had the authority to act on information,
rather than just forward it to someone.

Just before leaving for home Killham briefed Mainland on what Captain Dahlgren had told him. He told Mainland he had advised Dahlgren not to encourage a defection, and that in a later conversation (after Captain Brown's 4 P.M. call to Admiral Hammond) Dahlgren had called back and reported that a defection probability had evaporated.

Captain Brown had said as much to Admiral Hammond and Hammond asked Captain Dahlgren to pass it on to the State Department. None of the men forwarding the information was even remotely conscious of the fact that a desperate man could do desperate things regardless of office hours or how dark the sky was. The men involved had neatly spaced the possibility of a defection within normal working hours. Ironically, Kudirka had jumped aboard the *Vigilant* almost to the minute when Captain Brown and Admiral Hammond were blindly agreeing he had changed his mind. Now, Killham had passed that thought to his colleague Mainland and Mainland had gone home without advising the Duty Officers in the Operations Center.

McGuire and his superior would thus forward information about the defection and not attach any particular significance to it. There had, over the years, been other cables about returning defectors, and this one did not excite them.

McGuire called Edward Mainland soon after he realized what Lieutenant Tritbough had been talking about. Mainland was on the line.

"I've received word from the Coast Guard that the possible defector incident that was signaled earlier has been resolved by the return of the man to his vessel," McGuire said.

Mainland was surprised. The information seemed vague and he knew that a decision-making step had been left out somewhere. "Would you go through that again?" he asked.

"The Coast Guard says the possible defector incident has been resolved by the return of the man to his vessel," McGuire repeated.

Mainland was an eight-year veteran of the State Department and from 1968 to 1970 had served in the Bureau of Intelligence and Research and in the Office of Soviet Union Affairs. His latest position—Desk Officer in the Bilateral Section—was brand new. He had been there just over a month.

He knew perfectly well that something somewhere had gone wrong. Mainland was unsure whether the Office of Refugees and Migration had been contacted or the State Department's Office of Legal Affairs. Both of them dealt with defectors. From his own recent tour in the Bureau of Intelligence and Research, he knew that a colleague, Lawson Moyers, worked with defectors. But he did not know whether Moyers was involved in the case, nor did he call him to find out.

Knowing that something had gone amiss, he did not even bother to make the most routine inquiry into the matter. Mainland testified: "Since the case looked like it has been wrapped, one way or the other, in my mind I assumed that the Coast Guard skipper would then be drawing up more details and putting them into an amplifying report which we would receive in due course."

Mainland simply waited for further details, which would come "in due course."

In the State Department's Operations Center McGuire listed in his log:

> 1945 Coast Guard DO informed the Watch that the possible defection case reported in Coast Guard tel 231850Z Nov. 70 had been resolved by the return of the Soviet seaman to his vessel. Alerted EUR/DO, Mr. Eastman, and EUR/SOV/DO, Mr. Mainland.

(Actually, the time was not 1945 [7:45] but 2045, an hour later. The time error was cleared up in the ensuing investigation.)

McGuire then returned to monitoring other world events. Five hundred thousand East Pakistanis had died in a massive typhoon and tidal wave, and the State Department was in the midst of relief operations. There were troubles in Ghana. And Secretary of State Rogers was preparing for a trip.

In Flag Plot at Coast Guard Headquarters Lieutenant Tritbough listed in his log:

2030   RCC Boston advised that man in question had come aboard the CGC VIGILANT requested to stay and is being returned at this time at written request of his ship's Master. VIGILANT will escort vessel to beyond the Contiguous Zone. RCC will give press no comment unless advised otherwise. Passed to O,CCS,CA,C, State Ops. DO and A not in. DO will call. CA says RCC no comment posture is approved at this time.

There was nothing more of any significance in Flag Plot that night. Things were so slow that Tritbough would add: "2400 End of Day" shortly after 10:30, anticipating that nothing would happen in the next hour and a half before he went off duty. It was at 10:30 that the pathetic climax of the incident would just begin.

In RCC Boston Lieutenant Ryan was calling Captain Brown on an unrelated matter when Brown asked if he had heard anything more about the news media inquiries concerning the defection.

"No, sir. I have not heard a thing. I just talked with Flag Plot and I mentioned this press thing to him and he said he would get back to me on it."

The tapes at RCC were recording them.

"In the meanwhile," Brown said, "I guess you might say that we do have . . . that there was a possible defector from a Russian factory or mother ship or a trawler or something like that. Oh, dear! How the hell am I going to phrase this!" He paused briefly, then, "This individual had contacted us about the defection and, uh, however, the master of the vessel had requested his return and it was effected at the master's request due to a situation beyond our control."

"All right, sir."

"I think that is just about what you might . . . that's about the only thing you can say," Brown started, then stopped short. He sensed the wording was inadequate, but he could explain the return in no other way.

The wording was, in fact, suggestive. If the situation was "beyond our control," then it was under the control of the Soviets; an outrageous thought when considered with the fact that the *Sovetskaya Litva* was anchored a little more than 800 yards off Tissbury Beach in the clear view of summer homes on Martha's Vineyard.

Aboard the *Vigilant* Commander Eustis was going from the bridge to his cabin to return Kudirka to the Soviets.

While officers in Boston and Washington and officials in the State Department closed their books on the case, Eustis was just entering its most sordid part.

CHAPTER

21

"Set mooring stations, Paul," Eustis told his Executive Officer as the group filed from the Communications Room. Lt. Commander Pakos went up to the wheelhouse as Eustis led Gordon and Obolensky down one flight and into the passageway. Just before they reached the cabin, the ship's turbines were beginning to turn. Their whine was subdued, but inside the cutter's passageways the hum of the metal told the crew they were leaving. A lifted mood, rising with the pitch of the engines, spread throughout the *Vigilant.* Brieze, Burt, and Nickerson, who were in the Captain's Cabin, looked at each other in anticipation. The Soviets looked confused. Only Kudirka, looking out the small porthole of the Watchstander's Head toward the lights of the *Sovetskaya Litva,* remained near panic. Only Commander Eustis, walking down the passageway, remained tormented about the action he would have to take.

All eyes were again on him when he walked into his cabin. "I have orders from Boston to return him," he said resignedly to no one in particular. Obolensky said nothing, so the Soviet interpreter translated the remark.

"I request that you take measures to return the sailor to our ship," Burkal replied.

"Will you return to the ship without him?" Obolensky asked, hoping to persuade him on his own. He remembered Burkal from the Rhode Island seminar as a pleasant and reasonable man.

Before Burkal could even answer, the man in the gray sweater retorted, "No! He is a criminal and will be tried by Soviet law!"

None of the Americans addressed themselves to the statement or took steps to see if the charge was valid. Obolensky kept talking to Burkal, telling him the issue should be settled by diplomats, but Burkal deferred to the man in the gray sweater, who was adamant.

After a quick word with the commissar, Burkal again asked Eustis if he could see Kudirka.

"No!" Eustis said. Turning to Obolensky, he asked if he could persuade the defector to return on his own.

Obolensky glanced at the Captain with a look of a man who had been handed a distasteful assignment, but he agreed to try. He went alone out of the cabin.

"Captain, can I make a call home?" Brieze interjected from where he was sitting. "It is late and my wife will be worried." He explained later that he actually wanted his wife to call the Latvian or Lithuanian legation in Washington to inform them about what was happening.[1]

"I'm sorry, Bob, there are no private calls," Eustis replied.

Obolensky began formulating what he would say to Kudirka as he walked down the passageway. The Captain had asked him to do a difficult thing, but perhaps, he thought, he could better persuade Kudirka in a language they both spoke fluently. Maybe Kudirka would better understand the situation and leave. But how could he tell Kudirka he was a burden? Obolensky slowly climbed the stairway and looked at the door to Kudirka's refuge guarded by a young seaman.

"The Captain asked me to talk with him," Obolensky said, and the seaman moved aside. The interpreter slowly turned the knob, opened the door, and saw Kudirka facing him and breathing excitedly. He knew that Kudirka knew. Though the defector was surprisingly controlled, the fear in his eyes and the bulky life jacket pulsating with his heaving chest told Obolensky what was going on inside him.

As gently as he could, Obolensky said in Russian, "Asylum has been refused you and the Captain has orders from his superiors to return you to your ship."[2]

"I will not return! I will not return!" Kudirka seemed irritated that another person who spoke Russian could not understand why he would not return. "The Captain has told me there is a small boat waiting for me. I told you I will jump into the sea and drown before I go back! I would rather die from the cold!"

Obolensky stated much later that he did not remember all the specifics of his brief conversation with Kudirka, because he himself was "terribly upset" that night.

"What about your family? What about your wife and children?" he remembered asking. "You know the consequences they will suffer because of this."

"I know that. I am aware of that," Kudirka told him. "My decision is irrevocable! I cannot return! Do you understand? I cannot return!"

This exchange convinced Obolensky that Kudirka's decision to defect was not a spur-of-the-moment action precipitated only by the fact that the two ships were moored together. Obolensky knew Kudirka had thought of escape for some time. He explained long afterward: "I think the decision was not sudden, because he was not startled when I told him what might happen to his family." He theorized that had Kudirka jumped impulsively, he would have at least momentarily been taken aback when Obolensky reminded him of consequences to his family. "He had obviously thought this out before," Obolensky would say, "so he didn't react to that."

On the verge of tears, Kudirka said, "The Soviets asked me

to be an informer. They wanted me to denounce my compatriots who had taken to the woods. I refused to do that and have
suffered many years because of it. All other crew members have
mariner's certificates and passports. Do you know what it
means not to have them? They do not let me leave the ship in
port. I am a radio technician, but they do not let me do the work
I am trained for. They make me clean latrines and empty
garbage. They discriminate against me, because I refused to
denounce my compatriots. I have no rights!"

Caught up in the emotion of the moment, Obolensky would
simply not think to ask some follow-up questions about Kudirka's political references. Only the personal griefs and statements stuck in his mind and these he briefly discussed with the
defector. "I just didn't think to follow that up," Obolensky
would lament. "He was talking and I was just asking questions
based on what he said next. I just didn't think to ask him more
about that ['compatriots who had taken to the woods'] or to
search him to see if he had really stolen those rubles."

Generally, Obolensky's amiable attitude toward Burkal
prompted him to take the Soviets at their word, so he did not
outrightly reject the notion that Kudirka had stolen 3,000 rubles from Captain Popov's safe. The others, including even
Admiral Ellis, saw the charge as a frame-up. But Obolensky,
maintaining what seemed a neutral attitude, never entirely rejected the notion that Kudirka was guilty. Later actions bore
out the fact that he could not have stolen any rubles, but more
than a year after the incident, Obolensky would still say: "I
don't know. I just don't know."

At the moment, other things were going through Obolensky's mind.

"Now that I have escaped they will kill me," Kudirka told
him. "My life is no good over there." He repeated that the
Captain had promised a small boat would be waiting for him
when he jumped into the water. "I will jump into the sea! I
would rather drown than go back!"

Kudirka still maintained a tenuous hold on his self-control, but his muscles quivered and he seemed to be shivering. Obolensky knew that he was determined to jump into the water and that he still had a shred of hope for salvation. He could not convince him to go back—he had not put his heart into trying.

Obolensky returned to the Captain's Cabin and reported his conversation to Eustis. All the Americans turned to the three Soviets standing together on one side of the room, as if waiting for some sign of confirmation from them.

"There may be some validity to . . ." Burkal began, but the man in the gray sweater spit out "*Stoj!*" ("Stop!"), and Burkal stopped in mid-sentence.

"The defector refuses to go back by himself. Will you return to your ship and let this be handled by diplomatic channels?" Eustis asked once more.

Burkal refused to leave and again asked to speak with Kudirka.

This time Eustis felt he had to consent. He agreed and led Burkal, the man in the gray sweater, and their interpreter out the door. Obolensky followed them.

They all quietly filed down the passageway and up the stairs to the Watchstander's Head.

When Kudirka saw the Soviets standing outside the doorway he cringed toward the far corner of the little room and almost stumbled over the stool.

"They just want to talk to you," Obolensky said reassuringly. He stepped to one side of Kudirka, while Eustis stayed on the other. Burkal was facing him. Outside stood the man in the gray sweater and the interpreter, flanked by the seaman who had been guarding the door.

"Semion Ionovich. Why have you taken this action?" Burkal asked in Russian, using the patronymic.

"Ivan Nikolaiovich," Kudirka shot back. "You know why I have taken this action." Kudirka had been terrified, but now, in encountering Burkal, his fear was turning to rage. He spit out

to Burkal what he had told Obolensky earlier. "You discriminate against me! You give me menial jobs! You don't give me
identification papers! You know I have trouble with my stomach! You give me food that only aggravates it!"

"I know, I know," Burkal replied, trying to stop the outburst.
Then he continued in a low tone, "Semion Ionovich, Remember
what you are doing. Remember you have a wife and children.
Remember the punishment they will be facing."

"I know, I know," Kudirka retorted, mocking Burkal's
words.

"What about your mother . . .?" Burkal continued, but
Kudirka cut him short.

"I know this, you fool!" Kudirka hissed. His rage was mixed
with the frustrated knowledge that Burkal meant what he said.
They would take reprisals not only on his family but on his
friends as well.

Burkal told him he would fail in the United States, but
Kudirka answered that he was willing to do the worst possible
work rather than go back.

Abruptly, Burkal switched to Lithuanian. Obolensky knew
that Burkal was saying something he did not want the Americans to know. The tone to Obolensky sounded ominous.
Kudirka automatically replied in Lithuanian and the two exchanged some heated words. Obolensky would recall that by
replying in Lithuanian, Kudirka probably was drawn into Burkal's game and so revealed to the Americans nothing more
about his condition or perhaps further reasons for defecting.
Was Burkal threatening Kudirka? Did he say something that
would have led to a different decision from Brown or Ellis? Did
he say something that would have moved Eustis to risk his
career and take Kudirka into port? These are tantalizing questions that must remain speculative.

Obolensky would only wistfully recall the exchange and say
Kudirka was unconsciously maneuvered by Burkal into the
Lithuanian language.

Still in Lithuanian, Kudirka began to harangue Burkal and his associates with a vehemence that suggested a catharsis of years of subjugation, of hidden thoughts and ideals, of fear of expression and freedom of action. It did not matter anymore how openly he spoke to Burkal. His leap had already condemned him. Burkal retorted in kind, and his phrases were interspersed with stern words by the man in the gray sweater. Neither Obolensky nor Eustis understood what he said, but both sensed that Burkal's and the commissar's remarks were threatening.

His face red and the veins of his neck and temples bulging, Burkal stormed out of the head, followed by Eustis and Obolensky. As they descended the stairs to the passageway, the seaman closed the door on Kudirka, who was taking short quick breaths and trembling.

"The only way to get him back will be by force," Burkal declared as they filed back along the passageway.

"I wouldn't subject my men to such a thing," Eustis replied with a sudden realization that he held a trump card. As soon as they were in the cabin he went to an intercom located on a wall and ordered "secure mooring stations."

Within a minute the pitch of the turbines decreased and soon the engines were shut down completely. Ensign Hughes wrote in the log: "2125 [9:25] Secure all engines and turbines." It was just a notation, but with the winding down of those engines the officers and crew suspected a hitch in developments. They interpreted the silence as something bad for the defector. Otherwise, they would have left long ago. But Commander Eustis had stopped the engines for another purpose. He knew this would take some time, but believed that the Soviets might leave without Kudirka after all. Force would have to be used to get him off, he thought, but certainly he was not about to subject his men to something like that. If the Soviets were suggesting that the Coast Guard force him back, they would just have to leave without him.

Burkal repeated, "Force will have to be used to get him back to our ship."

Before Eustis could say anything, Obolensky replied, "What you suggest is against the civilized behavior of human beings." He asked Burkal again to leave without Kudirka, feeling that somehow Burkal was reacting more favorably to him than to the others.

Burkal turned to the man in the gray sweater—they had similar ruddy looks, except for the difference in clothes—and conferred with him a moment. "We would like to call our Embassy in Washington," he said when they finished.

John Burt, already upset over the turn of events, stood up and addressed Eustis in his gruff, Bostonian accent. "If Robert Brieze and I protest giving this man back, will it do any good? Will it do any good to protest? We can hold him until we find out if he's a thief and everything else." Burt's comment was theoretically the most logical, and a search of Kudirka was something they should have done in any event, but Eustis was beyond any more maneuverings. He was standing by his own final effort: If the Soviets did not take Kudirka back themselves, he would not do it for them.

"I think the State Department should know about this before you let them call the Soviet Embassy," Lieutenant Morehouse suggested. It was one of the few remarks he made that evening. Eustis would remember his role in the phrase: "He sort of faded into the background as the day went on."

Though he did not entertain Burt's question or the suggestion of Lieutenant Morehouse, Commander Eustis was intrigued with the idea of a call to the Soviet Embassy. If he did not use his own men to return Kudirka and the Soviets seemed reluctant to use force themselves, maybe their Embassy would advise them to leave the defector with the Americans.

"You can use my phone," he told Burkal, "if I can get a phone patch through for you." Eustis sent for a radioman who was soon at the door.

"Yes, sir."

"Can you get a phone patch to the Soviet Embassy?"

"Yes, sir," the radioman replied and left.

"What's up?" asked Lieutenant Burke, the Communications Officer, when the radioman returned to the radio room.[3]

"The Captain wants a phone patch with the Soviet Embassy."

"Oh. Well, maybe I'd better make that call myself," Burke said. Communications on the frequencies they had used for earlier phone patches were becoming riddled with static, so he hailed the Boston marine operator and asked her to call the Soviet Embassy in Washington. She did.

"This is the Embassy of the USSR," a voice answered when the patch was complete.

"I have a call from the U.S. Coast Guard Cutter *Vigilant*. Stand by, please," the operator said.

"Soviet Embassy, Coast Guard Cutter *Vigilant*. Uh, stand by, please," Lieutenant Burke repeated. He did not know what to say.

There was silence on the line. Finally the operator interrupted, "Isn't anybody going to say anything?" No words had been exchanged for several minutes.

"This is an important call, operator, over," Burke explained.

About five minutes later Lt. Commander Pakos walked into the room. He had heard the request for a radioman over the loudspeakers and had come down from the wheelhouse out of curiosity.

"Who is the call to?"

"The Soviet Embassy, sir," Burke told him.

"Cancel it," Pakos ordered without hesitation.

"Yes, sir, Mr. Pakos," Lieutenant Burke replied and terminated the call.

Meanwhile, in the Captain's Cabin, Obolensky was heatedly pleading with Commander Eustis. Sweeping his hand along his long hair, as he habitually did, Obolensky said, "If Burkal can call the Soviet Embassy, William Gordon should be able to make another call to Washington." He suggested the Office of the Special Assistant to the Secretary for Fisheries and Wildlife or the Secretary of State himself. Obolensky was convinced that someone along the line had botched the situation, which called for inquiries at the top if need be. He was visibly agitated, but did not confront Eustis; he could only sympathize with the Captain's dilemma.

But the civilians were sour over the fact that the Soviets should be able to freely consult with their Embassy, while Eustis grappled with an order they were sure was illegal.

Feeling pressured from all sides, Eustis called his Executive Officer to the cabin. The civilians' opinions rang true, but Eustis was already reconciled to what he felt he had to do. He now needed moral support, not lessons on what he should really do. His Executive Officer had given support in every action thus far and Eustis would warmly remember: "Paul was the only one who was really close to me that night."

When Pakos arrived, he motioned him to the adjacent wardroom where Eustis summarized for him the events of the previous half hour—Obolensky's conversation with Kudirka and Burkal's confrontation with him.

"They said force will have to be used, but they didn't seem too willing to use it themselves. I told them I wouldn't use my men to take him back, and then they asked if they could confer with their Embassy."

"Ralph, I don't think the Soviets should be allowed to call their Embassy until the State Department hears about it first. Mr. Burke had an open line to the Embassy a little while ago, but I cancelled it."

He explained to Eustis that the issue of force was a new factor and they could possibly do something with it to evoke a different decision.

"Well, let's look at it this way," Eustis replied. "He's going to escape from them and we're going to recover him, so the situation will be different."

"Yes," Pakos agreed. "It's different than if he escaped from us and we caught him ourselves."

"Then we can get a review of the situation," Eustis said, desperately looking for an exit from the maze in which he found himself.

"I would recommend we send another message telling them about the latest developments," Pakos suggested.

Commander Eustis agreed.

Pakos searched a desk for some paper, found a legal pad, and taking out his pen began printing: "FM VIG . . . TO CCGDONE [Coast Guard District One]." Then, very purposefully, Pakos added: "INFO COMDT" in order to ensure that the message reached Headquarters in Washington. Earlier messages had been headed only to the First District, but Lt. Commander Pakos intuitively knew the situation now warranted a guarantee that the First District be bypassed and that the command in Washington see what was happening. Without openly questioning the Captain's procedures up to then, Pakos was doing something that was in effect a maneuver around Commander Eustis. Indeed, it was also a maneuver around Captain Brown and Admiral Ellis in the First District. Pakos testified: "I felt proper authority [the First District] could not possibly fully appreciate the circumstances aboard the *Vigilant.* And I felt that maybe the 'Info Commandant' would stimulate more discussion in the matter [at Headquarters]."

Under the heading the Executive Officer hastily printed the following message:

1._____, Radio Officer, jumped from the Soviet vessel *Sovetskaya Litva* to rail of CGC Vigilant at approx 2310630R and requested political asylum. Vigilant was moored alongside Soviet vessel in posit   within territorial waters of U.S.

2. Escape was detected by Soviets and they have formally requested return of crewman. CGCDONE directed compliance and Vigilant has complied. However, it is clear to Soviets that force will be required to remove Simas. Simas has threatened to jump overboard at the earliest opportunity for fear of his life if returned. Soviets reluctant to use force and plan consultation with Soviet Embassy, Washington.

3. Understand that alternate solution is to keep—

Pakos stopped and thought a moment. He was implying they would keep Kudirka, but that was flirting with insubordination and he did not want to go that far. He crossed out several words and began again.

3. Recommend alternate solution by bringing Simas in custody to U.S. while Soviets achieve release through diplomatic channels.

The Executive Officer was sure the message would change the decision. Even though it was addressed directly to the First District the wording was for Washington. He showed the draft to Eustis who quickly read it, then rejected it.

"No, Paul. We'll call Captain Brown and discuss it with him personally." Eustis told the Board of Investigation: "I would have considered this [Info Comdt] a normal proceeding if I had done it on previous messages, and I did not now want to in any way go directly to the Commandant, even as an info addee on a message." Though the situation had developed into something extraordinary, Eustis still preferred very narrowly to interpret his duties (going through channels) and did not risk adding the words "Info Comdt."

Commander Eustis reminisced on that moment more than a year later and said: "I don't think he was trying to maneuver around me. I think he was trying to do the same thing I was trying to do with Captain Brown. I was trying to buy time, provide more information to somehow get a different decision. I think Paul was trying to do the same thing." But just as Captain Brown had frustrated Commander Eustis's efforts, Eustis now frustrated his Executive Officer's efforts. Blind duty was still stronger than their human compassion—they had been trained well.

Instead of clearing the message with the "Info Commandant," Eustis told Pakos, "Why don't you just summarize the three points and I'll tell them to Captain Brown. Maybe there's still some way I can get across to him directly that I'm very concerned for this man's life." His instinct to save Kudirka was strong, but he would only let himself express it through channels.

"Okay, Captain," Pakos replied. He was disappointed, but deferred to his Commanding Officer; maybe Captain Brown could still be convinced.

Pakos tore the paper off the pad, flipped it over, turned it lengthwise, and wrote in large, widely spaced print that suggested speed and urgency:

1. Soviets apparently reluctant to use force.
2. Soviets want to consult w/Embassy.
3. Rec. alt solution take into custody & let U.S.S.R. get thru diplo channels.

Eustis glanced at the notes and was satisfied that they covered the salient points of the proposed message. He took the paper and both officers went up to the radio room to call Captain Brown and persuade him to reverse his order.

About the same time Captain Murphy telephoned Lieutenant Ryan in RCC. It was one of three inquiries made that night by the Acting Chief of Operations of the District. He was curious, but had no influence in the case. Commander Curry, the Intelligence Chief, called once that night to check on the progress of the case. He, too, felt that since his superiors were handling it, he could do nothing to change the outcome. Commander Flanagan, the other officer who had taken part in the afternoon staff conference in Captain Brown's office, did not bother to check with RCC after he left his office. Captain Brown had casually convinced him that the defection would not occur.

As soon as Captain Murphy said "Hello," Lieutenant Ryan knew what to report.

"Yes, sir, uh, this thing is all set. Uh, the Captain wanted the man back, so we gave him back to them, and it looks like they will be getting underway and escorting them out of the waters."

"Mmmm, hmmm," Murphy muttered.

"And that's the last we heard. I haven't heard since then. That was about a half hour or so ago."

"I see."

"But, uh, the Captain did want the man back. He put it in writing. So . . ."

"Was there anything surprising about this?" Murphy retorted.

"No, no. And the *Vigilant* said they were going to break off, you know, and escort the guy out of, uh, territorial and contiguous zone. That's the last we heard."

"I see," Captain Murphy replied. "Good luck to the Red Sox."

CHAPTER

22

Commander Eustis had reached the radio room. He raised the Boston Radio Station and asked the operator to have RCC relay Captain Brown's home phone number to the *Vigilant*, so he could call Brown through the regular marine operator. There had been too much static on the relays via the Coast Guard's own radio station.

Lieutenant Ryan called Captain Brown, and the tapes at RCC recorded the following exchange (which seems flippant considering the gravity of the situation).

"The *Vigilant* is attempting to contact us again," Ryan said when Brown came on the line. "They wanted your telephone number so they could contact you via the marine operator."

"Yeah?"

"I told him I wasn't going to give it out unless you said it was okay."

"Yeah, it's okay," Brown replied wearily. He saw no reason to quibble about a telephone number at a time like this.

Ryan then relayed the number to the *Vigilant*, and Eustis called Brown. Several minutes later, Brown again answered his telephone.[1]

"Captain Brown, this is Cutter *Vigilant*."

"This is Captain Brown. Go ahead, over."

"Uh, Captain, the situation at this time is that we are still

moored alongside the Soviet vessel." Eustis glanced at his outline and continued, "The Soviets have suggested the use of
force, but appear reluctant to use force at this time. Uh, the
Soviets want to . . ."

"Commander Eustis!" Brown cried. "You have no discretion! You have your orders! Use whatever force is necessary! Do
not let an incident occur!"

Brown had dropped the familiar "Ralph" and in a demanding tone had given Eustis a direct order. Commander Eustis
acquiesced without even mentioning the other two points in his
notes. "Uh, roger. Does that include use of Coast Guard force
if necessary? Over."

"*Vigilant*, this is Captain Brown. Use whatever force is
necessary! Over."

"Roger on that. This is Cutter *Vigilant* standing by this
frequency."

Eustis knew he had no more room for maneuvering and he
would no longer equivocate. This final order had galvanized his
resolve to obey his order. He and Lt. Commander Pakos
stepped outside the radio room and once more went through
the pros and cons of the dilemma.

"For some reason the bigger picture means that this has to
be done," Eustis finally declared to his Executive Officer. "I
don't know what it is, but we have to have faith to do what we
are told." He explained in an interview: "I realized that I was
aware only of the situation that existed aboard the *Vigilant* and
must count on the wider knowledge of my superiors of the total
United States diplomatic position to make the best decision for
our government."

Reluctantly, Pakos agreed. He himself had planted that alternative in Eustis's mind during the discussion with Gordon and
Obolensky. Eustis had committed himself to it, rather than risk
censure or worse from the Coast Guard.

Pakos was drained and his light frame looked even more
gaunt from the strain, the maneuverings. "Ralph," he said, "If

we are really going to do this terrible thing, we should get on with it."

Eustis wordlessly agreed. Deep within him he appreciated his Executive Officer's support and that he had made the suggestion to proceed. "Okay, Paul, pipe mooring stations. I'm going back to tell the Russians."

He was resolved to carry out his order, but that did not settle his mind as he walked down the stairway and into the passageway. Silently, his feet fell on the carpeted floor as he approached his cabin. His conscience assailed him and it showed on his face. He knew he was willfully doing something he believed was wrong and his muscles tensed in protest.

As he walked into his cabin Gordon asked that he call the Office of the Special Assistant or the Secretary of State.

"I can't," Eustis replied. "I've spoken again with my commanding officer in Boston and have orders to return him. I have orders to use force if necessary."

Further argument by the civilians was futile. They could try to persuade him to ask for a change of orders, but they knew they could not convince him to commit mutiny, nor did they try. Burkal and the man in the gray sweater wore looks of silent content in their victory, while their interpreter remained passive. In what was by now a familiar ritual, Burkal and his commissar conferred again in Lithuanian.

Eustis was hoping they would leave, because he was determined to refuse any request for force.

"I need six men to take him back," Burkal declared. Obolensky, upset and disgusted, remained silent, so the Soviet interpreter had to translate the phrase.

"Gee, if a couple of you can't handle him, you really need six men," Eustis thought to himself, but out loud he answered, "You and your skipper should take him back."

"No. We cannot do it," Burkal said. "We are officers and we cannot do it. We need six men."

"The three of you should be able to take him back," Eustis persisted.

"No, Captain. Three are not enough."

Brieze would remember the conversation as a bargaining for a man's life, while the other civilians would not recall specifics about it. Brieze's own experiences had etched a sensitivity to such matters deep in his soul.

Eustis and Burkal were still bargaining, but finally Eustis said, "Are two more enough?"

"No," Burkal replied. "I need two more besides."

Eustis gave in. "Okay, you can bring three additional men from your ship." Seeing Burkal only as a fellow-officer, Eustis sympathized with his position; obviously, Burkal's dignity as a leader would be compromised if Burkal himself had to take Kudirka back.

Burkal's face spread into a wide smile. Uttering phrases in Russian, he briskly stepped up to Eustis, grabbed his hand, and started pumping it vigorously. Brieze closely watched the scene from his seat. To him it formalized a betrayal—this sickening shaking of hands. He had both pity and contempt for the Captain, who he felt was stupidly being manipulated by the Russian.

Eustis himself was self-conscious about the handshake and quickly drew back his hand.

The man in the gray sweater was showing no emotion; but, when he heard the agreement for three additional men, he scurried out of the cabin.

During the bargaining, Lt. Commander Pakos had come into the cabin. He waited for it to end, then asked Commander Eustis to come with him to the adjoining stateroom. When they were alone, the Executive Officer told him that mooring stations were set and preparations were being made to lower the launch. Pakos told the Board of Investigation: "We fully expected the man to go into the water and we were going to get him."

Their compassion for Kudirka was not stifled, even though their actions were by now fruitless gestures aimed as much at mollifying their own consciences as saving Kudirka.

Eustis was painfully aware that everything, everything now depended on what he himself would do.

Pakos returned to the bridge, and Eustis went back to his cabin to tell Burkal he would try once more to convince Kudirka to return on his own.

Minutes before that, Lt. Commander Pakos had piped "mooring stations" and was looking out the wheelhouse windows to see crewmen take their positions.

The turbines were again coming to life with their eerie whine.

"Mr. Pakos, are we leaving?" Lieutenant Lundberg asked as he came into the wheelhouse. It was the third time "mooring stations" had been piped that evening.

"Yeah, we'll be getting underway in a few minutes," Pakos replied.

Lundberg returned to the port boat deck and positioned himself in the doorway from where he could look up the stairway to the Watchstander's Head and down the deck to the flight area.

The stage was being set for tragedy.

Ensign John Hughes was on the flight deck as Gunnery Officer, accompanied by two gunner's mates. In after steering on the fantail, Engineman Third Class Santos was leaning out a hatch waiting for the unmooring. Nearby stood Boatswain's Mate First Class Towne.

No light from the Soviet ship reached their station, because the flight deck overhung part of the fantail. Joseph Jabour, Commissaryman Third Class, was fumbling in the dark by a rear bulkhead looking for the jack to plug in his telephone. In the haste someone had ordered him to be the phone operator on the fantail. He finally located the jack, plugged in the phone, and walked back to the stern railing trailing a long cord behind the phone apparatus strapped to his chest. He wore large earphones and a mouthpiece extended from his chest pack. He would be relaying orders from the bridge to mooring details nearby.

As Jabour waited for instructions, he heard over the phone to be prepared to throw off all lines and leave. Lt. Commander Pakos was making ready for a quick rescue of Kudirka when he jumped. Pakos had ordered the boat crew to stay near the launch without arousing attention. They were to be ready to lower the launch at a moment's notice. Boatswain's Mate Third Class Maresca and several other crewmen had drifted slowly toward the boat davits and were milling idly around them, exchanging remarks with Ensign Hughes and the gunner's mates.

When everything was set, Pakos had gone below to report that mooring stations were set and preparations had been made to grab Kudirka from the water. He had heard at that point that three more Soviets would be allowed to come aboard to get Kudirka. When Pakos returned to the wheelhouse, he sent Lieutenant Lawrence Hale to guard the Soviets who would be coming aboard, then went out to the port bridge wing to observe the proceedings. Just then, the man in the gray sweater hurried out the hatch and to the flight deck. He leaned over the railing, shouting something to a group of men at the rail of the *Sovetskaya Litva,* then hurried back inside the *Vigilant.*

There was sudden movement on the Soviet ship as shadows outlined by the vessel's lights jostled each other to get onto the tire rig. They clung precariously to the wire and to each other as the rig lifted off the deck and swung toward the cutter like a ball on a wrecker crane. No crewman was steadying the rig this time. It was just a dark mass swinging freely over the empty space between the two ships. When it was just a few feet above the cutter, it split into seven dark forms which landed on the flight deck of the *Vigilant.*

Seven menacing faces looked at the American crewmen on station. Ensign Hughes recognized one of them—the second mate who had entertained him and Lieutenant Lundberg that afternoon. Next to the mate stood the engineer, wearing a scowl. Towering above the other six was the first mate of the *Sovetskaya Litva*. The rest were anonymous, dressed in work clothes, each one of them husky, each looking like the others. The mates and the engineer had taken off their uniforms and all of them looked ready for some kind of dirty work. One of them held a thick coil of rope. Another had a tan blanket bunched in his arm and in his other hand held a sock that appeared to have something in it. He put the sock toward his mouth, indicating it would be used as a gag. But the gesture was too voluntary and out of character with the hostile mood of the seven men. Some *Vigilant* crewmen would later interpret the gesture as a cover for some other, more hurtful, use of the sock —a sock perhaps filled with metal.

Crewmen gravitated toward the intruders as if building a wedge against an expected onslaught. They stood on deck facing each other in the dark—the Americans and the Soviets— waiting.

As soon as Lieutenant Lundberg saw the Soviets lifted across, he came running down the deck. He stepped between the Soviets and Americans and ordered a search for weapons. The Soviets seemed passive and compliant when confronted with Lundberg's demand and submitted easily to a frisk by Lieutenant Lundberg and Lieutenant Hale. When his turn came, the stocky man with the blanket and sock lifted his hands, raising the sock out of sight.

Having seen all the Soviets come aboard, Lt. Commander Pakos ran onto the flight deck. "Only three or four of them will be allowed to go forward to get him," he declared. "Keep the others where they are." Pakos had heard Eustis allow three more Soviets to come aboard, but took no steps to order the other four—who were uninvited—off the ship. He turned away and went back to the wheelhouse.

"Only three or four can go forward," Lundberg repeated to Lieutenant Hale and returned to his vantage point in the boat deck hatchway.

No sooner had Lundberg left when all seven Soviets began pushing their way forward. Hale and several crewmen bodily pushed them back.

There is no question that the Soviets felt they had the upper hand in the matter, even to the extent of acting at home aboard the *Vigilant* and disregarding directives from the American officers.

"Hey, are we going to be armed?" a crewman asked as they shuffled in the dark. "I don't know. I sure hope so," came a reply. Other crewmen echoed approval, but neither Lieutenant Hale nor Ensign Hughes entertained the idea of asking for arms for their men. They were still able to control the Soviets on deck —barely.

The Soviets were feeling out the Americans, checking for the type of reaction. After the first jostle, the first mate muttered something to his men and four of them charged in the direction where Lieutenant Lundberg had disappeared, while two others took off across the flight deck with the obvious intent of charging the bridge from both port and starboard hatchways. Shouting warnings to each other, Hale and three crewmen jumped in front of the four just as they were even with the boat davit. Grunting and cursing, they pushed the Soviets back, struggling hard to restrain them.

Seaman Maresca, who was standing on the starboard side of the flight deck, leaped in front of the other two Soviets with another crewman, but the Soviets were pushing past them.[2]

"Hey! Martin!" Maresca shouted, and another crewman came up behind him. Together they leaned into the two Soviets and pushed them back to the port side of the flight deck.

After forcing them all to the spot where they had landed,

Lieutenant Hale ran forward to the boat deck hatch. "Mr. Lundberg! I can't keep 'em! If this keeps up I'm not going to be able to hold 'em! They're really anxious!"

"Get some help!" Lundberg exclaimed, "but keep 'em there!"

Lieutenant Hale returned to the boat davit where Ensign Hughes was talking to his acquaintance, the second mate. "Listen, you have to stay on the spot until I receive orders that you can go. And you aren't going anywhere until I receive the word."[3]

The mate listened perfunctorily to Hughes's exasperated command, turned to his companions, and relayed what the officer had said. The Soviets complied, but kept looking obstinately at the Americans assigned to control them.

Lieutenant Lundberg observed the scene from where he stood, hoping the crew would be able to hold the Soviets back. He noticed them settle down but several moments later observed another flurry of activity and heard noises and shouts. The intruders were again trying to muscle their way to the hatch where Lundberg stood.

Again the crewmen pushed them back.

At this point, Commander Eustis was walking out of his cabin, having just told Burkal he would try to persuade Kudirka once more to return voluntarily. Lundberg watched him come down the passageway with a grave look on his face, a look he had never seen his Captain wear before. Eustis said nothing as he turned in front of Lundberg and walked up the stairway. The door to the Watchstander's Head was clearly visible from Lundberg's hatchway. Forgetting momentarily the jostling by the boat davits, Lundberg watched the Captain open the door and go inside.

Commander Eustis walked in on a man who knew his time had come. Kudirka looked apprehensively at the Captain, his fear-stricken eyes saying everything.

With a quaking voice Eustis spoke, hesitating between phrases. "My personal sympathies . . . as a man . . . are with you . . . for your personal desires. But I hope you recognize that I have my authorities above me . . . I have to do what is required of me . . . You will have to return to your ship."

"Please! No send me back! I will not go back! They will kill me! They will kill me!"

Eustis knew Kudirka would not leave by himself, but if he had to give him back he would have to let the Soviets take care of the distasteful details. He did not want to take part in an exercise that would make him feel like a warden leading a condemned man to the death chamber.

During this conversation, Eustis apparently said something to Kudirka which the defector interpreted as a chance for escape. Because of something Eustis said, Kudirka followed him out of the Watchstander's Head. That something could only have been an assurance to Kudirka that he would be able to jump overboard before the Soviets laid a hand on him. Nothing else did, or could have persuaded Kudirka to leave the head on his own. Commander Eustis never admitted offering Kudirka a chance to escape, but indirectly let it be understood that that was the case.[4]

Kudirka cautiously followed Eustis down the stairway still wearing the life jacket. Meanwhile, Burkal and the man in the gray sweater had come out of the Captain's Cabin and were walking down the passageway, apparently wondering what was keeping Eustis.

When Kudirka reached the bottom of the stairs he spotted them. "No! No! No!" he cried, realizing there was no escape in the narrow passageway. He turned, charged up the stairs taking two at a time, and leaped back into his refuge.

Eustis glanced resentfully at Burkal and his commissar and went back up the stairs himself. The two Soviets returned to the cabin.

Back in the head, Eustis once more told Kudirka that if he

did not go voluntarily, the Soviets would be allowed to come and get him.

Simas Kudirka despaired.

With a resolution that subdued his fright he asked, "Oh, oh, please Captain, give me a knife. I will kill myself." The words would haunt Eustis for months and he would never forget them. In making his request, Kudirka had suddenly become the master of his fate. If the Americans could not help him, he would solve his destiny himself.

Eustis was stunned, but not entirely surprised by Kudirka's fatal bent. He had told him all along that he feared for his life and now was ready to die by his own hand rather than undergo whatever tortures he had envisioned.

"No! You know I can't let you do that," Eustis told him. He knew the obvious repercussions of such an act and did not want to be held accountable for Kudirka's death—indeed, he did not want him to die at all. The whole idea was just incomprehensible to Eustis.

There was nothing more to say. There was nothing more to ask. Kudirka's last and ultimate proposition had been rebuffed. He was now in a vacuum, aware of it, but never knowing how it came to envelope him. He would never know that his destiny —so foreboding—was a hodgepodge of appeasement, lethargy, naiveté, callousness, and bureaucratic clumsiness.

The Captain stood before him, sympathetic, compassionate, but Kudirka now saw him only as an instrument that would deliver him to his fate. He was deep in the metal innards of an American ship, but he might as well have been floundering in a wind-tossed sea.

He was forsaken.

Slowly and with trembling hands, Kudirka took off the life preserver that had given him a measure of hope and comfort and put it on the stool. Then he reached into his shirt pocket and took out the notebook with his papers and photographs. He handed it to Eustis. Digging into a hip pocket, he took out a small dictionary and handed it over also. Eustis looked sullenly at the notebook in his hands. It was soft and pulpy from constant use. A few papers stuck out of the edges.

Kudirka unbuttoned his flannel shirt, removed it, rolled it up, and gave it to Eustis. He stood there in a sleeveless undershirt and shuddered.

The Captain could stand no more. He turned away and stepped out of the head. Eustis was choked up as he climbed down the stairs. Tears began welling in his eyes as he walked down the passageway toward his cabin, clutching Kudirka's belongings.

"He's all yours," he said when he walked in. The words came with difficulty and his voice quivered. His eyes were glistening with tears. Brieze, Gordon, Obolensky, and Nickerson watched in helpless silence, feeling deep pity for Eustis, who they knew was stifling his conscience.

Burt had gone out with Lieutenant Morehouse to see what was going on.

As the Soviets started for the door, the man in the gray sweater told Eustis that several crewmen were waiting outside to get Kudirka. Eustis did not reply, but led Burkal, the commissar, and their interpreter back to the Watchstander's Head.

In his refuge Kudirka was moving back and forth as if looking for more space. He looked down at Lundberg through the open doorway and cried, "Please! Give me a board, anything!" Impulsively, Kudirka dropped to his knees and with clenched hands implored, "Please! Please! No send me back!"

The plea sent chills down Lundberg's spine.

He was sickened by the pathetic scene, but felt utterly powerless to do anything. His Coast Guard uniform was like a straitjacket. Glancing to his left, Lundberg saw Commander Eustis leading the Soviets along the passageway.

Kudirka was still on his knees in the head.

"Three more men can come and get the defector," Eustis said when he came up to Lundberg.

Lundberg leaned out the hatchway, held up his hand with three fingers extended for Lieutenant Hale to see. "Three!" he called out mechanically.

Three of the Soviets pushed past their guards and came running down the deck. Lundberg stopped them at the hatchway and recognized them immediately. They were the same ones who had so jovially entertained him aboard the *Sovetskaya Litva*—the first mate, the second mate, and the engineer, the curly-haired, dimple-cheeked engineer. Their mood now was different, and Lundberg could feel viciousness emanating from their stares.

Commander Eustis turned and started walking back to his cabin completely overcome with bitterness, humiliation, and grief. He had unceremoniously given up Kudirka.

Now, Lieutenant Lundberg stood alone between the man on his knees at the top of the stairs and the six Soviets eyeing him virulently.

Ivan Burkal glared at Lundberg, puffed out his chest and, pointing to it with his inturned thumb, boasted, "I Captain. Me Captain."

CHAPTER

23

Kudirka was still on his knees when five Soviets ran up the stairs to get him. "Oh, God! Help me!" he cried pitiably, looking at his attackers.

Burkal, the man in the gray sweater, and the first mate jammed into the room. Burkal, who had told Eustis it would be improper for him, an officer, to get Kudirka himself, was the first to smash his fist into the side of Kudirka's head. All three then pommeled him as he kneeled. Unable to ward off the barrage of fists and kicking feet, Kudirka began to scream above the shouts of the Soviets.

Frozen with shock, Lieutenant Lundberg stood in the hatchway watching. He was the only American on the scene. Normally he would have gone to his mooring station, but now Lundberg stood transfixed, as if his presence was the only thing he could offer Kudirka.

The first three Soviets dragged him screaming out of the head, and two more fell upon him. They beat him and kicked him incessantly as they dragged him to the stairs. At the top of the landing Kudirka went limp, apparently stunned by the blows. Two of the Soviets, both propping him up by the arms, began leading him down the stairs. But as soon as they reached the bottom, Kudirka suddenly wrenched free and pleading, "Help me! Help me! Help me!" ran down the passageway toward the Captain's Cabin.[1]

John Burt and Lieutenant Morehouse had appeared at the opposite hatchway and watched in surprise as Kudirka ran toward them. Burkal and his commissar were right behind him, flailing at him and shouting in Russian.

Still crying, "Help me! Oh, God, help me!" Kudirka grabbed the knob of the door to the Captain's Cabin and opened it. With one hand on the doorknob and the other grasping the doorway, he tried to pull himself inside, but Burkal was already upon him, battering him and trying to break his hold.

The men in the cabin were thunderstruck. Eustis was leaning on the doorway to his bedroom. His head was bowed and tears were rolling freely down his cheeks—he was weeping. Brieze leaped from his couch and charged toward the door with Gordon at his heels.

"No! No! No! You cannot do this!" he yelled at Burkal as he brushed past Kudirka whose body was glistening with sweat. He would say later that an ugly streak of blood was streaming from his nose onto his lips. Brieze shoved Burkal, trying to break his grip on Kudirka's arm, but to no avail. The four other Soviets were jostling around behind Burkal.

"Bob, please don't get involved," Gordon pleaded just as the Soviets pulled Kudirka back into the passageway. Gordon was trying to keep his voice as even-tempered as he could. "It has now gone so far that we can no longer reverse this. Bob, please sit down!"

In the passageway the Soviets were again battering Kudirka and pushing him toward the port hatch where Lundberg still stood. Bending his body to protect himself from the continuous blows, Kudirka swung his elbows wildly back and forth trying to keep his attackers from grabbing a firm hold. He was totally surrounded. In the commotion, Burkal had found time to close the door to the Captain's Cabin to hide what he and his comrades were doing.[2]

A feeling of utter incredulity overwhelmed Burt as he stood in the starboard hatchway. "This can't be happening here!" he intoned to Lieutenant Morehouse as he watched the fists of five men pounding on Kudirka. "I had to restrain myself. Did you ever see Americans stand by when an underdog was being beaten?" he would tell a reporter the following week. "I bit my lip so hard I could taste the blood."

Inside the cabin an enraged Brieze was yelling at Commander Eustis. "You see! You see! You let them beat the man!"

"Bob! Bob! I can't do anything!" Eustis moaned as he grabbed the sides of his head and swayed back and forth in agony. Tears continued rolling freely down his cheeks as he hunched over in helplessness, trying to block the noises from his mind.

"This is wrong! They should not be allowed to do this on the ship!" Brieze continued excitedly.

"Bob, sit down!" Gordon implored as he tried to calm him. "We're all aware this is wrong. We can't do anything else. We have to let Eustis carry out his orders."

"You're on a military ship. You can be arrested," Brieze remembered someone telling him.

At the hatchway, Lieutenant Lundberg backed off as the strugglers pushed through. "In Russia, Russians beat Russians," he said deridingly.

The second mate heard him, said something to the others, and they eased off, apparently humiliated by Lundberg's remark.

In that instant, Kudirka wrenched free again and dove under the launch which hung several yards away from the hatch. Crouching in the small space under the launch he looked fearfully at five pairs of feet shuffling around it.

Using those few precious moments, Kudirka vaulted the wire railing and lowered himself along one wire, than another, until Lundberg saw only the tips of his fingers clinging to the lip of the boat deck. Kudirka was dangling precariously between the two ships.

Suddenly the fingers disappeared.

"Man overboard!" Lundberg cried and reached for a life preserver hanging on the bulkhead.

From his cabin, Commander Eustis heard only a muffled cry. He perked his head, listening. "Man overboard!" he heard someone yell and exclaimed, "We've got to get the hell out of here!" It was the moment to overcome his paralysis. He ran for the door—this was the chance to save Kudirka, because he was in the water.

When Lt. Commander Pakos heard the cry he also grabbed a life preserver hanging on the bulkhead of the wheelhouse. He tossed it between the two ships and ran to the end of the bridge wing where a signal lamp was attached. Turning it on, he opened the shutters for most light and aimed the beam back and forth between the hulls of the two ships.

He saw nothing.

Upon hearing the cry, Ensign Hughes ran to the rail of the flight deck and noticed the five Soviets by the launch in apparent confusion over what to do. "Take off your life jacket and toss it in there!" he ordered to a gunner's mate at his side, "And go get a battle lantern!" Hughes peered into the water, but saw only the fenders made shapeless and eerie in the beam of the searching light.

Several more life preservers splashed into the water, but there was no one to grasp them.

Kudirka knew exactly what to do. He had carefully studied the conformation of the *Vigilant* for hours that day and knew every stanchion, every rail. Seconds after Lundberg saw his fingers disappear from the lip of the boat deck, Kudirka's searching feet had found the rail of the main deck (port air castle). He had snapped his body forward and pitched himself onto the main deck, landing heavily and bouncing into the bulkhead. He straightened up, looked quickly around him, and dashed toward the stern. As he ran, he heard loud shouts to his right. Turning his head, he saw Russians on the deck of the *Sovetskaya Litva* running along with him, shouting and pointing at him. They had seen his maneuver.

Burkal and his men, still milling around the launch, saw their crewmen running and pointing at the *Vigilant*'s air castle. They charged into the passageway, down a flight of stairs, and out a hatch on the main deck.

At the same time Commander Eustis was running along the passageway for the same stairway, but leading up to the wheelhouse.

Kudirka ran frantically down the port air castle to the fantail and jumped onto the .50 caliber gunmount grid; a small, elevated metal stand from which he glanced around him.

There was nowhere to turn.

Suddenly he saw he was not alone.

His eyes met Jabour's who was looking at him curiously. It was the first time the telephone talker had seen the defector. Kudirka was a curious figure dressed only in a tattered undershirt and dark slacks. Seamen Towne and Santos by the rear bulkhead saw him only from a distance, but they could physically sense his dread. Wide-eyed, Kudirka moved back and forth on the grid. His mind was paralyzed with fear and he was uncertain about his next move.

Then, pleading to Jabour, he pointed to himself and to the water. He wanted to go overboard. Jabour continued staring at Kudirka. He could see the fright controlling his trembling body and tried to think of something he could do to help, but everything was happening too fast.

Several eternal seconds went by as Kudirka, Jabour, Santos, and Towne stared at each other in frozen curiosity. Then they heard the stomp of running feet on the metal decks.

Kudirka's hunters were coming.

New alarm went through him, and he jumped off the grid, dashed to the stern railing, and started to climb it. Santos and Towne instinctively followed. Kudirka boosted himself a little, lifted one foot over the rail, then the other, and taking a deep breath, prepared for the shock of the cold sea as he let go of the rail to fall backwards into the water.

Instead, he felt a steellike grip on his right wrist. Kudirka looked incredulously at Towne and an instant later felt Santos grab his other wrist. He wanted desperately to go into the water where the small boat would be waiting, but the young seamen were betraying him. He spoke to them gently—in stark contrast to his anxiety—trying to convince them to let go. Neither of the seamen understood what Kudirka said, but they knew he wanted to go overboard.[3] Still, they held on and unknowingly foiled the only chance he had left.

Santos would explain in testimony before the Board of Investigation: "Normally people don't jump in the water."

As Towne and Santos held him, the first mate and engineer ran onto the fantail. Without changing stride, they leaped onto the two Americans and reached over their bent bodies for Kudirka's neck. He gasped for air as the two Soviets started pulling him aboard, one holding his neck, the other grabbing for his mid-section. Towne and Santos managed to extricate themselves from the pile and backed off. They stood by and watched.[4]

Kudirka's arms were free, and he grabbed for the hands pressing his neck, trying to regain his breath.

They pulled him aboard on his side, his ribs grating along the top of the rail like a stick along a fence. His whole body throbbed with pain and he was visibly weakening.

As they pulled Kudirka aboard, the man in the gray sweater ran up to the group. In unison, the Soviets battered him as Jabour, Towne, Santos, and several other crewmen at mooring stations farther along the deck looked on.

The sailors testified later that word had been passed to them shortly before "mooring stations" to "stand back." No one recalled who passed the word, and no one would admit passing it, but the sailors did recall such instructions and considered them orders.

The three Soviets chopped at Kudirka's sides and his neck with karate blows. He screamed in pain while the *Vigilant*'s crewmen listened to the thuds against his body. Kudirka was weaker, but in his desperation, adrenaline continued pouring into his bloodstream. He struggled, trying to break free from his attackers, trying to fend off their blows. As the fists continued smashing into him, Kudirka imploringly looked at Jabour who was now about five feet from him and tried to say something to him amid the yelling.[5]

Jabour felt a chill down his spine—he was frightened for the ill-fated man.

Suddenly, one of the Soviets grabbed Jabour's telephone cord to wrap it around Kudirka's neck. Jabour tugged at his end, pushing the mate away at the same time and tearing the wire from his hands. The mate looked at him, actually surprised by Jabour's resistance.

Meanwhile, Burkal had run onto the fantail and joined in the beating. Four Soviets were now trying to batter Kudirka into submission. He continued fending off the blows, occasionally lashing out and landing a punch himself, but his struggle was useless. They swept him off his feet and three of them held him horizontally, carrying him to the rear ladder.

Kudirka moaned. He tried kicking his feet and squirming free, but to no avail. The Soviets held on as they cursed and shouted. One of them grabbed Kudirka's head and began to rhythmically smash it against the steel rail.[6] Kudirka screamed and, with another desperate surge of energy, tried to double himself up so his head would not be vulnerable. But his moves were by now futile.

The mate kept smashing Kudirka's head against the rail of the ladder.

Standing on the flight deck about eight feet from the ladder was Lieutenant Morehouse. He saw the Soviets coming up and stood watching the assault. Ensign Hughes ran to the area from the port railing. He had just realized the defector had not gone overboard. The beam from a spotlight held by Seaman Maresca on the flight deck illuminated the incredible scene; punches were landing all over Kudirka's body as the Soviets brought him up the ladder and stood him up at the rear of the flight deck.[7]

Kudirka could barely lift his arms to ward off the blows.

Hughes noticed his acquaintance, the second mate, battering Kudirka and ran up to him. "Stop! Stop! You can't do that on an American ship! You can use force, but you can't beat him!"

He glared at the second mate, who then turned to his comrades and told them to stop. They pulled their punches and shoved Kudirka toward the tire rig, but still continued chopping at him sporadically with karate blows on the neck and around the kidneys.

Maresca and several other crewmen ran toward the group, ready to assist Kudirka.

"Stay clear! Stay out of the way!" Ensign Hughes shouted as he motioned them back. "It's none of your business!"[8]

The crewmen stopped short and obediently backed off.

Hughes then left the Soviets with Kudirka and ran for the ladder leading to the bridge to report what was going on.

Meanwhile, Commander Eustis had come running breathlessly into the wheelhouse. "Throw off all lines!" he relayed to the telephone talker, then turning to the helmsman ordered, "Back dead astern!" He did not want to turn the ship for fear of crushing the defector between the hulls. He ran out to the port bridge wing and leaned over the coaming, looking down at the decks of the *Sovetskaya Litva*. Recalling the scene, he would say months later: "I was concerned then over many things. One, my people, being typical Americans concerned of human rights, might get in the act one way or another . . . I had a 200-foot ship alongside a 400-foot ship, 50-man crew alongside a 200-man crew, with their people lining the rails watching the scuffle, my people watching the scuffle. I decided, whether

I had Soviets on board or not, it was time to get away from there."

Jabour on the fantail was still looking up the ladder where the Soviets had carried Kudirka. He heard instructions over his phone and ordered, "Throw off three and four." He could hear the struggling above him, but reported nothing about the brutalities he had just witnessed, even though he was in direct contact with the bridge.

Lines were belayed on the *Sovetskaya Litva,* so mooring details in their haste let them go by their bitter ends. Bow and stern lines were winch-operated and could not be detached, so the crewmen hastily chopped them away with axes.

As soon as Ensign Hughes left the Soviets to report to the bridge, they again started beating Kudirka incessantly and chopping at him with karate blows. He squirmed with pain, but could no longer fight. Mustering his last reserves of strength, he could only wearily lift his hands to ward off the blanket which one of the Soviets tried to throw over his head.

Nine men now surrounded him at the end of the flight deck; the first bunch had been joined by the other four who had been kept at the boat davits. They had pushed their way to their comrades when Kudirka was brought up the ladder.

Five of them were throwing punches and chopping him with karate blows—to the back of the neck, the kidney area, the back of the neck, the kidney area.[9]

While they did this they shoved him toward the tire rig. Crewmen on the flight deck were enraged. They were poised, ready to pounce on Kudirka's assailants, but their fury was mixed with frustration and uncertainty. Ensign Hughes had ordered them to "stay clear." The crewmen were ambivalent, felt helpless and confused by their conflicting emotions. Should they obey the order or exercise human compassion and pull the Soviets off Kudirka?

The Americans could have stopped them at any time, but did nothing.

At about that time, the whine of the turbines reached its screaming pitch, and the Soviets abruptly stopped beating Kudirka to look around for the source of the unfamiliar noise; they were startled by the power plant. No human had stopped them, but the *Vigilant* herself—her engines screaming as if in protest over the violation on her decks.

Water churned furiously at the cutter's stern as she backed off from the *Sovetskaya Litva*. The Soviets had resumed beating Kudirka, and from the opposite side of the flight deck Lieutenant Morehouse, standing with Burt, saw four or five more blows land in Kudirka's face while another man chopped at him three or four times across the neck.

Lieutenant Morehouse, an officer and a gentleman, would testify before the Board of Investigation: "Maybe they were hitting the man over the head with a lead pipe, but I didn't see them beating him to an extreme, so I had no feelings for the man."[10]

Kudirka by then could not stand by himself, so his assailants held him up themselves and continued pommeling him.

Suddenly, Ivan Burkal stopped punching, looked at his ship, and saw it receding into the darkness. He was stunned. He stepped back from the pack and hurried toward the boat deck hatch.

The man in the gray sweater also noticed the ship's movement, but his reaction was entirely different. He yelled orders, and his henchmen quickly pushed Kudirka to the winch of the boat davit and started tying him to it. One of them made a hasty loop around Kudirka's neck. He took the loose end and brought his arm back to heave the rope to a shipmate on the *Sovetskaya Litva*. They were going to hang him as the ships separated.[11]

CHAPTER

24

Shortly after he had thrown a life preserver from the bridge wing into the water, Lt. Commander Pakos heard noises on the fantail and noticed dark forms struggling up the ladder to the flight deck, where a single beam from a spotlight illuminated the wild scene.

"There he is!" someone yelled inside the wheelhouse.

Lieutenant Lundberg, who had come up to take the watch, turned to the rear window and saw Kudirka being stood upright and pommeled. The officers watched wordlessly as the captors struggled with their prey across the flight deck. Commander Eustis was still at the corner of the bridge wing watching the cutter starting to pull back from the *Sovetskaya Litva*.

Then everyone heard loud scraping noises and the twangy sound of steel lines snapping. In backing away, the *Vigilant*'s mast had struck one of the booms of the *Sovetskaya Litva*. The collision tore away the cutter's port whip antenna and two other antennas attached to the mast, while four stanchions along the port bow—the ones onto which Kudirka had leaped —were bent out of shape by the tire rig, which seemed to crawl forward along the cutter's deck as the ship backed away.

Eustis looked up. He saw the boom extended over the *Vigilant*'s deck moving towards him and cowered in the corner of the bridge wing, his hands over his head to protect himself from the inevitable falling objects. Pakos was still standing outside the wheelhouse, casually looking upwards—as if expecting rain. Lundberg thought the noise was the mast falling and seeing Pakos outside, unprotected, grabbed him by the shoulder and violently jerked him inside. The Executive Officer stumbled in backwards; he was not as heavy as Lundberg had expected.

"I'm sorry, Mr. Pakos, I thought the mast was coming down," he sheepishly explained as Pakos straightened himself. Lundberg wondered if he could be court-martialed for manhandling an officer.

Just as the *Sovetskaya Litva*'s boom and the cutter's mast collided, Ensign Hughes was climbing the ladder of the signal bridge to report what was happening on the flight deck. He scurried over the top and ran to the protection of the wheelhouse. Hughes did not see the Captain anywhere, so addressed the Executive Officer.

"Mr. Pakos! The man is still aboard! They found him and they're beating him! I stopped them, but when I turn my back, they hit him again! What should I do?"

"Stop it as best you can," Pakos replied. "And take them down to the mess deck."

"Yes, sir," Hughes replied breathlessly and ran back outside.

The boat winch where the Soviets had tied Kudirka was aft of the cargo boom, so they were little affected by the collision. The Soviets looked up momentarily, then prepared to watch Kudirka hang by the movement of the *Vigilant.*

Just then Ensign Hughes returned. He saw the grisly scene and lunged for the hand of the executioner, tearing the rope from his cocked hand. Kudirka stared at Hughes blankly with the other end of the rope still tied around his neck.

"You can't do that on an American ship! You have to stop doing that!" Hughes yelled. "I have orders to take you to the mess deck! Come with me!"

They refused.

Exasperated, Hughes again started for the bridge to report.

He did not know what the Soviets would do in his absence, but he needed instructions. When he left, the Soviets resumed punching Kudirka who was still tied to the winch and completely helpless.

Crewmen on the deck were appalled, but dared not disobey their orders. At one point, a gunner's mate approached the group and urged the men to stop, but they ignored him.

Ensign Hughes once more rushed into the wheelhouse. "Mr. Pakos! Mr. Pakos! They have a rope around his neck! They're trying to kill him!"

"Well, stop it!" Pakos shot back in his own frustration.

"They're trying to tie him up. Should I use Coast Guard people to help tie him up?"

"Yes, but only if necessary," Pakos said, recalling Captain Brown's order to "use whatever force is necessary."

Ensign Hughes hurried back to the flight deck.

Meanwhile, Commander Eustis, feeling that the danger from the collision was over, got up from his corner on the bridge wing and ran into the wheelhouse. Pakos quickly told him what was happening.

"Pipe all hands below deck!" Eustis ordered.

Seconds later, a voice intoned over the loudspeakers, "All hands to the skin of the ship. All hands to the skin of the ship."

Everyone on deck started drifting inside, leaving the Soviets alone with their victim.

Robert Brieze, William Gordon, and Alexis Obolensky had been sitting in silent horror after Kudirka had opened the door to the Captain's Cabin pleading for help.

Their thoughts were interrupted by noises of the collision, and moments after that, Ivan Burkal burst into the cabin. He was a frightened man; pale, confused, apparently thinking the Americans were taking him and his comrades into port. He no doubt thought that he had finally overstepped their bounds of tolerance and had evoked reaction.

"Please. I need assistance," he said through his interpreter, who had returned to the cabin when the beating began.

Gordon felt it was necessary to maintain a surface atmosphere of cordiality throughout the bizarre happenings, so he reassured Burkal.[1] "We will do everything possible to keep the situation steady," he said. "The situation will not deteriorate. Arrangements will be made to return you to your ship. We're extremely sorry that this had to occur." He was apologizing to Burkal.

"I am sorry also," Burkal replied in kind, no doubt pleased by Gordon's suppliant and unexpected attitude, and left the cabin with his interpreter, smug with satisfaction.

Shortly after that, the loudspeakers had intoned "all hands to the skin of the ship," and Lieutenant Morehouse walked in with John Burt.

"When the Captain comes back, he'll want to be alone," the lieutenant from Washington told the civilians. "You'd better go below to the Officers' Wardroom." They all silently filed out of the cabin and followed Morehouse to the wardroom.

Several junior officers were there when the group walked in. Dishes set for mess earlier were gone. No one had bothered to come and eat that evening. The men looked at each other in embarrassed silence—all of them aware something insidious was happening aboard ship. They stood around, paced the wardroom, sat down, stood up again. They were uneasy and could still hear muffled shouts and noises outside mingled with the steady whine of the turbines.

"Maybe they'll take the whole bunch of them to New Bedford," Burt said hopefully to Brieze.

"Maybe we are going home," Brieze agreed.

Burt was fidgety, nervous, and suddenly had a craving for a cigarette. He had not smoked in six weeks, but what he had just witnessed on the flight deck was too unsettling. No one in the wardroom seemed approachable; so he went into the galley and asked a seaman for a smoke. Several minutes later he asked for another, then again, and finally the seaman gave him the whole pack. It did not settle his agitation.

The wardroom was conspicuously quiet.

Ensign Hughes returned the second time from the wheel-house to see the gunner's mate vainly trying to persuade the Soviets at the boat winch to stop hitting Kudirka. Hughes intervened once more with the second mate, asking him to stop. The assailers paused.

"Would you please step inside there," he said, pointing to the helicopter handling shack at the base of the signal bridge.

The second mate motioned his comrades toward the shack. They untied Kudirka from the winch and pushed him across the flight deck with the rope still around his neck. He walked heavily and several of the Soviets jabbed him as they shoved him along.[2]

He barely lifted his feet over the short lip of the hatchway, then stepped inside followed by five of the Soviets. Kudirka was sapped, and no longer struggled.

The shack was a long, narrow work shed with tools and other gadgets strewn over a long, gray work table.

They shoved Kudirka into a corner and stood facing him, speaking to each other. One of them took the rope off his neck while Hughes watched from outside. The second mate turned to him. "He will be returned to his ship," he said in English. "He will have to be tied up."

Hughes felt tying him was no longer necessary, but he still replied, "Okay, you can tie him up."

The five grabbed Kudirka and cudgeled him, as the man with the blanket, assisted by a comrade, wrapped it tightly around him from his neck to his ankles.

"Hey, this can't go on at all on an American ship!" Hughes warned once more. "You can't beat him! If you have to tie him up, tie him up! Force him to let you tie him up, but don't beat him on this ship!"

They stopped hitting but continued binding and jostling him. Soon Kudirka was tied tightly in the blanket. He was completely immobile.

The chasedown and battering had lasted forty-five minutes. It was now almost 11:30.

The *Vigilant* was cruising a half mile from the *Sovetskaya Litva,* and Commander Eustis was conferring with Lt. Commander Pakos in the wheelhouse about how to get the Soviets back to their ship. He did not want to go near the Soviet ship, because of an inordinate fear that the Russians would attack them.

By then, Eustis was too emotionally overcome to have anything more to do with the affair and, after instructing Pakos to use the launch to return Kudirka, went alone to his cabin.

Pakos rushed to the radio room to report the latest developments. While the marine operator placed the call to Captain Brown, he wondered whether he should personally appeal to him to review the order. But Pakos could no longer resist—he was drained physically and mentally and decided to obey to the letter what Eustis had instructed.

"Captain, this is Cutter *Vigilant,*" Pakos said when the phone patch was complete.[3] In the turmoil, he did not say, nor did Brown ask, why Commander Eustis did not initiate the phone patch as he properly should have.

"We had some problems aboard ship. I believe we have lost an antenna on the port side in getting underway. We thought the man had gone overboard, but he did not. He's still aboard." Pakos explained as much as he knew at the time—Soviets had come aboard, they beat Kudirka, they chased him down, they were ready to take him back.

Brown listened wordlessly. He himself had believed Kudirka was headed for an ill fate, but was resigned to his own instructions from Admiral Ellis.

Pakos was still talking. "He is still aboard, and the two ships are apart at this time. Uh, request permission to send Russian party over in the boat. I don't know how many Russians we have aboard, seven or eight or nine, but there are quite a lot of them, over."

"*Vigilant,* this is Boston. How are the weather conditions? Uh, are they satisfactory for operating a small boat? Over."

"Boston, this is Cutter *Vigilant.* The weather is not adverse, and there should be no problems, over."

"This is Boston. Uh, very well. Get the Russians aboard their own ship using your boat, over."

Pakos terminated the conversation.

It was 11:30 P.M. and the *Vigilant*'s last communication with Captain Brown.

Pakos would recall long afterward: "In retrospect, this may have been another lost opportunity [for a change of orders], one which is my fault."

After the phone patch, the Executive Officer hurried from the radio room to the flight deck to see what was going on.

He saw Kudirka wrapped from the neck down in the blanket, surrounded by the ten Soviets near the boat davit. He was sagging, and several of his assailants were holding him upright. One of them gave Kudirka a karate chop across the neck just as Pakos approached.

"If you hit him again, I'll . . ." he began and stopped short. What would he do if they hit him again? "At that point I felt very frustrated," he told the Board of Investigation.

Nearby stood the boat crew. They had been on station to get ready to save Kudirka. Now the boat would be used to facilitate his journey to his doom.

"Get ready to take the Russians back to their ship," Pakos told Seaman Maresca. He turned and went back to the bridge, unable to stomach the scene.

Maresca was worried and frightened. He addressed Lieutenant Hale. "There is no way in the world for me to take that boat without an officer," he declared. Maresca explained in testimony: "The way the Russian crew members were allowed to beat and stomp the defector gave me doubts of any security in the boat." The rest of the boat crew also balked at going without an officer. They feared the Soviets might turn on them en route.

Lieutenant Hale spoke with Ensign Hughes, and they assured Maresca and the others that an officer would accompany them—Hughes himself would go along.

Maresca then wondered out loud if they would be armed.

"No. We don't need anything," Hughes assured him.

As they were speaking, the Soviets laid Kudirka flat on the deck. He could no longer stand by himself.

The Soviets milled impatiently, waiting for the ride back to their ship.

Lights from the *Sovetskaya Litva* were glistening in the darkness off the port beam. The wind was still blowing briskly, and a cold drizzle had begun falling on the decks.

Out of the darkness came Commander Eustis and Alexis Obolensky. The interpreter, fully disgusted, had not even wanted to come on deck, but had reluctantly agreed to perform his duties. Lt. Commander Pakos had also come back, accompanied by Lieutenant Burke.

Lieutenant Lundberg was still in the wheelhouse, emotionally drained. He no longer cared what happened. It was too late to care. He stood at the conn, his only concern being to get the small boat safely away. Glancing out the rear window, he checked to see if it was ready for lowering.

The officers stood around the Soviets in the mounting rain with a certain curiosity and apprehension. No one spoke.

Then Eustis curtly announced, "We'll return you to your ship."

He bent over the bundled form on the deck and, looking into Kudirka's eyes, tried to speak. His words were broken.

"As a man, I'm aware of what's happening and I'm personally concerned for you—for the fact that you have to go—back

to a way of life you obviously don't want. I hope—that—
somehow—things will come out all right for you in the end."

Kudirka was conscious and stared at him blankly, and Eustis
interpreted it as an unemotional expression of fatalism. "That's
the way it has to be," Eustis interpreted in the look.

The Captain straightened up and, without saying anything
more to Burkal or the others, left with Obolensky.[4]

A crew member activated the winch and hydraulic lifts
slowly lowered the launch outward and downward until its
gunwales were even with the deck.

The launch looked like an oversized polyethylene bathtub
and had the notation "VIG 1" on the prow. A molded spray
shield shaped like an archer's bow protected a narrow cockpit
where the helmsman steered the craft with a wheel similar to
one in any car, except that it was perpendicular to the deck.
Located amidships was the engine, which was covered by a
rectangular cowling that reached almost level with the gunwales. There were small cockpits with planks for sitting on
either side of the cowling. It was a utility boat, stubby, but
seaworthy.

First in the launch was the boat crew.

"Follow only my orders," Ensign Hughes said worriedly
across to Maresca at the wheel. "Don't do the obvious, just
follow my orders." Hughes was afraid for his own safety and
that of the boat crew. He suspected the damage to the *Vigilant*
during the collision had been deliberate and felt the Soviets
would do something to the launch when it pulled alongside the
Sovetskaya Litva.

When the Americans were aboard, two of the Soviets
grabbed Kudirka by his feet and shoulders and heaved him like
a sack from the deck into the boat. His body dropped three feet
onto the engine hatch—head first—landing with a muffled
thud.[5]

American officers and seamen on deck and those in the boat
watched in embarrassed silence.

Seaman Maresca looked at the blanket-wrapped, bound figure lying motionless next to him on the cowling. Kudirka's eyes were closed. His brain, jarred beyond endurance by his attackers, had drifted into the merciful blackness of oblivion.

CHAPTER

25

At the same instant when Kudirka's battered and blanket-bound form was being heaved into the launch, Edward Mainland, the Duty Officer at the Bilateral Section of the Soviet Desk in the State Department, was beginning to wonder about the case. It was 11:30 and he had not received any more word about resolution of the affair. The entire matter, in fact, was starting to nag him.

He called Kevin McGuire, the Duty Officer in the Operations Center, and asked if they had any additional information about the defection.[1]

"No," McGuire replied. "Did you check with the Coast Guard Duty Officer?"

Mainland said he had not.

"Why don't you call him and see if they have anything new?" McGuire suggested.

"Do you have the number?"

McGuire found the number for him, and Mainland called Flag Plot. He asked a yeoman about the case.

"I don't know anything about it, sir, and the Duty Officer is asleep."

Mainland did not bother to inquire further. He thanked the yeoman and hung up. He would explain to the Board of Investigation: "Well, my initial assumption, at the first moment there, was that if the yeoman had no knowledge of the case at all ... and the watch officer was asleep then, and nothing had been transmitted to the State Department, obviously there was nothing further beyond the 7:45 [sic] report."

Still, he was uneasy. He did not think he should put the matter to rest solely on his own volition. Something was still nagging him. Something was unusual about the whole thing. He called back McGuire.

"I called the Coast Guard," Mainland told him, "but they told me the Duty Officer was asleep. Do you think I should insist on speaking with him?"

"Yes, I think you should insist on speaking with him," McGuire replied.

Mainland said he would. He again dialed Flag Plot and this time asked the yeoman to awaken the Duty Officer.[2] Lieutenant Tritbough was soon on the line.

"Do you have any more information about the defection case?" Mainland asked after announcing himself. Tritbough recognized his voice from calls on other matters dealing with the Soviets.

"Didn't you get any word from your Operations Office?" Tritbough asked. He had presumed McGuire would pass on the information.

"Yes, I did," Mainland said. "But could you repeat the briefing for me?"

Tritbough would tell the board: "I was left with the impression that he didn't quite understand this. He didn't quite understand what was told to him at this time [when McGuire first reported the return to Mainland]."

The Duty Officer recounted for Mainland the information Lieutenant Ryan had passed from Boston. "The man came aboard, had requested to stay aboard the *Vigilant,* and was returned to his own vessel at the request of the ship's master. The *Vigilant* then escorted the vessel outside the twelve-mile limit."

"Was it necessary to use force?" Mainland asked him.

"The indication that I had at the time was that the man was in the process of being returned, and I had no other information in that regard," Lieutenant Tritbough explained.

"Was there any indication of the man's attitude at that time?" Mainland pressed. Things were not looking too good.

"No, sir. There was no indication of that either, except as I already told you. He had requested to stay aboard."

"Well, is this information available?" He told Tritbough he wanted to have it for the next morning.

"This is fine," Tritbough replied. "I'm sure we'll probably have a complete report on it by that time. I'll be glad to call you in the morning at about seven-thirty."

Mainland thanked him and hung up. He was satisfied that he would have a complete report in time to brief his superiors when they came in to work the following morning.

CHAPTER

26

Having tossed Kudirka into the launch, the ten Soviets climbed in themselves, two of them grabbing his inert body and pulling it from the engine cowling to the stern cockpit. He landed face down and the engineer sat heavily on his neck.[1]

Seconds later the launch slipped toward the black water below with only the muffled whir of the hydraulic system breaking the silence on deck.

John Burt strained to catch a glimpse outside the window of the Officers' Wardroom. "Gee, they got him all wrapped up like a mummy." Several others looked outside to see the launch pass in view and just as quickly disappear.

The launch settled deeply in the water and rode gently in the troughs. As soon as it was under its own power, the engineer, who was sitting on Kudirka's neck, began pounding the sides of his head with his fists.[2] Ensign Hughes turned around.

"Hey! I don't want the man roughed up!"

The second mate said something to the engineer, who got off Kudirka and sat down next to a comrade along the gunwale. But as soon as Hughes turned his back, the engineer again pounced on Kudirka's neck and continued beating at his temples.[3]

Ensign Hughes did not turn around again.

Instead, Seaman Maresca at the wheel heard noises and

turned to see what was happening, only to be met by a menacing stare from the engineer. Maresca was too frightened to say anything and turned his back. He would turn around several more times in order to say something, but each time was cowed into inaction by the menacing stares from the engineer.

Seamen Gonzalves and Morin, who were in the stern, also saw what the engineer was doing, but were afraid to speak up. Six Soviets surrounded them, each giving menacing looks that froze the young seamen.

When the lights of the *Sovetskaya Litva* loomed near, Hughes spoke apprehensively to the second mate. He asked where the best spot would be for a landing and insisted that he did not want to moor to the Soviet ship.

The second mate assured him everything would be all right.

Meanwhile, the man in the gray sweater, noticing the sailors view with shock the pounding on Kudirka's head, created a chilling moment that challenged the coldness of the sea wind and drizzle by declaring in English: "If he is not dead now, he will be dead in a few minutes."

It was the one and only English phrase uttered that day by the political commissar.

The launch continued on, the only sounds coming from the engine, the waves slapping on the bow, and the muffled thuds of the engineer's fists landing on Kudirka's head.

Twenty agonizing minutes went by for the boat crew as the launch plodded to the *Sovetskaya Litva.* When it finally pulled along the starboard bow, it was but a dot on a piece of paper compared to the factory vessel.

"Don't take any lines!" Maresca cautioned the crew and, looking across at Ensign Hughes, knew that the officer agreed.

Hughes told the second mate only he would be allowed off the launch while the rest of the party stayed behind. He had to get assurances that the Soviets would do the Americans no harm.

Acceding to Hughes's wishes, the second mate shouted to deckhands aboard the *Sovetskaya Litva.*

The tire rig swung over the deck and was lowered to the launch. The second mate jumped onto it and was hoisted aboard, while the rest of the Soviets looked up at the decks. Several of them shouted to their comrades. They seemed pleased.

Two of them grabbed Kudirka's body by the shoulders and feet and heaved it onto the engine hatch. Seaman Maresca looked at his face: the lines of tension were gone, his eyes were closed, face expressionless. Was he already dead?

After several minutes the second mate was lowered down again. He gave something to Ensign Hughes and assured him everything would be all right, there would be no trouble. He was again the jovial man who had entertained him and Lieutenant Lundberg aboard the *Sovetskaya Litva* that afternoon.

The Soviets grabbed Kudirka from the engine hatch and heaved him face down into the rig. Then all ten jumped on top of him and clung to the netting as the rig was slowly hoisted aboard. As the Americans watched it swing over the deck, they caught their last glimpse of Kudirka, an inert, undefined, blanket-bound form at the bottom of ten pairs of feet.

It was the last time they or any other Westerner would ever see him.

When their part was over, Maresca turned the launch and headed back to the *Vigilant.* En route, Ensign Hughes asked Seaman Gonzalves if the Soviets had stayed off Kudirka.

"No, sir," Gonzalves replied. "The man sat back down on him. He sat back down on the defector's neck."

They continued the rest of their return trip in silence, each wondering what the Soviets could be doing to Kudirka now—when they had him all alone.

Commander Eustis was waiting in the wardroom with his officers and the civilians. They were all numb with shock, their minds assaulted by what they had seen. Guilt lay heavy in the wardroom.

Burt was pacing back and forth, chain-smoking. Brieze could not imagine how the Soviets had managed to control the entire situation while anchored in U.S. waters. Gordon felt pity for Eustis. Obolensky was recapping in his mind his conversations with Burkal; he just might have persuaded him to leave without Kudirka had the commissar not butted in. When told more than a year later that Burkal was the first to hit Kudirka, Obolensky would register surprise. Burkal did not seem the type of man, but Obolensky knew his opinion was based on a very brief acquaintance with the Acting Fleet Commander.

Eustis stepped up to the table and laid Kudirka's belongings on it—the notebook, the papers, a dictionary. A seaman had already come in with another dictionary that Kudirka gave him while he was guarding the door to the defector's refuge. Some of the men thumbed through the papers, curious to know more about the stranger who had so deeply affected them.*

They heard the whir of the hydraulic lifts and caught a glimpse of the launch being hoisted up past the windows. Aboard it were a handful of sailors. The blanket-wrapped figure and the ten Soviets were gone.

It was over.

Lieutenant Lundberg had watched from the wheelhouse as the boat returned, but he did not care to see who was aboard. He explained much later: "All I had to do was ask and I would have known. But I knew if the defector was still aboard, that was the end of Eustis, and if he was not aboard, that was the end of the defector." Lundberg did not want to entertain either alternative.

Ensign Hughes had clambered out of the launch and hurried to the wardroom with something for the Captain.

He walked in, went over to Eustis near the table in the center of the room, and handed him a bottle of scotch with compliments from the Captain of the *Sovetskaya Litva*—Johnnie Walker Red Label.

*See Appendix B.

Eustis exploded. "What a hell of an exchange! What a hell of an exchange! A bottle of booze for a man's life!"

Everyone around him sheepishly looked at this symbol of ultimate humiliation. Johnnie Walker, Red Label. Eustis would say long afterward that he did not remember what he did with the bottle.

Still, fuming, he announced that he would have to escort the *Sovetskaya Litva* out of territorial waters. "Have they weighed anchor yet?" he asked Lt. Commander Pakos.

"No, Captain," Pakos replied after a glance out the window.

"If they don't leave soon, I'll take the whole boatload back to New Bedford," he declared in his frustration. But his new resolve was belated.

When the *Sovetskaya Litva* finally got underway, the *Vigilant* dutifully accompanied her southward into Vineyard Sound and then past No Man's Land into international waters.

Each man wondered about only one thing as he watched that mammoth, dark outline speckled with lights move through the rain.

Behind which of those lights . . .? Was he still alive or already a cold cadaver? Would they throw his body overboard? Would they put it into a refrigerated hold with their fish to dispose of when they returned? What made it come to this?

At the twelve-mile limit the cutter halted, and soon the *Sovetskaya Litva* disappeared into the rain.

Gradually, crewmen drifted into the wardroom to break the dumbfounded silence with words of support for their Commanding Officer.

"We'll stand up for you, Captain," a junior officer told him. "We had all we could do in restraining ourselves from jumping in and beating the hell out of the Russians."

"On behalf of myself and the crew in the Engine Room," said an enlisted man, "I'd like to say we stand up for you and think this was a horrible situation."

Another officer came in. "It was a terrible situation, sir. If we had been allowed an opportunity or had a word of encourage-

ment, we would have taken on the whole crew. It's horrible that
something like this can happen on an American ship."

"Gee, we didn't know what to do," a sailor told Lieutenant
Morehouse. "We didn't know whether to jump in and help the
guy and stop them."

Commander Eustis made no reply. He walked out and went
alone to his cabin.

Several moments after he left, members of the boat crew
walked in. The others wanted to know what had happened.

"They were kicking the man during the ride over to the
Russian ship," one of the sailors said.

Another continued, "One of the mates said the man will soon
be dead."

More silence.

Then a sailor intoned, "Now I know what freedom is worth
and how good it is to live in this country."

Commander Eustis sat at his desk in his cabin, with deep
bitterness his only companion. It clutched physically at his
throat and seemed to squeeze his chest. During his entire year
and a half tour on the *Vigilant* he had never received a direct
order as he had tonight. It was always "today, why don't we
do this, and we did it." He felt no animosity toward Admiral
Ellis or Captain Brown, but he was bitter against the "system";
a "system" that would force him to do what he had just done.
He knew the decision had been wrong. It had been forced upon
him by the "system." He had acted against his moral grain. But
was he bitter because of what happened to Kudirka or because
he knew that he was afraid to risk his career on something that
challenged his character, his Christian upbringing? How would
members of his Congregational Church look at this? What
would they do in his position?

There had to be some reason for that order. He knew the
decision was very much against Paul Pakos's moral grain as

well; yet Paul had finally said, "You have to trust someone." There had to be a reason for that order. What happened was a small part of U.S.–Soviet relations. There must have been a larger, more encompassing reason. Who was he, after all, to know that the decision was wrong? Wasn't this very kind of thing the ultimate test of a good officer who obeys orders regardless of his personal feelings? Hadn't he just passed that test admirably?

"The system has to function," Eustis thought to himself. "It has to function on all of us having respect for our superiors."

He got up and went back to the wardroom.

Brieze would remember Eustis coming in and, after some soul-searching moments, saying: "I wish you would keep what happened on the ship secret."

Eustis would not deny he had asked for secrecy, but months later would put the request this way: "It was a tense situation, details unpleasant, but each person will have to live with them personally and not let everybody else know."

He then left the wardroom and went to the wheelhouse where he found quiet solace among his officers. Pakos was looking out a window into the darkness. Lundberg was at the conn. No one spoke.

The *Vigilant* had escorted the *Sovetskaya Litva* to international waters and was heading for home. It was past midnight as the cutter churned toward New Bedford, her turbines whining deep within her.

Eustis stood near the helm gazing out into the darkness. "The beating—what about the beating?" His mind was still nagging him. "It was force necessary to subdue a violent man," he thought then, as he would testify later.

Looking into the darkness, Eustis caught a faint glimpse far ahead of the night lights of New Bedford. Would he really have been a hero if he had brought Kudirka into port? What would have happened if he had seized the entire ship, or Burkal? A sensation? A court-martial?

He thought of Burkal. "Here was another man, another
officer in charge of a ship, and he had responsibilities. He was
concerned for what he was doing as it related to his chain of
command as I was concerned for my chain of command." He
had no stereotyped feelings toward Burkal or any of the others.

Eustis sensed something would happen. Something like this
could not just fade into the background. He would have to call
his wife and tell her not to worry if she heard something on the
news.

What about Simas Kudirka? Eustis could only hope everything worked out for him, but he suspected otherwise, and that
is what tormented him the most. Had he really given a man over
to his death? What really made him jump in the first place? One
of the items Eustis had seen in Kudirka's belongings indicated
an answer, but Eustis did not understand the language in which
it was written. Kudirka had jotted in Lithuanian: "A man born
in a cave does not know what freedom is. To die for freedom
is worth the risk."

Eustis looked out the wheelhouse window toward the lights
of New Bedford. Only the whine of the turbines reverberated
through the *Vigilant* as she approached the hurricane dike
protecting New Bedford harbor. Deathly silence reigned among
the men on board. They knew she was coming home disgraced.

Eustis remained in the wheelhouse, desperately trying to
justify in his tormented mind what he had done. Had he been
able to understand another notation Kudirka had copied—in
German—Eustis would have had in retrospect a standard for
his own actions.

Simas Kudirka at one time had jotted: "One should sacrifice
everything for humanity, except humanity itself."

The Aftermath

CHAPTER

27

The *Vigilant* docked at State Pier at three in the morning. Self-consciously shaking hands on the dock, the civilians went their own ways. Commander Eustis remained in New Bedford. After dawn he simply shoved off for routine patrol as Captain Brown had instructed in his last phone patch with him the night before. Eustis had done his duty and felt no need to call the District office.

John Burt returned home looking "white as a sheet," told his wife what had happened, and cautioned her not to say anything, "because this might not get out." She replied she had already heard about the defection on the radio. Robert Brieze was restless at home after he told his wife and daughter. He knew he would have to do something about the outrage aboard the *Vigilant* and tossed sleeplessly in bed the remainder of the night.

Soon after daylight, Brieze, Burt, and Howard Nickerson met at the Action House on Pier 3, a small, red-brick building where fishermen had gathered for more than a century to sell their fish and hear news of the fortunes and misfortunes of their fleets.

A reporter for the New Bedford *Standard-Times* was there covering his regular beat. Brieze approached him and soon he, Burt, and Nickerson were in Nickerson's office near the famous

Whaling Museum telling their story. Burt and Brieze were anxious to get the facts off their chests, but Nickerson seemed reluctant to pursue the issue and would only say: "I was an innocent bystander to something I would not like to see again."

Their account appeared the same day in the *Standard-Times* and was the impetus for all news that was to follow.

William Gordon had stayed overnight in New Bedford and early that morning called his superiors at the National Marine Fisheries Service in Washington. NMFS was at a loss for an official stance, so in turn it contacted the Office of the Special Assistant to the Secretary for Fisheries and Wildlife; it was the same office Gordon and Alexis Obolensky had wanted to call while the case was in progress. William Sullivan, Jr., the Special Assistant, replied he would get more information and would call NMFS back with "guidance." Sullivan—on his own volition—would pursue these facts all day.

Captain Brown came into the District office that morning in Boston looking "like death warmed over." During the regular morning "coffee conference" Commander Flanagan asked him what was wrong, and Brown replied, "I think I sent a man to his death last night." He explained what happened to the utter astonishment of Commander Flanagan. The Legal Officer was doubly surprised to learn that Admiral Ellis had been involved in the decision. Flanagan immediately suggested that the District convene a one-officer informal board to look into the matter and requested that either Commander Eustis or Lt. Commander Pakos be flown in by helicopter to give a first-hand account of what happened. Flanagan saw no immediate need to recall the *Vigilant* to port, and Brown, understandably, was not too anxious to pursue the matter much further.

When Brown phoned Ellis, the Admiral was shocked at what had happened. He had visualized a very simple situation: a gangway, Coast Guard people putting Kudirka on one end, Kudirka civilly walking across, and the Soviets gentlemanly accepting him at the other end. Now things were taking on a very different and foreboding tone. "I had a feeling that this was not the end of it," Ellis said in an interview long afterward. "I was told the man had been beaten, Russians had come aboard and took him. They were invited aboard. This didn't sound right . . . I wouldn't have condoned it. Nobody should be treated like that."

Meanwhile, in the State Department, Edward Mainland, the Duty Officer of the Bilateral Section who had taken a belated interest in the developments the night before, reported to Edward Killham. Killham would lament to the Board of Investigation: "I was surprised, shocked, and I didn't understand what happened. I spent most of the morning trying to find out what happened, and everything I found out kept getting worse and worse." He informed his superior, Adolph Dubs, Director of the Office of Soviet Union Affairs, who smelled trouble and asked for a meeting with his own superior, Richard T. Davies, Deputy Assistant Secretary for European Affairs. They agreed to get more information on the matter.

During this time Sullivan, out of his own concern and curiosity, called the Law Enforcement Branch at Coast Guard Headquarters, the office his group usually contacted, for information. Lieutenant Michael Reed, a staff member, replied that he had no information, but would get it and call back.

Sullivan then called Killham, and Killham told him to refer all inquiries to the State Department.

When Lieutenant Reed returned Sullivan's call, he put Lieutenant Morehouse on the line. Morehouse had taken an early plane to Washington and was back at his desk. Morehouse related what he knew. The official State Department memorandum on the incident would characterize his report as "not complete since he had not been present during the entire matter, and had not taken part in it directly." Morehouse, in fact, was a witness to much of the incident, but would let those directly responsible handle it. He would not even write a routine report on the matter, although it had been the most serious situation he had encountered in his career.

Coast Guard Headquarters that morning was buzzing. Admiral Hammond had called the First District to find out more about resolution of the case and by now knew what had happened, as did Captain Dahlgren. Both were surprised to learn from Captain Brown that Kudirka had been forced back and beaten. They conferred with Admiral Bender, the Commandant, and decided to let Captain Dahlgren, the Intelligence Chief, continue handling the case as he had the day before. They called the District again and learned that Pakos was coming into Boston for a debriefing. No one in Washington bothered to get a direct account from anyone aboard the *Vigilant,* even though Commander Flanagan had suggested that Pakos fly to Washington for a debriefing as well. At Headquarters, the officers had begun drafting a news release with Captain T. McDonald, Chief of Public Information.

It was by then past noon.

Captain McDonald informed Dubs and Killham in the State Department that a news release was being drafted for release by Commander Eustis who had been ordered by Headquarters to return to port so he could read the statement and answer reporters' questions himself.

Early that afternoon a State Department press officer called the White House with the news. He discussed the case with a staff member named Houdek, but Houdek did not pass the information to the President, who was preparing for a Thanksgiving weekend at Camp David, his Maryland retreat. The incident was over and did not seem critical enough for the President to be burdened with it.

Meanwhile, Lt. Commander Pakos had been whisked to Boston and was being debriefed by Commander Flanagan. The Legal Officer considered what Pakos reported serious enough to warrant immediate action by Coast Guard Headquarters and told Brown accordingly, much to the Captain's embarrassment.

Headquarters made no response to Flanagan's call for action, because it believed the matter would fade away with barely a visible sign left in its wake. They were prepared to issue a news release, but only if anyone specifically asked about the incident. Otherwise, the case was closed. No one involved had as yet seen any news about the defection, no reporters were waiting in the halls of the First District or at Headquarters, and that tended to make them feel they were in the clear.

But William Sullivan of Fisheries and Wildlife that Tuesday afternoon kept pressing Captain Dahlgren for more details so NMFS would know what to say if queried. Covering his own trail, Captain Brown had told Captain Dahlgren what he had heard from Lt. Commander Pakos, but in such a way as to give credence to the Soviet accusations that the defector had been drunk, was mentally unstable, and had stolen 3,000 rubles. Dahlgren passed that on to Sullivan, but the information was accepted with a grain of salt. A subsequent State Department memorandum would view the information Dahlgren gave Sullivan this way: "The information failed to substantiate a Soviet officer's allegations that the seaman was drunk, or that he was mentally disturbed."

On the basis of the facts collected throughout the day, Killham, Sullivan, a public information officer of the Bureau of European Affairs, and Captain Webb, the Coast Guard liaison officer, agreed on the text of a press briefing to be released by the State Department. Copies of the briefing had the proviso: "If *asked* about reports that a Soviet seaman attempted to defect to a Coast Guard vessel yesterday."

The briefing confirmed the unsuccessful defection attempt and gave the reason for the meeting of the two ships. It ended with: "Other members of the Soviet crew under the command of their Executive Officer obliged him to return to his own vessel."

"Obliged" was an interesting euphemism, but would never be used, because more explicit accounts by Brieze and Burt and

Commander Eustis himself would force the State Department to speak more openly.

Toward the end of the working day, Captain Dahlgren called Adolph Dubs of the Soviet Desk for more guidance. Dubs gave him the standard condolence, saying the return of the seaman was "unfortunate," but that he could appreciate the thoughts going through Commander Eustis's mind at the time, including questions of the fishing negotiations.

The negotiations in fact had been the farthest thing from Eustis's mind.

Dubs told the Coast Guard to keep referring all inquiries to the State Department until Eustis returned to port, and Headquarters relayed Dubs's reply in message form to the First District, which simply legitimatized Admiral Ellis's reasons for returning Kudirka:

1. CONFIRMING FONECON CONTINUE TO RE-FER PRESS INQUIRIES TO STATE DEPARTMENT UNTIL VIGILANT RETURNS TO PORT. UPON RE-TURN AUTHORIZE COMMANDING OFFICER TO ISSUE PREPARED STATEMENT TO PRESS RE-COUNTING FACTS IN CASE. REQUEST YOU PRE-PARE STATEMENT FOR HIS USE AND PHONE COPY TO US PRIOR TO RELEASE.

2. RATIONALE FOR PERMITTING REMOVAL OF MAN FROM VIGILANT WAS PROGRESS OF DELICATE INTERNATIONAL DISCUSSIONS BE-ING CARRIED ON REGARDING FISHING PROB-LEMS AND WHICH COULD HAVE BEEN ENDAN-GERED BY OTHER COURSE OF ACTION.

The talks had been raised conveniently to the category of "delicate."

By the end of that day, positions in the Coast Guard and the State Department had solidified. State Department officials considered themselves blameless and magnanimously informed the Coast Guard it could "release detailed information." For its own part, the Coast Guard was ready to take responsibility for the order based on Admiral Ellis's hastily construed opinion of why a man should summarily be refused political refuge. But the rationale would not hold up.

At 9 A.M. Wednesday, the *Vigilant* docked in New Bedford with Commander Eustis ready to give the account prepared for him by the District's Public Information Office. The press release outlined circumstances leading to the meeting, described the defection, and confirmed that the defector was returned.* The explanation was a little comical, because it was really a solicitation for the Soviet master to ask for the defector and it set up the Coast Guard as a target for ridicule. Not a word was mentioned about the beating, and the phraseology was designed deliberately to give the public a sense of some important behind-the-scenes political maneuverings or crucial diplomatic negotiations that made Kudirka's return inevitable. The public did not buy it.

Demand for news was heightened by the speedy formation in Boston of a pressure group called "Citizens Concerned for Simas," which publicized Kudirka's name after learning it from Brieze, whom they had contacted by phone after reading his account in the *Standard-Times*. Brieze even agreed to join the group in a protest demonstration planned in Boston. Two Boston newspapers, the *Herald-Traveler* and the *Record-American* each ran sketchy items about the incident, even as Eustis was giving the version prepared for him by the Coast Guard Public Information Office. Eustis added on his own that Kudirka was treated "very rough and far beyond the standards our life styles would allow."

"He must have been quite a guy to make a decision like this," he added and was quoted the following day.

*See Appendix C.

In Washington, a legal adviser for the Bureau of European Affairs Wednesday afternoon called Arthur T. Downey, a young member of the National Security Council and aide to Henry Kissinger, the President's principal adviser on foreign policy. The State Department's legal adviser told Downey "informally" of the incident, but Downey did not pass it on as a significant piece of information for consideration by the President. The incident was over and done with, and no one at the time could foresee the furor it would cause.

Late in the working day an information memorandum was prepared by Killham and addressed to the Acting Secretary of State, U. Alexis Johnson, in the absence of Secretary Rogers, who had gone on a trip. The next day was Thanksgiving and the nonchalant attitude of high-ranking officials toward the incident was reflected in the fact that no one bothered to give Johnson the memorandum until after the holiday. Everyone involved still felt sufficiently insulated and presumed the incident would fade away.

That Wednesday evening a State Department press officer again called the White House to give what more information he had about the case, but the information remained with staff member, Houdek, since the President had already left for Camp David.

Thanksgiving Day, the *Herald-Traveler* and *Record-American* had follow-up stories of the incident with more details, while the New Bedford *Standard-Times* published further accounts by Brieze and Burt. "Public Raps Refusal of Asylum" ran the headline of the *Record-American,* with the accompanying article noting that the Nixon Administration was acknowledging "a flood of protests." This report was a little premature, but could not be criticized for lack of enthusiasm. "Citizens Concerned for Simas," made up mainly of persons of Baltic descent, had organized a demonstration in front of Boston's Federal Building demanding an investigation of the incident. The *Herald-Traveler,* quoting Captain Brown, ran a story under the headline, "Coast Guard Returned Red Defector When State Dept Failed to Act." In the story, Brown acknowledged that he and Admiral Ellis made the decision to return Kudirka when they received no guidance from the State Department. It was done "in consideration of delicate international discussions."

Nothing of the defection attempt was mentioned in the prestigious *Boston Globe* until Friday, when it was apparent that reaction was taking on major proportions.

Nationwide attention was focused on the incident that Friday far from where it occurred, through the efforts of the Lithuanian Student Association of North America, which was in the midst of its annual convention in Cleveland, Ohio. Colleagues from Boston had telephoned news of the incident to student leaders Wednesday night; and the students, in turn, planned a peaceful demonstration for Friday morning. They marched several hundred strong from their hotel to Cleveland's Federal Building with a black facsimile of a coffin marked "Human Rights," and burned it in the plaza of the Federal Building. City authorities had given them full cooperation, even though the students did not have time to apply for a permit. The authorities told organizers that their relations with students of East European descent had always been amicable and that local demonstrations throughout the years—mainly on behalf of subjugated nations in Eastern Europe—had always been somber and peaceful.

A delegate read aloud a statement outlining the Student Association's position, and specific points were wired to the State Department and the Coast Guard. Calling the return of Kudirka "tantamount to murder," the Association demanded the resignation of Admiral Ellis, called for a Congressional investigation of the incident, wanted assurances by the government that such a violation of traditional U.S. policy not occur again, and demanded that Kudirka be returned to the United States. As it turned out, all points covered in the demands were eventually realized, except the return of Simas Kudirka. In a wire to Admiral Bender, the Student Association called the incident "nauseating" and added, "We demand that you initiate a full investigation of the atrocious violation of traditional American policy of political asylum."

The students' demonstration was covered extensively by the news media and syndicated nationwide, creating a public furor that remained in the headlines for a full month and more. Although the spark of indignation was lit by people of Baltic descent sensitive to the neglect by the U.S. government of the plight of nations subjugated by the Soviet Union, the incident itself assaulted the public morality of the nation and evoked universal sympathy for Kudirka.

That same Friday in Washington, Secretary Volpe asked for a full report from the Coast Guard and conferred with Acting Secretary of State U. Alexis Johnson, looking for ways to avoid such embarrassing incidents in the future. Considering the facts they had, Volpe and Johnson concluded that some Coast Guard units did not have standing instructions and procedures for dealing with political refugees and defectors, and that the Coast Guard had inadequate understanding of the most effective channels for reaching the State Department.

Johnson told Volpe that the State Department would immediately send the Coast Guard interim guidelines for future behavior, suggested the Coast Guard join interagency offices dealing with refugee and defector cases, and agreed with Volpe to set up a special communications link directly between Coast Guard Headquarters and the Operations Center of the State Department.

Massive demonstrations were held Saturday in Boston, New York, Chicago, Los Angeles, and other U.S. cities, continuing throughout the weekend and into the following week, heightening public rancor. Newspapers everywhere—in the U.S. and abroad—were castigating the incident as one of the biggest U.S. blunders in memory.

At Camp David that weekend, President Nixon was reviewing the press and happened upon accounts of the defection. He was surprised that no one had told him about it and was disturbed over what he read. The return of Kudirka was distasteful and appeared to touch the sensibilities of the American public in general, and nationality groups, whose votes he had always counted on, in particular. A potential embarrassment loomed before him, because John Volpe, under whose jurisdiction the Coast Guard belonged, had been in charge of rallying nationality votes in the 1968 election, which Nixon had won by a very slim margin. Nixon instructed his staff to get preliminary reports from the State Department and the Coast Guard by Monday morning. Reaction was reaching such proportions that he knew he himself would have to make a statement on the incident.

Early Monday, both the Coast Guard and the State Department gave separate but simultaneous accounts of the defection. Speaking at the State Department, press spokesman Robert J. McCloskey repeated circumstances surrounding the defection, blamed the Coast Guard, and concluded: "Now, we naturally and deeply regret that this incident occurred. Let me say on background that if the Department had been told that a defection had actually occurred, I am confident that things would have been handled—or things would have developed differently."*

McCloskey assured reporters that the State Department and the Department of Transportation were continuing an investigation and "will promptly institute procedures to prevent a recurrence of this type of incident." The State Department that same Monday sent interim guidelines to Volpe. They were an elucidation of a policy that had been taken for granted for years and would be announced publicly the following Wednesday.

At the Department of Transportation, a straight-faced Ad-

*See Appendix D.

miral Bender was giving a deliberately misleading statement about the incident to the press, and his rationale left him defenseless before journalists.* Bender intimated that Kudirka ruined his chances by jumping directly from one ship to the other rather than into the water, as he had originally told *Vigilant*'s officers he would do. This prejudiced his case, because the Coast Guard had instructions on what to do if he jumped into the water, but had no instructions on what to do if he jumped directly aboard. Actually, Admiral Ellis had ordered the return before Kudirka even made his jump, and, aside from the juvenility of Bender's rationale itself, Killham had made no distinction when he advised "call us when he is aboard."

When pressed by reporters whether the Coast Guard searched Kudirka for the stolen money Bender had mentioned, he admitted it had not, adding lunacy to the explanation that Kudirka was given back because he had been accused of stealing money. On a more serious level was his statement that the Soviet ship had been invited into U.S. waters; however, this was a falsehood, which Bender was most likely unaware of.

In all, Admiral Bender's statement was inept, and he was badgered for it in the press. The "man in the water" and the "2,000 [sic] rubles" would follow him around for a long time.

President Nixon by then had returned to Washington and was looking over the preliminary report of the incident given him that morning. Some Congressmen were already clamoring for an official investigation of their own. Nixon was appalled by the report and, in an unusual step, ordered in writing an "immediate and full report" to be given him within two days. The President was particularly upset that he had learned about the incident through the newspapers, rather than normal government channels. "At best, there appears to have been some error in judgment, and after the President reviews the investigation's

*See Appendix E.

findings, appropriate action will be taken," his press secretary announced.

"Appropriate action" was already being taken that Monday, exactly a week after the incident. Technicians were installing a special teletype machine in the Communications Center at Coast Guard Headquarters and at the Operations Center in the State Department. The teletypes—a hotline—for some time after the incident would be tested every half hour to make sure they worked. It was an extreme and unrelated reaction to the embarrassing breakdown of communications machinery between the *Vigilant* and the First District. Meanwhile, the Coast Guard, without fanfare, repaired the machinery aboard the *Vigilant* and at the Communications Center in the First District.

To avoid any future misunderstanding of U.S. policy towards refugees and defectors, all Coast Guard commands and units were receiving copies of "Summary Interim Procedures for the Handling of Requests for Political Asylum by Foreign Nationals," issued by the Secretary of State.*

In the wake of the President's demand for a full report, Admiral Bender, having earlier in the day unconvincingly told reporters why "it could be understood" that Kudirka was returned, found himself compelled to order a full Coast Guard investigation to begin the following day, December 1. He appointed Vice Admiral Thomas Sargent, III, the Assistant Commandant, to head a one-man Formal Board of Investigation and named Rear Admiral Ellis, Captain Brown, and Commander Eustis as parties. The board was to investigate "allegations of improper conduct." That evening Coast Guard Headquarters abruptly informed the three officers that they were relieved of their commands and duties pending the outcome of the investigation.

Eustis took his suspension philosophically, but still felt puz-

*See Appendix F.

zled why he should be taken to task for obeying orders. Brown was rattled by the curt manner in which he was informed and said long afterward that he suspected the investigation was started "on a whim."[1] Ellis, who had just returned to active duty that same day, immediately consulted his lawyers. He was a flag officer, and his suspension was unprecedented in recent military history.[2] Although flag officers and generals have been suspended before—which is rare in itself—it was only after specific charges had been placed against them. There is little question that Ellis's suspension, particularly, was due to public furor over the return, since the Coast Guard had already admitted in statements to reporters the previous week that Admiral Ellis gave the order; and the Commandant, State Department officials, and the President himself had expressed "disturbance" and "regret" over it. Ellis's professional fate was already sealed and the investigation for him would only unfold the type of punishment he would get.

That same day—exactly a week after the incident—Prince Sadrudin Khan, United Nations Commissioner for Refugees, called on the U.S. Ambassador, Charles Yost, and gave him a copy of a note he had sent to Secretary of State Rogers protesting the failure of the United States to grant Kudirka asylum. Khan reminded him that the U.S. had always shown what he termed "unswerving importance" to the principle of asylum and "has always championed the sanctity of this concept." Khan asked for details in the case. Yost assured him that "there was consideration and concern for the case at the highest levels."

News of the incident had reached international proportions, with accompanying derision of U.S. behavior. In order to assure the world, especially countries of Eastern Europe, that U.S. policy toward political asylum was unchanged, the Voice of America beamed daily broadcasts about the incident in twenty-two languages, including Lithuanian, with the assurance that it would never happen again. On Tuesday, the State

Department reiterated U.S. policy in a public statement read by McCloskey. He gave a brief background of United Stated efforts to take in more than one million refugees since World War II and ended with: "I just wanted to make it clear that there has been no change in that policy."

Wednesday, President Nixon received official memorandums from the State Department and the Department of Transportation. They detailed the incident and included several eyewitness statements by crew members of the *Vigilant.* What he read repulsed him. "This is outrageous," Nixon said and instructed Ronald Ziegler, his Press Secretary, to announce that guidelines listed in the State Department memorandum were being implemented to prevent a recurrence of "such a shocking incident." Ziegler told reporters the President felt the return of Kudirka was "completely contrary to every principle this country stands for and contrary to international procedures."

Procedural guidelines were made public the following day, together with the memorandums from the State Department and the Department of Transportation.

While Ziegler was speaking to reporters, the Assistant Secretary of State for European Affairs, Richard T. Davies, called Minister-Counsel Yuri M. Volontsov of the Soviet Embassy in Washington and told him the case was "very regrettable" and should have been handled through the U.S. judicial system to determine Kudirka's status. Volontsov told Davies that Kudirka was "a criminal," and that, as far as the Soviet Union was concerned, "the case was closed." Davies then told Volontsov to postpone the visit of a Soviet oceanographic vessel to Boston Harbor. The visit, according to Davies, "would be inopportune at this time."

When House Speaker John McCormack heard of the exchange between Davies and Volontsov, he rejected the Soviet claim and termed the incident "disgraceful."

Meanwhile, Congressmen of both parties were going on record against the return of Kudirka, calling the entire affair "shocking," "outrageous," "a fiasco," "a ruinous act written in our history." They continued demands for a Congressional investigation and an official U.S. request for the return of Kudirka to the United States. For the next month and more, the Congressional Record would be filled with official statements decrying the incident, and a resolution would be put before the House calling for the renaming of the *Vigilant* to the *Simas Kudirka.*

Public reaction was so intense and widespread that President Nixon spoke out again on Thursday, supplementing the interim guidelines issued by the State Department with an order for all federal agencies never to "arbitrarily or summarily turn a would-be defector back to foreign control until determining whether the request for asylum was legitimate." The same day the guidelines on defector policy were announced publicly.

Not to be outdone, Representative Wayne L. Hays, a Democrat from Ohio, and Chairman of the House Subcommittee on State Department Organization and Foreign Operations, announced that his committee would hold public hearings into the incident. "I have never trusted any organization which is investigating itself," the peppery and outspoken Hays told newsmen on announcing the hearings.

The suspensions of Admiral Ellis, Captain Brown, and Commander Eustis were announced Friday, mollifying the public to some extent.

Meanwhile, the Coast Guard investigation was in its third session, conducted under a pale of universal criticism of the incident.

Newspapers throughout the United States, representing both liberal and conservative outlooks, were castigating the return of Kudirka. In one of several editorials, *The New York Times* stated that the forcible removal of Kudirka from the *Vigilant* "is surely one of the most disgraceful incidents ever to occur on a ship flying the American flag." The *Times* called the Coast Guard's explanation "almost as bizarre as the incident itself."

The *Times* said the real explanation "is surely craven stupidity in high places, possibly accompanied by lethargy." The editorial had touched the heart of the matter. In another editorial, the paper stated: "The United States Coast Guard sinks into ever-deeper waters as it tries to explain its incredible cooperation with Soviet seamen in the forcible return of a defecting Lithuanian to his fishing vessel . . . The Commandant now says the hapless defector would have had a better chance of receiving sanctuary if he had leaped from his ship into the water rather than directly onto the Coast Guard Cutter *Vigilant.* This unbelievable comment is matched by the simultaneous excuse that the defector was accused by the Russians of stealing ship's funds—as though such an unproved charge would have automatically forefeited his right to asylum. These explanations are as ludicrous as the Coast Guard's initial excuse that to have given him asylum would have imperiled 'delicate' discussions with the Soviets over the take of yellowtail flounder."

The *Washington Post* declared: "No more sickening and humiliating episode in international relations has taken place within memory than the American government's knowing return of a would-be Soviet defector to Soviet authorities on an American ship in American territorial waters . . . The mind clogs, the heart clogs at contemplation of this fantastic parable of our times."

In Boston, near the scene of the incident, where emotions were particularly deep, the *Record-American* stated editorially a reaction that was typical throughout the U.S.: "Nothing that has happened since the surrender of the *Pueblo* has so shocked and aroused the American public." This paper—and it was no exception among the media—has been flooded with letters, telephone calls, and telegrams from indignant, unbelieving, ashamed people. To them it was inconceivable that a boarding party of a foreign nation—and a none-too-friendly one, at that —would be permitted to invade the sovereignty of a U.S. armed

vessel to kidnap by brutal force a helpless political refugee
. . . No wonder a veteran sea Captain, in a letter of protest,
described it as 'the most heartless act' he had heard of during
his thirty-seven-year career."

The *Cleveland Press* called the incident the "most shameful
in the long and valiant history of the U.S. Coast Guard." West
Coast newspapers called the incident: "Shocking, disgraceful,
literally sickening"; "there is a strange and distasteful aura
about the incident"; "the nation sees a shocking exhibition of
governmental timidity and muddleheadedness."

"The U.S. Coast Guard officer who returned a Lithuanian
defector . . . was not, I venture to think, pro-Communist or
anti-Lithuanian," wrote columnist Robert McClure. "He was
just a typical American dummy who had been taught that the
Russians are pretty good people who won't do us any harm if
we do right by them." Though McClure was somewhat vindic-
tive, he gauged Admiral Ellis's thinking very accurately.

In a characteristically wry commentary, William F. Buckley
noted: ". . . Driven to search for an explanation of the Coast
Guard's behavior, the admiral [Bender] simply had to make up
a story and lacking the talents of, say, Rube Goldberg, failed
to come up with anything better than he did."

Editorial comments were the most forceful, even vehement,
in years.

Giving Congressman Hays full leeway, the Senate held no
hearings of its own. Senator Edward Kennedy, Chairman of the
Judiciary Subcommittee on Refugees, in whose state the incident took place, said nothing via the news media, but did make
some comments for the Congressional Record and sent a letter
of inquiry to the Secretary of State. In statements on several
different days, Kennedy called the incident "shameful and
humiliating and sickening." It was "an incident which right-
fully registered shock and dismay among all Americans, and
among people throughout the world who look to our country
for comfort and hope."

Citizens of New Bedford reacted more forcefully and directly in the wake of the incident. Storekeepers refused to cash checks of Coast Guardsmen, they were refused service in various facilities, and people jeered them in the streets. The *Vigilant* herself was placed under guard when persons began calling in bomb threats. Commander Eustis's home in Mattapoisett was placed under twenty-four-hour guard, and his telephone had to be changed to an unlisted number. His two sons were harassed in school; and one unthinking teacher even put one of them in front of a class, demanding to know: "Why did your father return that man?" The burden of such guilt by association was too much for the fourth-grade boy, who burst into tears, but nevertheless kept the ordeal to himself. Eustis only found out about it indirectly.

Harassment of Coast Guardsmen in New Bedford became so heated that the City Council had to pass a resolution giving the Coast Guard its vote of confidence. In the resolution, the Council stated the necessity to "speak out strongly against the harassment being shown those whose only crime was to be stationed on this ship at a fateful time." The resolution urged citizens to "treat the officers and men of the *Vigilant* as the friends and protectors they have always proven themselves to be." The resolution was met with mixed feelings among the embittered population. Emotions were still high as the public waited for the findings of the Coast Guard investigation, which would continue until December 10.

In a news conference on December 10, President Nixon responded to a reporter's question on the incident: "I can assure you it will never happen again. The United States of America for 190 years has had a proud tradition of providing opportunities for refugees and guaranteeing their safety, and we are going to meet that tradition."

CHAPTER

28

The Formal Board of Investigation heard testimony from most of the men involved in the incident except Alexis Obolensky and William Gordon. Obolensky was in Moscow for routine talks on international fisheries and could not be located by the Coast Guard, while Gordon went on vacation. Obolensky's presence was important, because as an interpreter he was the only one who really knew what the Soviets were saying, aside from Robert Brieze, who was not privy to everything discussed. But pressure for the hearings was so high that the Coast Guard did not bother to hold them up because of Obolensky's absence.

The board met in three sessions from December 1–3, 1970, at the Transportation Systems Center in Cambridge, Massachusetts, and reopened the hearings December 9 at the Department of Transportation Building in Washington.[1] At that time Lieutenant Kenneth Ryan, the RCC Controller, was also designated a party on suspicion of "dereliction with respect to the passage of erroneous information."[2] However, after hearing his testimony, the board withdrew the designation the same day. All testimony was completed by December 10, when the board gave its opinions and recommendations to the Commandant.

A high-ranking officer involved in the investigation said in an interview that he believed the probe was "superficial." This opinion was also held by the attorney for Robert Brieze, who was present during one session. He called it "shallow." Nevertheless, the investigation was adequate in uncovering the critical roles and where responsibility lay.

The crux of Admiral Ellis's defense was that Captain Brown and Commander Eustis solicited his advice, and he gave it reluctantly, because he did not want to leave his officers in the lurch, even though he was on sick leave and had no legal right to get involved. As for the decision itself, he steadfastly maintained that he ordered Kudirka returned because the Soviets were moored in territorial waters. He testified: "The Soviet vessel had been invited into territorial waters of the U.S. and the Soviet vessel had invited the members of the U.S. visiting group aboard for discussions of the fishing situation. This presented to me a special situation." Ellis gave the Soviets every consideration and would say months afterward: "We were going to have to, under any rules of decency, send him back."

In character, he stuck to that idea obstinately, even though Captain Brown had told him he was searching for advice from Washington and that staff members in the First District did not agree with his decision.

Ellis did not know that the Soviets had not really been invited into territorial waters. Captain Brown had presumed the ship was invited, because it was anchored in Menemsha Bight; and he had no way of knowing from the *Vigilant*'s first message that they had sailed in on their own volition. Only Commander Eustis was aware of that, but thought it of no consequence at the time.

Even allowing for Ellis's mistaken belief, his reasoning lacked depth and sophistication. He would reveal in an interview something he did not tell the Board of Investigation: "We shouldn't accept this man. He's a deserter no matter what he is . . ." Ellis failed to make a distinction that day between a common deserter and a man seeking refuge from oppression, because he saw no distinction. He told the board he had no specific knowledge of national policy regarding defection and added in a subsequent interview that he had little specific knowledge about the Soviet Union. Ellis was not aware, among other things, that the U.S. did not recognize the Soviet occupation of the Baltic States and that Kudirka technically was not a Soviet subject. "I'm not sure if he [Captain Brown] said the man was a Lithuanian. I don't think it would have meant anything if he had. He was still a Soviet citizen," Ellis said long after the incident, still holding a mistaken belief about Lithuanians under Soviet control. One can legitimately presume that a high-ranking military officer should be familiar with the general makeup of Soviet Russia and the nations under its control, and their status in U.S. eyes. Particularly relevant to Coast Guard officers is the fact that Soviet fleets constantly ply the waters inside and outside their areas of jurisdiction and patrol.

A number of Coast Guard officers involved in the incident displayed an almost comical ignorance of the Soviet Union. Certainly, they don't have to be required to know the Russian language, but those officers who constantly report Soviet ship movements to Headquarters should at least know the vessels' designations are not written in "acrylic" or "Gaelic." In discussing Brieze's role in the incident, one high-ranking officer in the First District said Brieze probably escaped from Latvia in 1944, "because he wanted to avoid the draft," likening the situation during the Soviet takeover of Eastern Europe to the American draft-dodging phenomenon of the late 1960s. This is an appalling ignorance of a most tumultuous time in modern history and is a definite clue to the depth of historical knowledge imparted at the Coast Guard Academy. It is a clue also to how Admiral Ellis could have made the decision that he did that November day.

Under questioning at the hearings, Ellis stuck to one and only one reason for Kudirka's return and he expanded on it later in an interview: "I was thinking purely of the position of the United States and not only in that conference, but in future conferences . . . I believe that if we went to a meeting like that and allowed our ship to be a haven of refuge, pretty soon there wouldn't be any more meetings." The Soviets know full well that they risk losing people when they meet in international forums with democratic nations, and still have not shut themselves off from such meetings. Admiral Ellis, however, elected to put the Soviets' own responsibility on himself and the United States.

He knew his opinion on the return was counter to accepted beliefs, but found solace in comments by the late Dean Acheson, former Secretary of State, whose own ideas about the Soviet Union had sometimes been controversial. In an article appearing December 17, one day before the Coast Guard hearings ended, Acheson wrote in the St. Louis *Post-Dispatch* that Kudirka would have been returned regardless of who made the decision. Acheson based his statement on what he interpreted as the postwar threat of nuclear conflict and the resultant stalemate between the United States and the Soviet Union. This stalemate, according to Acheson, had made it imperative for the U.S. and the USSR to placate each other. But Acheson's connection in the article between the threat of nuclear war and Kudirka's return was a little farfetched. Ellis did not go so far as to say the Soviets would have threatened dire consequences if Kudirka was not returned, but he did order the return in that spirit of placation that Acheson described.

His connection with the case was the most brief, but also the most decisive.

Captain Brown was taken to task for following Admiral Ellis's instructions. Brown was the Acting District Commander according to provisions of Article 13-3-4 of U.S. Coast Guard Regulations which state in part:

Succession to Command of a District

A. The district chief of staff shall act as district commander . . . when there is a vacancy in that office, when

the district commander is absent from the district office
because of leave, sickness, or temporary duty outside the
district . . .

Brown had acted accordingly since November 4 when Ellis
went on sick leave. He kept in touch with the Admiral, keeping
him abreast of developments and giving him non-official letters
to sign, such as letters of appreciation from well-wishers. When
he first called Ellis that afternoon, he found himself in a
dilemma. He had to either challenge him on a technicality and
possibly ruin his own position in the District when the Admiral
returned, or obey Ellis as the real District Commander. Brown
hopped back and forth between his position as Chief of Staff and
Acting District Commander throughout the afternoon until he
finally decided to carry out Ellis's orders. This equivocation on
Brown's part had much to do with the reaction, or lack of it,
from Coast Guard Headquarters.

During the 4 P.M. telephone conversation with Admiral
Hammond in Headquarters, Brown did not tell him of Admiral
Ellis's instructions to return the defector, because he intended
to inform Headquarters when Kudirka was aboard. He would
say in an interview almost two years after the incident: "I did
not discuss [with Hammond] that Ellis said give him back. I
didn't believe in my own mind that that was the way it should
happen." Little did Brown realize during that 4 P.M. conversation that he would two hours later be knuckling under to Admiral Ellis's desires. Brown told the board: "I did not feel that I
had any authority to refuse Admiral Ellis's orders on that day."

The board never questioned Brown as to why he felt he had
to obey Ellis's orders and never considered the implications of
his dilemma. Those implications raise several interesting legal
points that are beyond the scope of this book. Brown indirectly
alluded to some of those points when he discussed his actions
in several interviews.

Captain Brown explained his interpretation of his role: "He

[Ellis] was in charge of all his faculties, reading *Sports Illustrated* all day long, doing jigsaw puzzles, but he was not in his office. He had not officially returned. The fact remains this: had I made a complete and total decision, it would have affected his continued performance of duty when he came back to work in a couple of days. I felt obligated, it was essential that I call him as my immediate designated superior . . . His name is still up there as Number One. Officially, I was in command, but you can read the regulations a couple of ways and make your own interpretations . . . They said I had no business following his orders or . . . forceful suggestions. I was not looking at the moral aspect of this thing at the time. My actions were governed solely by my deep-felt belief that I was carrying out orders of the District Commander, regardless of what the book says in so many words about the succession of command . . . Admiral Ellis had in effect given me orders, and that is what I'm paid for. It's my job. If it's an illegal order, that's one thing . . . I do not feel as if it was an illegal order."

Brown insisted that had he refused to obey Admiral Ellis he would have been relegated to some minor desk job to shuffle papers. This, however, is unlikely, because he actually had the weight of Headquarters behind him with instructions to notify Flag Plot as soon as Kudirka was aboard. Knowing what he did, Brown, in fact, had an obligation to protect Ellis by overriding his instructions.

Commander Eustis's maneuvers to keep Kudirka were commendable and bordered on insubordination, but when he finally decided to obey his orders, he did it in a way that produced the maximum sense of outrage. The inviolability of U.S. ships has been an honored tradition since the War of 1812, prior to which British naval forces used to board U.S. vessels and impress sailors into their own service. Though there were several other immediate reasons for the war, one of the most publicly sensitive was that issue—the inviolability of U.S. vessels.

Eustis shattered that tradition with very simple reasoning.

He told the Board of Investigation: "During my career I have more than once gone down to the police station to pick up a Coast Guardsman that has been held . . . They [the Soviets] were trying to bring one of their men back. I felt it reasonable for them to bring him back, but most important, I realized that this was a man that was going to be very desperate when he was to be returned to the vessel. I was sure that considerable force was going to be needed to be used to restrain this man to insure his safe return to the Soviet vessel."

Eustis did not want to order his own men to force Kudirka back, so he simply let the Soviets do it.

He would say in an interview that the political implications of that act did not occur to him at the time. Eustis was aware of the concept of the inviolability of a U.S. ship, but did not consider that point in his emotional state on the night of November 23.

The board never questioned Eustis about details of the beating and was satisfied with his reply that force would have to be used to return Kudirka, whether the Soviets applied it or the Coast Guard did. This, however, was pure conjecture, and Eustis had no way of knowing how Kudirka would have reacted if the Coast Guard had taken him off the ship. It must be remembered that Kudirka had an innate fear of the Soviets and saw the Coast Guardsmen as friends. In fact, when Seamen Santos and Towne grabbed his wrists just as he was about to leap into the water, he did not struggle at all, but talked very gently to them. Kudirka knew they were frustrating his last chance for escape, yet he did not react violently at all. This had to be considered in any speculation on whether Kudirka would have struggled with Coast Guardsmen, but it was not.

Admiral Ellis would say of Eustis's actions: "I think he had good reasons, but there were better reasons for not letting the Russians come aboard." Captain Brown also expected Coast Guardsmen to return Kudirka, but said he did not recall his reaction when he found out the Soviets had done it.

In order to vindicate his decision, Eustis and his attorneys had to show that the alternative to Soviet force would have been worse—namely, Coast Guard force. Yet, the only actual contact Kudirka had had with Coast Guard force had proved that he did not resist it.

Admiral Hammond's role centered on the question: Why did he not take a more active part in the decision-making process?

As Chief of Operations, Admiral Hammond dealt mainly with planning Coast Guard activities. He testified that about fifty percent of the task of Operations was to answer questions from the field, but they were almost always questions that did not require an immediate response. Those that did he characterized as "law enforcement type questions."

"And they fall within the division of Law Enforcement and Intelligence?" Counsel appointed for the board asked him.

"Yes, I would say so," Hammond replied.

So when Captain Brown asked for advice, Hammond relegated the task of getting it to Captain Dahlgren, Chief of the Intelligence Division. "I felt he knew more about who to contact than I did," Hammond testified.

He said he never considered calling the *Vigilant* directly: ". . . I have never done it . . . and I certainly didn't consider it at this time. By not considering it, I mean I would not have called them had I considered it . . . The First Coast Guard District has command and knows the situation better than I— the local situation. If they call and ask for assistance, then we'll give them that assistance if we can, but fully they're an operational command."

Hammond that day was not speaking officially for the Commandant, so the District Commander or Acting District Commander was technically on an equal footing with him. Hammond felt no real compulsion to take over responsibility in the case and, in effect, left that responsibility in the First District. He could have done more than just instruct Captain Dahlgren to get advice from the State Department, but he did not, because he simply felt no need to.

When asked if anyone at Headquarters knew of U.S. policy regarding defectors, Hammond replied, "I think our legal office would be the only one that would." He added: "I'll tell you exactly, it never entered my mind to call our legal office. This I realize was a mistake. I thought by going to the State Department we were getting first-hand knowledge and it just did not occur to me to call our legal office."

Admiral Hammond may have been thrown off by the fact that Captain Brown did not ask him for a policy statement regarding defectors, but for advice on procedures to get Kudirka out of the water.

From his own experiences Hammond knew that the State Department was not always helpful. In fact, he expected little help from the State Department, because he knew it often lagged on decisions. But feeling that the men on the scene—in Boston and aboard the *Vigilant*—knew the situation better than he did, he offered no advice of his own.

Hammond was reluctant to get personally involved in the case. Even when he learned from Captain Dahlgren that the State Department had been of little help, he still did not counsel Captain Brown, because he felt it was not in his competency to give instructions on how much force to use while competing with the Russians to get Kudirka out of the water. This was already a political decision.

The Admiral had no inkling that the guidance Brown sought included the basic question of whether they should keep the defector when they did get him. Had Brown told him Admiral Ellis had ordered the return, Hammond might have reacted differently, but in their 4 P.M. telephone conversation, Hammond simply told Brown to let Headquarters know when the defector was aboard the *Vigilant* and Headquarters would pass that information to the State Department. Brown agreed to do that, thus precluding the necessity of revealing Admiral Ellis's own instructions to Admiral Hammond.

Hammond admitted to the board that he may have discouraged Brown during their 4 P.M. telephone conversation when he reiterated Captain Dahlgren's message that the State Department had been of little help.

When asked whether he instructed Brown, Hammond replied: "I don't know that I used the word 'instruct.' I certainly gave him the information we had from the State Department."

As Chief of Operations of the U.S. Coast Guard, confronted by a request for assistance from one of the Districts, Admiral Hammond was, at best, too aloof. For this reason some officers and former officers of the Coast Guard claimed Admiral Hammond committed a sin of omission—he did not consult with the Legal Office at Headquarters for an alternate channel into the State Department or for an opinion on the status of the case as a whole. He himself admitted that he did not "instruct" or "advise" Captain Brown, but maintained that the First District was perfectly capable of handling "the local situation."

No official action was taken against Admiral Hammond, sparking some controversy within the Coast Guard—some officers felt justice was unevenly applied in the case.

However, the burden of responsibility in this particular instance weighs heavier on Captain Brown, because he admitted he understood from his 4 P.M. telephone conversation with Hammond that he was to contact Headquarters as soon as Kudirka was aboard.

Edward Killham of the Bilateral Section of the Soviet Desk was the only substantive link the Coast Guard had with the State Department, and his role focused on the advice he gave Captain Dahlgren.

When Killham read the *Vigilant*'s first message, he immediately suspected a provocation and told Captain Dahlgren nothing should be done to encourage the defection. But Dahlgren was more concerned with getting an answer to a particular question: how much force could the Coast Guard use against the Soviets to get the defector after he jumped into the water? Killham said he could not answer that kind of question without getting advice from his own superiors. In order to avoid an international confrontation, Killham had suggested the obvious. He testified: ". . . If the Coast Guard moved fast enough in accordance with its traditional efficiency in these areas [rescue from the sea] then there would be no issue [competing with the Soviets], because we would simply have picked the man up before anyone recognized that that issue exists. That's what I had in mind, yes."

Captain Dahlgren did not catch the implication and translated that part of Killham's advice to mean simply that if the man was in the water he could be rescued. He passed that idea on to Captain Brown, who quite naturally scoffed at it.

When Dahlgren asked: "What if he's already on the American ship?," Killham told the board he said: " 'Well, if he's on the American ship let us know immediately, and we'll send you further guidance on how to handle the situation.' " He claimed he was thinking of the possible complications alluded to in the *Vigilant*'s message—the possibility that Kudirka might jump aboard the *Vigilant* while the U.S. delegates were still on board the *Sovetskaya Litva*. Killham would have to confer with his superiors if that contingency arose, because it might have meant "taking a series of political tactics" that he alone was not authorized to initiate. It would be a problem that would have to be faced if and when it occurred, so Killham did not speculate on it with Dahlgren.

He told the board: "He [Captain Dahlgren] was not satisfied with the advice . . . He wanted something harder and firmer, and we went over the ground several times, but came out essentially the same place every time. But it was too complicated and difficult for me, I felt, to decide on. And to get him a decision it would take too long to do him any good. And again, the Coast Guard, with its tradition, should be able to handle this."

Counsel for the board then asked him: "Did you feel that the advice you gave him was satisfactory advice?"

Killham replied: "Yes, I think it was quite adequate, and if it had been followed, we wouldn't have any problems. However, in hindsight I might say that it was not imaginative enough. As I said, I couldn't imagine this thing could be permitted to develop the way it was, it did. In fact, I still find it hard to believe."

Killham said that if he had gotten the message from Boston to the *Vigilant* which included the instructions to "give USSR every opportunity to recover," he would have seen the case in a different light and been able to gauge the thinking of the officers involved.

He only saw that message a week after the incident.

CHAPTER

29

On December 18, 1970, three and a half weeks after the incident, Vice Admiral Thomas R. Sargent, III, President and sole member of the Formal Board of Investigation, gave his findings and recommendations to the Commandant based on testimony completed that same day.*

He recommended that Captain Brown be awarded a General Court-Martial on charges of Dereliction of Duty "for his failure to inform the Commandant of the progress of the case and for his failure to retain the defector aboard the VIGILANT until having advice from proper authority."

Sargent noted that Brown failed to rely upon the advice of his principal staff officers and instead referred the matter to Admiral Ellis, thus failing to exercise his command powers and accepting his command responsibilities as Acting District Commander.

Sargent did not recommend a court-martial for Admiral Ellis, but did advise that he be issued a Punitive Letter of Reprimand from the Commandant for "offering instructions or advice without having informed himself of the fact and policy necessary for a proper decision, all to the prejudice of good order and discipline in the service." He added that Ellis should

*See Appendix G.

be removed from command and asked to retire no later than six weeks after the hearings. His recommendations for Ellis were much milder than for Brown, because Sargent took at face value Ellis's contention that he offered advice "reluctantly" by virtue of the fact that all the phone patches were initiated by Brown and Commander Eustis, who sought his advice. The Board of Investigation never questioned Ellis's contention, although the testimony of Captain Brown showed his advice was, in fact, quite forceful.

According to the findings, Ellis "should have known that CAPT BROWN and CDR EUSTIS were treating his remarks not as advice, but as orders." Sargent determined that Ellis "infringed improperly upon the command prerogatives of the Acting District Commander."

Admiral Sargent decided that Commander Eustis "was not in sympathy with the orders he had received to return the defector." He recommended that Eustis be issued an Administrative [non-punitive] Letter of Reprimand from the Commandant "for allowing Soviet crew members aboard his vessel to remove a Soviet defector without exercising upon [them] the proper restraints; and that he be immediately reassigned from the VIGILANT."

Sargent pointed out that Eustis would have "avoided or refused to return the defector" if he had had the opportunity, but accepted the finality of his orders when it became apparent they were "past reconsideration." Under such conditions, Sargent continued, Eustis "cannot be faulted in his decision to allow Soviet crew members aboard his ship to remove the defector if he went willingly." But Sargent added the stipulation: "his failure to impose and exercise effective restraints on these Foreign Nationals to prevent a breach of discipline on an American Military Vessel cannot be condoned."

In light of other facts in the case, he found that the State Department "did not furnish the Coast Guard with adequate, helpful, or timely advice to deal properly with this defection.

The quality of liaison and communication between the two agencies was not satisfactory and contributed to the unfortunate result that occurred." In order to perform their duties as representatives of the nation's maritime law enforcement agency, Coast Guard commanders and commands, according to Sargent's conclusions, have to have "ready access to current State Department policy and procedures."

He recommended that the Office of Operations confer with the State Department to inform itself of those policies and procedures and suggested that the Office of Personnel confer with the State Department to upgrade the existing exchange of billets.

Although the Coast Guard had filled its billet in the State Department—at the time of the incident with Captain Webb in the Office of International Scientific and Technological Affairs —the State Department had never reciprocated, and its billet at the Coast Guard had been empty ever since the exchange program had been initiated two and a half years earlier. Soon after the board made its recommendations, Coast Guard Headquarters created the post of Political Adviser for Foreign Affairs, and a former professor and veteran State Department official, Ben F. Dixon, was assigned to it. Dixon had direct access from Coast Guard Headquarters to various offices in the State Department, making possible a closer working relationship between the Coast Guard and the State Department. Dixon's appointment was a direct result of the *Vigilant* incident.

As for technical shortcomings, Vice Admiral Sargent noted that Coast Guard communications were deficient in several respects: there were long delays in transmission of important messages because of equipment malfunction; important telephone conversations were not confirmed by written messages; and recording equipment in Flag Plot was inoperative.

He recommended the obvious, that the necessary equipment at Headquarters, in the First District, and aboard the *Vigilant* be repaired.

In addition to the hotline setup that had been installed at Flag Plot and the State Department Operations Center, the Coast Guard made other improvements. The Duty Officer staff was bolstered. Equipment that had been planned for future installation was installed immediately. All District offices were linked by means of facsimile machines, so copies of orders or important messages could be circulated without delay.

"We can justify this investment better after the incident than we could before," a Coast Guard spokesman explained after the equipment was installed.

On the same day that Vice Admiral Sargent made his recommendations, Admiral Bender acted on them. As Convening Authority for investigative bodies within the Coast Guard, it was his responsibility to take appropriate action, using the board's findings as a guideline.

He concurred with the need for instructions on defector policy and already had in his possession the interim guidelines issued by the State Department a week after the incident.[1]

The Commandant noted that "although not mentioned in the opinions or recommendations, hindsight indicates that more aggressive actions on the part of Coast Guard Headquarters might have altered the prosecution of this incident. Specifically, Coast Guard Headquarters might well have insisted on more definite guidance from State Department."

But the crux of Admiral Bender's action was in regard to the three officers who were the subject of the investigation. He concurred in the opinion concerning Captain Brown and in the recommendation for a General Court-Martial. Bender reasoned, however: ". . . regardless of the results of a trial, CAPT BROWN'S performance during this entire incident has seriously impaired his effectiveness as a senior captain on active duty." He therefore stipulated that if Brown immediately submitted a request for retirement, Bender would accept it and not refer the charge for trial, but instead would issue Brown a

Punitive Letter of Reprimand under Article 15 of the Uniform Code of Military Justice.

Bender concurred in the opinion regarding Admiral Ellis, adding that he "assumed authority not possessed by anyone in the Coast Guard." However, Bender did not concur in the recommendations against Admiral Ellis. He could not see how Admiral Ellis, who gave Captain Brown the order to return Kudirka, could be held less responsible than Brown. It would be hard to explain to the public how an officer who gave the order could get off with a lighter punishment than one of his subordinates who followed it. Indeed, it was a consideration the board should have pondered more deeply.

Accordingly, Bender reasoned that Ellis's actions "prompting the recommendation for a Punitive Letter of Reprimand were such as to make him no less responsible in the matter than CAPT BROWN . . . I direct the Board to embody the misconduct it found to exist in an appropriate charge or charges and specifications. I find such charges should be referred for trial by court-martial." As with Captain Brown, he concluded that Admiral Ellis's behavior during the incident "has seriously impaired his effectiveness as a flag officer on active duty." He stipulated that if Ellis immediately submit a request for retirement, he would not have to stand trial, but would be issued the Punitive Letter of Reprimand under Article 15 of the Uniform Code of Military Justice.

Admiral Bender concurred with most of the opinion regarding Commander Eustis, but he rejected the idea that Eustis "cannot be faulted in his decision to allow Soviet crew members aboard his ship to remove the defector if he went willingly." He sympathized with Eustis's moral dilemma, but said he could not "conceive of any commanding officer interpreting orders authorizing the use of necessary force so as to permit foreign nationals to exercise authority on board a Coast Guard vessel, whether or not proper restraints were imposed." He concluded that Eustis's error in judgment reflected "an inadequate understanding of the underlying principle of the sovereignty of a United States naval vessel."

Although his reprimand was not punitive, Eustis was ordered transferred to other duty, because he could "no longer serve effectively as Commanding Officer of the VIGILANT . . ."

Admiral Bender stated that in allowing Admiral Ellis and Captain Brown to avoid trial by court-martial through retirement, he was not "extending inordinate leniency or discounting the seriousness of their conduct."

Captain Brown immediately exercised his option and requested retirement. He was very bitter about the action taken against him, but the bitterness was mixed with an inner guilt over his role in the incident. "All the action served nothing, but to appease public opinion," he would say almost a year later. But at the same time he would admit: "Yes, I felt a pang of conscience. I did that night. I did the following day. I did not condone the action. And I was put in a position where no matter what I did, it was wrong."

Other officers who observed him during the investigation said Brown, of all three officers accused, was the most agonized over the incident. "He just looked like hell the whole time," one officer said.

Much later Brown steadfastly maintained that the entire issue was brought out in public to draw attention away from a U.S. military raid on a North Vietnamese prison camp in an unsuccessful attempt to free American prisoners of war. Brown claimed the raid occurred the same day the President first expressed his indignation over the incident—November 30— and that that indignation was designed to cover up the failure of the raid. However, the raid actually occurred the day of the incident—November 23—was mentioned in the press that week, mainly in a positive way as a morale booster for soldiers, and was over before public attention ever focused on the *Vigilant* incident. Still, Brown believes to this day that he, Ellis, and Eustis were "scapegoats" for the unsuccessful raid.

Admiral Ellis fumed when Admiral Bender overrode the board's recommendation and directed charges to be specified against him and that he stand trial by General Court-Martial. Bender and Ellis had been very close friends, but Bender's action in ordering a court-martial for Ellis terminated that friendship, and Ellis has not spoken to Bender since. Ellis said much later that he would have submitted his letter of resignation immediately if Bender had followed the board's recommendation and just issued the Punitive Letter, together with a stipulation for his retirement. He agreed that his continued effectiveness in command had been compromised by the incident. But now it would seem that he was retiring under threat of a court-martial, "retiring under fire," as he put it. This, Ellis could not bring himself to do, and he seriously considered submitting to the court-martial with a firm belief that he would be vindicated. "I had the option, but I wanted to see the charges and specifications first." He presumed the charges would center on his interposition in the chain of command.

Ellis quickly consulted his lawyers and they advised "if I threw in the towel, they could end the case right there."

Before he could decide which route he would take, Secretary Volpe solved the problem for him. In a letter to Admiral Bender on December 21, three days after the end of the investigation, Volpe said he did not concur in the award of court-martials for Ellis or Brown. Volpe stated: "It is my considered view that no purpose would be served by subjecting either RADM Ellis or Captain Brown to a court-martial. There is no doubt that both of these officers now appreciate fully their serious error of judgment in this case. It is also clear that they have been subjected to most extreme castigation from many quarters in this nation. This, indeed, is a severe indictment, for which both they and their families have already suffered."

Volpe directed Bender to withdraw court-martial charges for Ellis and Brown, but agreed that both should receive Punitive Letters of Reprimand. He approved of the action against Commander Eustis.

That same day Volpe announced publicly: "I regret very deeply that a young man had to lose his chance for freedom in order to bring to light the deficiencies in government procedure for welcoming victims of oppression to American soil. Also, I regret that the proud history of the U.S. Coast Guard, which has given shelter to hundreds of political refugees, was not upheld in this tragic incident." He declared that "errors in procedure" had been corrected and stated flatly: "We can now give assurance to the world that an incident such as that which occurred on November 23 can never occur again and that America remains the haven for the oppressed."

Both Admiral Ellis and Captain Brown retired. In a last maneuver, Ellis would send Secretary Volpe an appeal of his Letter of Reprimand, but it would be denied.*

It was not quite the final curtain for these officers. On December 29, the House Subcommittee on State Department Organization and Foreign Operations held hearings on the incident. Essentially it went over testimony given before the Board of Investigation and asked Ellis and Brown some additional, often heated, questions about their roles. The two former officers, sitting side by side, repeated what they had said before the Board of Investigation.[2]

More than a month later, on February 4, 1971, the Subcommittee made its report and presented conclusions in the gutsy, outspoken style of Congressman Hays, its Chairman. The conclusions are worth noting for their tone and are found in Appendix I.

In the aftermath, Ellis and Brown were extremely critical of the role Headquarters played in the incident. Ellis would say long after he retired: "The only bitterness I have is that people in Headquarters did not live up to their responsibilities by sending us guidelines and accepting their responsibilities in the whole situation . . . If Captain Brown had received any kind of instructions from Washington he would have followed them

*See Appendix H.

explicitly." Brown was even more forceful: "I don't think there was anybody sufficiently stirred up at Headquarters level to really get on the phone and call somebody and say, 'Now, God darn it, I want some answers and who am I going to talk to and get some answers . . .' Not one of them in Headquarters said 'Well, what's the story? What's the situation? Has the State Department given back any information? . . . Have any orders gone out to the First District?' But there was not one single iota of response or responsibility."

What Ellis and Brown said was, of course, true, but it did not absolve them from their own responsibilities.

Ellis took a long vacation after he retired, then returned to his home in Beverly, where the sudden idleness of retirement forced him to keep thinking back on the incident. Finally, in the fall of 1971, he again found work—as an administrator at North Shore Community College in Beverly.

Brown retired to his home in Gloucester, where ensuing months brought back the days of "Halcyon." He sees the incident now as "water over the dam, just water over the dam." He and Ellis have grown much closer after the incident and meet socially on frequent occasions, playing bridge, visiting each other's homes. "We never mention the incident," Brown said.

Admiral Hammond, the Chief of Operations, retired in April, 1972, and moved to California.

Captain Dahlgren, Chief of the Intelligence Division, was transferred to Honolulu, Hawaii, where he became Chief of Staff of the Fourteenth District.

Lieutenant Ryan, the RCC Controller, a little more than half year later, was transferred to the Seventeenth District in Alaska.

Edward Killham, Officer in Charge of the Bilateral Section of the Soviet Desk, seven months after the incident, was transferred to the U.S. Embassy in Copenhagen, Denmark, where he assumed duties as First Secretary after having served as head of the Bilateral Section only one year. Neither Killham nor the

State Department would comment whether the transfer was a promotion or demotion.

Commander Eustis was transferred to Executive Base, New York, located on Governor's Island in the harbor off the southern tip of Manhattan. His new duties there as Executive Officer of the base were by no means a demotion. Six hundred Coast Guardsmen and their families live there in a self-contained community. "It's like being the assistant mayor of Governor's Island," he said about his new post. Somewhat self-conscious over what may be interpreted as a choice assignment in an idyllic, ninety-acre country setting minutes from the heart of Manhattan, Eustis explained that he only received the assignment because his superiors wanted to shield him from newsmen. (The island may only be reached by Coast Guard ferry.) He noted that disposition of the *Konrad* case—his seizure of the West German fishing trawler—was settled out of Federal Court, because the Coast Guard did not want to subject him to further public scrutiny and castigation. That may be true, but it is also true that the U.S. rarely prosecutes seizure cases anyway, in consideration of amicable relations with the home countries of the trawlers.

Since he was still in uniform at this writing, Eustis used cautious comments about his superiors and uttered cautious opinions about the action taken against him by the Board of Investigation and the Commandant. He did admit that his punishment was extremely mild, as, indeed, it was. An Administrative Letter of Reprimand does not stay permanently in an officer's record, and there were officers commanding ships with records that included Punitive Letters of Reprimand. Eustis said he was not bitter against Ellis or Brown, but against the "system" that compelled all three to act as they did. He would say of Ellis only: "That day Admiral Ellis, as very typical of him, he got in the middle of something. He was not the District Commander . . . I, as one of the men under his command, called, asked for help, so to speak, and he assumed the role of superior."

"There is a lot of criticism among people senior to me," he revealed almost two years after the incident. He said that the *Vigilant* incident remains a subject of heated controversy among Coast Guard officers and old graduates of the Coast Guard Academy. Eustis has felt repercussions of that. Though eligible for the rank of Captain, Eustis found that he had been passed up when candidates were announced in May, 1972. But he said he was heartened to learn that his old friend Lt. Commander Pakos, who was transferred to a LORAN Station in London, England, eight months after the incident, was selected for promotion to Commander a year ahead of fellow-officers with the same grade. Pakos had staunchly supported Eustis that night and made an unsuccessful attempt tactfully to add "Info Commandant" to a message that could have changed the outcome of the case by clueing Headquarters to the situation aboard the *Vigilant* late that fateful Monday night. "He was very much involved," Eustis said. "I'm sure it was discussed in the promotion board. At least it didn't hurt him that day."

Pakos himself was reticent after the incident, referring all questions to his testimony before the Board of Investigation. He was reluctant to talk, because he was still trying to unravel his role in the incident. Many months afterward he came to a very candid conclusion.

After a brief assignment in Greenland, he was waiting in a small coastal village for transportation back to England. In the quiet, white solitude of mid-September he penned his thoughts in a long, sometimes philosophical letter.

". . . I had visions of high-level officials in the State Dept. making the decision, so I placed my faith in the 'system'—it failed me badly and in my thoughts since the incident, I wonder about the fact that my military training was so strong that it evoked such a response in me." He had mistakenly thought that night that Kudirka was being traded for American prisoners of war in Vietnam. "Is one life in hand worth another in exchange? Is one life in hand worth the *possibility* (or even probability) of several hundred others (POWs, for example) being saved? Is it valid to 'trade off' like this? *During* the incident I could not answer such questions, so I eventually had to put faith in my superiors—*since* the incident I have come to the conclusion that the answer to those questions in fact rests with *me* . . .

"In the end I, too, was a good soldier, much to the dismal future of Mr. Kudirka and to the disgrace of our country."

But Pakos still had faith in the "system" that failed him and Commander Eustis on November 23, 1970. He called the incident an "aberration" except for one ever-present factor: "If each individual involved had been more aware of his personal responsibilities, the incident would never have occurred."

He recognized that he, too, was responsible for what happened, even though he did not have ultimate command: ". . . my contribution to the end result [returning Kudirka] can never be justified or rationalized away. I am now much more acutely aware of my personal responsibilities and hope that my future actions reflect this awareness."

The incident had matured him.

As for Commander Eustis, he has at this writing served almost twenty years in the Coast Guard. He is not sure if he will remain after that. "We'll know when the next promotion board comes up," he mused and smiled.

During pensive moments Eustis glances out his office window overlooking the harbor and skyline of New York and sees, less than a mile away, staring in perpetual irony, the Statue of Liberty.

CHAPTER

30

The fate of Simas Kudirka became a mystery. The day after the incident, Bob Couto of WBSM in New Bedford called the Soviet Embassy in Washington and asked chargé d'affaires Ippolitov what happened to Kudirka. In a phrase that sounded ominous, Ippolitov replied: "The incident has been resolved at sea." Couto repeated that over the air and may have contributed to some local speculation that Kudirka was dead.

Some of the *Vigilant*'s crewmen were telling their friends that he was "either dead or unconscious" when the Soviets hauled him aboard the *Sovetskaya Litva*. Robert Brieze repeated that to reporters who printed the remarks. Rumors spread that Kudirka had died.

These rumors persisted until February, three months after the incident, when official Soviet sources announced by telephone to foreign correspondents in Moscow that Kudirka was well, free, and living in a new apartment in Klaipeda. The sources added that Vladimir Popov, Captain of the *Sovetskaya Litva*, had been sentenced to fifteen years in a labor camp.

The information was printed without comment by United Press International and the Associated Press.

Members of Lithuanian émigré groups told reporters that although they believed Popov could have been punished for allowing the defection to occur off his ship, the news about Kudirka was ludicrous. In fact, it spurred rumors of his death.[1]

Then, in the second week of March, 1971, a person or persons unknown telephoned foreign correspondents in Moscow that Kudirka was in prison in Vilnius, the capital of Lithuania. The sources, apparently dissident nationalists, said official announcements stating Kudirka was free and in a new apartment were false and they insisted that Kudirka—at least up to about February 25—was still alive.

The sources said his wife had told friends she was able to see him once on New Year's Day, but had not seen him since. When first imprisoned, Kudirka had reportedly been very rebellious and had gone on a hunger strike. No information was known about his condition. The sources also told the foreign correspondents that soon after the incident about fifty of Kudirka's relatives, friends, and associates were interrogated by the secret police while thorough searches were made of their residences. This information was also gotten to various Lithuanian émigré organizations in the United States.

According to the information, Kudirka was being held under the Lithuanian equivalent of the Russian Republic's Article 64-A, which stipulated that leaving the Soviet Union without permission was treason. The offense is punishable by death.

These reports from the dissident sources were published in major U.S. newspapers on March 10, 1971, and their veracity seemed to be upheld two months later, on May 27, when a Soviet court official in Lithuania announced by telephone to correspondents in Moscow that Kudirka had received a ten-year sentence in a Soviet labor camp. Typically, the news lagged behind the event; the official said Kudirka's trial had taken place between May 17 and 20 before the Soviet Lithuanian Supreme Court.

The sentence was light according to Soviet standards and may have been influenced by the fact that Kudirka by then had become a world symbol. Related incidents and resultant public furor may also have played a part.[2]

News that filtered out of Vilnius nine months later from "reliable sources" was printed in the Lithuanian émigré press. The sources stated Kudirka was held in prison for a time in Vilnius and beaten by his guards.

His wife was not able to visit him nor correspond with him. The sources said she was thrown out of work and out of their residence with her two children. All their belongings were confiscated. A Lithuanian-language newspaper in Chicago quoted the sources as saying: "Genele and her children had no shelter and spent several nights outside. Later some good people sheltered them." The Soviets had demanded that she denounce her husband, but Mrs. Kudirka refused.

Nothing more of Kudirka was heard until early August, 1971, when his friends smuggled a brief account of his testimony during his trial to Anatole Shub in Paris. Shub was a correspondent formerly assigned in Moscow and had close ties with Soviet dissidents. In an article for the *Washington Post,* Shub quoted the testimony and brought the case to the headlines again.

The underground sources said that the trial was secret and Kudirka was allowed to speak for four hours. His statements were highly political, informed, and vehemently anti-Soviet. They went far beyond any other statements of earlier trials of Soviet dissidents and intellectuals, because Kudirka totally rejected Soviet rule over Lithuania, rather than just criticizing weaknesses that should be corrected. Other dissidents on trial in Russia had usually manifested an underlying loyalty to the regime. Using his trial to speak on Lithuania's behalf more than his own, knowing all along he faced a possible death sentence, Kudirka said:

"I do not consider myself guilty, since I did not betray my homeland, Lithuania. I do not consider Russia, called the Soviet Union today, as my homeland . . . By the decisions of the Teheran, Yalta, and Potsdam conferences, whole nations found themselves in slavery. In the eyes of the American military administration, I, as a Lithuanian, was the legal property of Brezhnev, the heir to Stalin, and should be returned to him . . .

"From the standpoint of international law, I am not a criminal. My decision to go abroad does not contradict the United Nations Declaration of Human Rights or even the Soviet constitution. Therefore I consider myself wholly innocent. However, I know very well that my fate has already been decided by the security organs."

According to Kudirka's testimony, secret police officials, some of whom had come especially from Moscow, tried to reeducate him while he was in solitary confinement awaiting trial. They hinted that if he condemned "bourgeois nationalism" in Lithuania and elsewhere he might get a lighter sentence, but Kudirka refused to cooperate, saying at his trial that he was foregoing his personal freedom for the sake of his homeland, Lithuania.

He then said: "The bravest and most resolute patriots of Lithuania were physically annihilated. But a new, young generation has grown up which intends to go the road of its fathers.

"I ask the Supreme Court not to persecute my mother, my wife, and my children. I ask you not to harm them."

Before being sentenced on May 20, 1971, Kudirka said: "I have nothing more to add to what I have already said, only one wish, more specifically a request, both to the Supreme Court and the government of the Soviet Union. I ask that you grant my homeland, Lithuania, independence . . . An independent Lithuania, in my opinion, has a sovereign government and is not occupied by any army. The government has a national administration, its own legal system, and a free democratic system of elections.

"The laws of other countries are not binding on this government, as the laws of Russia are here today. An independent

Lithuania wouldn't be dominated by the Russian language as it is today.

"I would like there to be no more trials such as mine in Lithuania . . . In a democratic trial anyone who wished would be permitted to attend. If I betrayed my homeland, then why are you afraid to show the public a traitor? Let the public itself judge me."

Soon after Shub's article appeared the Soviet underground, *samizdat* ("self-publishing"), gave credence to Shub's report by quoting it in its Chronicle of Current Events and providing added details of the testimony.[3]

In late November, 1971, *samizdat* informed Western correspondents in Moscow that Simas Kudirka was in a labor camp in Mordovia, deep in Soviet Russia. *Samizdat* reported that Kudirka had refused to participate in political indoctrination classes and as a result had lost the privilege to use the camp store. With the help of money sent from families and friends, prisoners were able to buy certain foodstuffs which were considered essential to supplement the starvation diet they had at the camp.

The last known reference to Kudirka appeared in early 1972 when a petition from the Potma Labor Camp was somehow smuggled to the International Red Cross protesting conditions at the camp. Of the eight signatures on the petition, one of them was purported to be that of Simas Kudirka.

Kudirka's actual fate remains a mystery, details sketchy, but one fact stands out: he remained a free-spirited rebel, refusing to "rehabilitate."

His deed had repercussions. Encouraged by world attention focused on Kudirka's plight, Estonia, Latvia, and Lithuania stirred. Local party leaders began to complain to Moscow about lack of various rights; seventeen members of the Latvian Politburo sent a petition to Moscow listing a number of political grievances; seventeen thousand Lithuanians signed a petition to Moscow and smuggled a copy to the United Nations protesting the suppression of religion in Lithuania. Starting in May, 1972, a series of political suicides in Lithuania—one of them accompanied by massive rioting in Kaunas, the second-largest city—centered new attention on the Baltic States.[4] All these rumblings, though motivated by separate grievances, could be connected to Kudirka's daring, but ill-fated leap from the *Sovetskaya Litva* to the Coast Guard Cutter *Vigilant* in the twilight of November 23, 1970.

While Kudirka by now has probably paid the supreme penalty for his attempt to find freedom, it may not have been entirely in vain. He sparked a searching reevaluation of U.S. policy and procedures in granting asylum to political refugees and aroused the conscience of the nation and the world. Countless others who follow in his footsteps may well have him to thank for their success.

Appendices

APPENDIX A

Commandant Instruction 3123.11

Subj: Initial Incident Reports

1. *Purpose.* This instruction promulgates a requirement for the Commandant to be informed immediately of transportation-related incidents which have potential national, international, or widespread local significance.

2. *Cancellation.* Commandant Notice 3123 dated 20 September 1969 is hereby cancelled.

3. *Discussion.* With the growing public concern over significant transportation-related incidents, it is most important that the Commandant and the Secretary of Transportation be aware of these events as soon as practicable.

 a. The Coast Guard, because of its traditional twenty-four-hour readiness posture, often receives information of an incident before other organizations. If this information can be quickly transmitted from the field unit which first receives the information, it may be of great benefit both to the Coast Guard and the Department of Transportation. In order for the Commandant and the Secretary of Transportation to respond to inquiries from members of Congress or from other branches of the Government, it is most desirable to have initial reports quickly transmitted so as to reach Headquarters before news releases or queries from parties with parochial interest.

 b. It is impossible to describe all incidents which are of such significance as to require immediate reports to the Commandant. For instance, a tanker or oil barge aground in U.S. waters may not be a particularly important SAR incident, but as a potential pollution case, it would be highly significant. On the other hand, an SAR case with a large number of persons in danger or an incident involving a high official of the government will usually attract a great deal of public attention. The potential significance of each event will depend on the facts and must be evaluated accordingly. When in doubt, a report should be made.

4. *Action.* Coast Guard commands, upon receipt of initial information concerning potentially significant transportation-related incidents, shall cause that information to be transmitted by telephone or other equally rapid means, to the cognizant RCC for evaluation and, when deemed appropriate, immediately relay to the Headquarters Flag Plot Duty Officer. In the interest of time, this report need include only those facts that are immediately available. Amplifying information should be provided when obtained, if appropriate. This procedure is not a substitute for the requirements set forth in current instructions.

/s/

R.W. Goehring
Chief, Office of Operations

APPENDIX B

Official U.S. Coast Guard Itemization of
Possessions Kudirka Left Behind

1. Short School German-Lithuanian and Lithuanian-German Dictionary published in Kaunas, 1963, by the Government Publishing House of Pedagogical Literature of the Lithuanian SSR.

2. Short School English-Lithuanian and Lithuanian-English Dictionary, published in Kaunas, 1966, by the publishing house "Sviesa."

3. Newspaper clipping from an unidentified Russian-language publication on the use of the English aircraft carrier LEVIATHAN to promote English exports during its visits to foreign ports. The article was apparently based on an article in *Quick,* published in Munich, West Germany.

4. Russian-language article entitled "Secretariat of the Directorate of Union Fisheries of the RSFSR," dated November 1969. It appears to be a political exhortation. One page.

5. Russian-language transliteration from the English of what appears to be news broadcasts, including temperatures in various cities throughout the world and items from such cities as Washington, New Orleans, Saigon, and London. Dated 1970. Two pages.

6. Pages 28–29 torn from an unidentified German-language magazine presumably published in East Germany. The article in question, on page 28, is entitled "Three Months—And You Can Speak a Foreign Language."

7. Two humorous snippets about a fence surrounding the fishing dock in the Port of Klaipeda that prevents the inhabitants from enjoying the beauty of the ships sailing into the distance and is so high

that even a witch could not surmount it with her magic broom; and an appeal to an imaginary captain to stop driving his men. He should use reasoning in lieu of poking fists in the faces of his men. All this is in the form of a holiday greeting.

8. Complaint by a correspondent about poor, unsanitary working conditions at a water-supply pumping station—no medical facilities, no waste disposal, no heating.

9. Lithuanian-language article clipped from an unidentified publication, probably a magazine. The article is about movie actor Spencer Tracy.

10. Untitled German poem in a romantic vein.

11. Russian-language article transliterated apparently from Spanish. Appears to relate to political matters involving Albania. One page.

12. Russian-language transliteration from the English of assorted short news items datelined from such cities as Washington, Tokyo, London, San Clemente, and Bonn. Two pages.

13. One half-sheet of paper containing two untitled poems in German in a romantic vein.

14. Russian-language radiogram, apparently a personal message to Kudirka from his wife. It says she received his telegram and letter, the house is as before, that she is awaiting a letter, and sending love.

15. Five items stapled together.

A. Small photograph of a young man. No identifying marks.

B. Russian-language radiogram from Zhenya saying that Evaldukasa has been brought home, everyone is well, and they are planning to go to Moscow. On the reverse is a handwritten series of notes in Lithuanian relating to the 1925 Scopes Monkey Trial. There is a second handwritten note stating that Prince Sihanouk commented on 18 March 1970 that he will remain in Moscow or Peking and form a temporary government-in-exile.

C. Russian-language transliteration from the German of short news items datelined from such cities as Kuala Lumpur, Frankfurt, and London. On the reverse side is a Russian-language transliteration from English of a warning about a floating mine and floating logs.

Also another German item from Hamburg and some handwritten notes in German.

D. Russian-language radiogram to Kudirka from Sasha saying everything is well, in fifty-five days has saved 800 rubles and already has a financial reserve.

E. Russian-language transliteration from German of news items, apparently from a West German station on 8 November 1968. Items are datelined from such cities as Berlin, New Delhi, and Prague. Two pages.

16. Pass booklet, Klaipeda Maritime Fishing Port, No. 11483, valid until 31 December 1970. Issued to Simas Ionovich Kudirka; with photograph.

17. (Enclosed in above.)

Miscellaneous union dues stamps (one is six- and three are eighteen-ruble denominations).

Pass issued by Captain Kazys Preiksas to Kudirka who is radio operator of ship. (No designation, no date.)

Pass issued by Captain of *Boyevaya Slava,* November 196(?), to Kudirka who is radio operator.

Pass issued by Captain of *Boyevaya Slava,* 12 December 1969, to Kudirka who is radio operator.

Pass issued by Captain of *Boyevaya Slava* to Kudirka, no date.

(NOTE: above passes are pieces of paper identifying Kudirka as being assigned to vessel, presumably used as ID passes aboard ship.)

18. Notebook (3½ x 5 inches), Russian alphabetical breakdown into Roman letters, various notations in Lithuanian, German, Russian, and English.

A. Lithuanian commentary, including a number of anti-Soviet statements, sayings, notes from various publications, statistics about Lithuania and other countries, names of authors of various books.

B. Three sayings in German, including: "One should sacrifice everything for humanity, except humanity itself."

C. Quotes from a book by Rudolph Abel, plus various other notes, including statement by Shirley Paige Manuel before a New York Court.

D. Various schematic diagrams of radio parts—EM 87 (five tubes), ECC 83, ECC 81, EF 93, EL 84, ECC 82, and ECH 81.

E. Comment on Morton Sobell; notes on Jan Palach; (fnu) Kardel, and Professor Vsemirov; Heinz Sutterlin, and Leonora.

F. Notes on earnings of various other mariners, prices of food.

APPENDIX C

Vigilant *Case—Press Release*

At 10:30 A.M., Monday, 23 November, the Coast Guard Cutter *Vigilant,* under the Command of Commander Ralph Eustis, home ported in New Bedford, Massachusetts, met the Soviet mother ship *Sovetskaya Litva* in United States territorial waters for the purpose of holding a joint meeting of representatives of the National Marine Fisheries Service, interested New Bedford fisheries industry representatives, and officials of the Soviet fishing fleet. In this latter group are included the Commanders of the *Lithuanian Kaliningrad,* the Latvian fleets, technologists, and a Russian interpreter. This meeting had been arranged through the normal State Department diplomatic channels as a means of coming to an agreement concerning conduct of the foreign fishing fleet in waters adjacent to the United States as concerns the yellowtail flounder fishing industry.

The two vessels met and moored together in an area just off Gay Head, Martha's Vineyard, Massachusetts. Throughout the day there was an exchange of courtesy visits between the members of both vessels. Small gifts, including cigarettes, and friendly talk were exchanged by the crews during the six-hour period that the two vessels planned to remain together. At the conclusion of the successful and harmonious meeting, and just prior to the planned separation of the two ships, at about 4:30 P.M., a crew member of the *Sovetskaya Litva* leaped from his vessel to the deck of the Coast Guard Cutter *Vigilant* with the obvious intention of requesting asylum. This fact was soon borne out when the crewman, Simas, who was later identified as the radio operator of the *Sovetskaya Litva,* confirmed his intentions in fairly good English as the two ships were preparing to separate. An interpreter-translator, who was a member of the American party, understood a call from the Soviet mother ship that they had discovered one of their crewmen was missing and they believed him to be on board *Vigilant.* It was at this point that *Vigilant*'s Commanding Officer notified the Commander First Coast Guard District in Boston of the situation that there was a defector on board and requested advice as to what procedures should be followed. These procedures consisted primarily of two points. First, that the presence of the crewman be made known to the master of the Soviet vessel and secondly, that the individual would be returned only upon receipt of a formal request from the master of the Soviet mother ship that he did in fact desire the crewman back aboard his vessel. There followed a series of separate consultations between Cdr. Eustis and representatives of the Soviet mother ship, and with the crew member himself, these meetings lasted a period of approximately five hours.

Meanwhile, a formal written notice from the master of the Soviet mother ship requesting that man be returned aboard was delivered. The information gathered at these various meetings plus specific information from my operational commander determined that the subject was to be returned to his own vessel. The man was subsequently forcibly returned to the mother ship at approximately midnight by members of its crew who were permitted to come aboard and to take the man into custody. At this point the Soviet vessel was escorted into international waters by CGC *Vigilant* in accordance with long-standing practice, and the *Vigilant* then resumed its patrol duties in the offshore areas adjoining Cape Cod.

APPENDIX D

Statement of [State] Department Spokesman
November 30, 1970

The Department of State was informed by the Coast Guard in Washington, by telephone, at about 2:30 P.M., November 23, that a seaman aboard the Soviet ship indicated to Coast Guard personnel that he wanted to defect. The Coast Guard at that point was told that we would not want to encourage a defection and that a provocation might be involved.

The Coast Guard was asked, however, to keep the Department informed of developments.

At approximately 3:30, or an hour later, another telephone discussion took place, again with the Coast Guard in Washington, in which the Coast Guard informed us that it appeared no actual attempt at defection had been made, but that the Coast Guard Duty Officer would keep the Department of State informed.

Nothing further was heard from the Coast Guard until about 7:45 [sic] P.M., when the Department was told by telephone that a defection had in fact occurred and that the seaman had been returned to his ship. The Department was further told that the Soviet ship was being escorted out of United States territorial waters.

Now that is the chronology—

Now, we naturally and deeply regret that this incident occurred. Let me say on background that if the Department had been told that a defection had actually occurred, I am confident things would have been handled—or things would have developed differently.

The Department of Transportation and the Department of State are continuing an investigation and will promptly institute procedures to prevent a recurrence of this type of incident.

APPENDIX E

Statement by the Commandant, U.S. Coast Guard
November 30, 1970

The Commandant of the United States Coast Guard makes the following statement with respect to the incident involving the Soviet defector to the Coast Guard Cutter VIGILANT on the date of 23 November:

The would-be defector had made direct contact with one of the officers on the Coast Guard Cutter VIGILANT on the morning of 23 November. He indicated at the time that he was contemplating jumping into the water upon the separation of the mother ship and VIGILANT, who were at the time moored side by side near Martha's Vineyard. There was continued visiting between the personnel of the two vessels during the day.

The information from the would-be defector was relayed through Coast Guard Headquarters to the State Department in Washington, and advice was given to the effect that if the man were to be brought on board the Coast Guard ship, further reference should be made to the State Department for advice.

The defector, in fact, did not wait for the two ships to separate, but jumped directly on the Coast Guard vessel. A decision was made soon thereafter by the Commander, First Coast Guard District, to return the defector to the Soviet mother ship, by force if necessary. It was further decided that any force required would be exercised by the seamen from the Soviet vessel.

As background for this decision, it should be noted that the Soviet ship had been invited into our territorial waters for a friendly discussion on fisheries in the North West Atlantic, and again the two ships were moored side by side. Furthermore, the Soviet Master alleged that the defector had stolen $2,000 [sic] from the ship's fund. Under these circumstances, the Commander, First Coast Guard District, felt that it was reasonable and proper that we not permit our ship to be used as a means of defection and that the man should be returned.

As Commandant of the Coast Guard I recognize that the Commander, First Coast Guard District, has not received specific advice from the State Department or Coast Guard Headquarters as to what action to take under these circumstances. While it is not yet clearly established whether or not he took the proper action, I believe it to be understood how he would make this decision on the existing circumstances. I do not approve of the use of force on a Coast Guard ship by personnel of another nation, but do recognize that considerable force was required, as the defector was resisting strongly.

It is my desire and expectation that the State Department will soon give us specific instructions as to procedures to be followed in the future under similar circumstances, which certainly could be repeated.

APPENDIX F

Summary Interim Procedures for the Handling of Requests for Political Asylum by Foreign Nationals

1. Application

These procedures should be applied by all agencies of the U.S. Government which do not now operate under established guidance. These procedures are effective immediately and should be followed until replaced by revised and amplified procedures now in preparation.

2. Policy Background

In accordance with American tradition and practice, foreign nationals who request political asylum from the United States Government due to persecution or fear of persecution should be given full opportunity to have their requests considered on their merits. Because of the wide variety of circumstances which may be involved, each request must be dealt with on a case-by-case basis, taking into account, among other factors, humanitarian principles, foreign policy considerations, and applicable laws.

3. United Nations Protocol Relating to the Status of Refugees

The United States is a party to the United Nations Protocol Relating to the Status of Refugees, which incorporates, by reference, all of the substantive articles of the 1951 Convention Relating to the Status of Refugees. Article 33 of the Convention reads as follows:

"1. No Contracting State shall expel or return ('refouler') a refugee in any manner whatsoever to the frontiers or territories where his life or freedom would be threatened on account of his race, religion, nationality, membership of a particular social group or political opinion.

"2. The benefit of the present provision may not, however, be claimed by a refugee whom there are reasonable grounds for regarding as a danger to the security of the country in which he is, or who, having been convicted by a final judgment of a particularly serious crime, constitutes a danger to the community of that country."

As a party to the Protocol, the United States thus has an international treaty obligation for the meticulous implementation of Convention Article 33.

4. Procedures

A. Agencies are requested to notify the State Department immediately by the quickest available means whenever a foreign national request for asylum is received by U.S. Government officials. Initial contact should be through the Operations Center of the State Department, which will refer the request to the appropriate offices in the Department for consideration and guidance.

B. The determination of whether or not a person seeking asylum is a *bona fide* refugee involves complex factual and legal considerations. Persons seeking asylum should be interviewed immediately to ascertain as fully as possible the basis for their asylum request and to establish the *bona fide* nature of their request. Information thus procured should be forwarded rapidly to the Department of State which will provide appropriate guidance in coordination with other interested agencies.

C. Under no circumstances should the person seeking asylum be arbitrarily or summarily returned to foreign jurisdiction or control pending determination of his status. Moreover, to the extent circumstances permit, persons seeking asylum should be afforded every possible care and protection.

APPENDIX G

Formal Board of Investigation into Allegations of
Improper Conduct in Connection with Recent
Defection Attempt of Soviet Crewman to CGC
Vigilant *near Martha's Vineyard, Massachusetts, on*
23 November 1970

OPINIONS

1. CAPT BROWN, although counseled by his principal staff officers that the defector should have been retained aboard VIGILANT until State Department could arrange disposition, failed to properly utilize or rely upon their expertise. In referring a matter of important decision to RADM ELLIS, and in acceding to, accepting, or adopting instructions provided by RADM ELLIS, CAPT BROWN failed to exercise his command powers and accept his command responsibilities as the Acting District Commander of the First Coast Guard District. Furthermore, CAPT BROWN failed to keep Coast Guard Headquarters informed of important changes in the case, even though he was asked to do so by Headquarters authorities, and was required to do so as a matter of general policy with the Coast Guard. It should be noted that although CAPT BROWN asked LT RYAN to call Headquarters about the case, he effectively rescinded that order without ever verifying whether or not Headquarters had been informed.

2. RADM ELLIS, although he was reluctant to offer advice while not in command, should have known that CAPT BROWN and CDR EUSTIS were treating his remarks not as advice but as orders. Instructing these men as he did, RADM ELLIS infringed improperly

upon the command prerogatives of the Acting District Commander. Furthermore, RADM ELLIS gave instructions on complicated and sensitive issues having obvious national and international import without first apprising himself of established national policy.

3. CDR EUSTIS was not in sympathy with the orders he had received to return the defector. Having the opportunity, CDR EUSTIS would have avoided or refused to return the defector. CDR EUSTIS accepted the finality of his orders, and he returned the defector once it became evident that the decision of the District Commander was past reconsideration. Under these circumstances, CDR EUSTIS cannot be faulted in his decision to allow Soviet crew members aboard his ship to remove the defector if he went willingly. On the other hand, his failure to impose and exercise effective restraints on these Foreign Nationals to prevent a breach of discipline on an American Military Vessel cannot be condoned.

4. The State Department did not furnish the Coast Guard with adequate, helpful, or timely advice to deal properly with this defection. The quality of liaison and communication between the two agencies was not satisfactory and contributed to the unfortunate result that occurred. Due to the increasing complexity of international relations and the status of nations, it is imperative that Coast Guard commanders and commands be provided with ready access to current State Department policy and procedure to perform their duties as representatives of the nation's maritime law enforcement agency.

5. Coast Guard communications were deficient in that: (a) there were inordinate delays in operational immediate messages due to failure in equipment, (b) telephone conversations of great importance were not confirmed by written messages, and (c) recording equipment in Flag Plot at Coast Guard Headquarters was inoperative. Although not conclusive, a more efficient communications procedure may have affected the outcome.

RECOMMENDATIONS

1. That CAPT BROWN be awarded a General Court-Martial for trial on charges of Dereliction of Duty for his failure to inform the Commandant of the progress of the case and for his failure to retain the defector aboard the VIGILANT until having advice from proper authority. An appropriate charge sheet is enclosed.

2. That RADM ELLIS be issued a Punitive Letter of Reprimand from the Commandant for offering instructions or advice without having informed himself of the fact and policy necessary for a proper decision, all to the prejudice of good order and discipline in the service; that he be removed from command and asked to retire as soon as his health permits but not later than 31 January 1971; and that in the interim he be assigned to a position of minimal responsibilities.

3. That CDR EUSTIS be issued an Administrative Letter of Reprimand from the Commandant for allowing Soviet crew members aboard his vessel to remove a Soviet defector without exercising upon them the proper restraints; and that he be immediately reassigned from the VIGILANT.

4. That the Office of Operations confer with the State Department to explore those areas in which the Coast Guard would benefit by having detailed guidelines on current State Department policy and procedure. Further, that the Office of Personnel confer with the State Department to explore the possibilities of making more productive the existing exchange of billets between the two agencies by filling the State Department officer billet at the Coast Guard and by creating regular liaison duties for the Coast Guard Officer assigned at the State Department.

5. That immediate steps be taken to repair the telephone recording equipment in Flag Plot at Coast Guard Headquarters with automatic time recording equipment, and that competent engineering personnel review the communications difficulties experienced by CGC VIGILANT and the office of Commander, First Coast Guard District, to determine what changes, if any, may be necessary.

6. That a Commandant Instruction be issued directing the confirmation by written message of important telephonic orders and instructions.

Action of the Convening Authority Regarding Rear Admiral William B. Ellis

RECOMMENDATION NO. 2 IS NOT CONCURRED IN.

It is true that RADM ELLIS disobeyed no orders; he was not, in fact, in the chain of command at the time of the incident. Nevertheless, he gave advice having the force of orders and adhered to his position firmly and even stubbornly in spite of the fact that he was informed that principal staff officers were not in agreement with his position and in spite of the fact that he knew advice had been sought from the Commandant. His actions prompting the recommendation for the Punitive Letter of Reprimand were such as to make him no less responsible in the matter than CAPT BROWN. Accordingly, I direct the Board to embody the misconduct it found to exist in an appropriate charge or charges and specifications. I find such charges should be referred for trial by court-martial. In this instance, however, as in the instance of CAPT BROWN, there is little doubt that regardless of the results of a trial, RADM ELLIS's performance during the incident has seriously impaired his effectiveness as a flag officer on active duty. For this reason, if RADM ELLIS immediately submits a request for retirement, I shall accept it and not refer the charge or charges for trial, but rather will issue a Punitive Letter of Reprimand under Article 15 of the Uniform Code of Military Justice.

APPENDIX H

Rear Admiral Ellis's Appeal of Letter of
Reprimand
and
Secretary Volpe's Denial of Appeal

5812
JAN 29 1971

From: Rear Admiral William B. ELLIS 1437, USCG
To: The Secretary of Transportation
Via: Commandant, U.S. Coast Guard

Subj: Appeal of nonjudicial punishment awarded by Commandant, U.S. Coast Guard on 23 December 1970

Ref: (a) Report of Formal Board of Investigation convened by
Commandant U.S. Coast Guard by Appointing Order
dated 30 November 1970
       (b) Letter of Reprimand issued under authority of Article 15
UCMJ by Commandant, U.S. Coast Guard to Rear Ad-
miral William B. ELLIS 1437, USCG dated 23 December 1970

1. Reference (b) which is a letter of reprimand issued under the
authority of Article 15, UCMJ by Admiral C. R. BENDER, Commandant, U.S. Coast Guard was received by the undersigned on 28
December 1970 at 1600 at Boston, Massachusetts.

2. This letter constitutes an appeal to the Secretary of Transportation
through the Commandant, U.S. Coast Guard in accordance with

Article 15, UCMJ, Paragraph 135, Manual for Courts-Martial, 1969 (Rev.) and Coast Guard Supplement to MCM, 1969 (Rev.). The Commandant granted an extension of the usual fifteen-day time limit on appeals on 7 January 1971, said extension to expire on 29 January 1971.

3. My appeal is based on three grounds, viz:

   a. The letter is too vague to properly inform me as to what offense I have committed.

   b. If the offense I am charged with having violated is an offense under Article 92, UCMJ, i.e. disobedience of an order or regulation, the evidence of record fails to establish the offense as a matter of law, and

   c. The letter fails to state any offense under the law.

4. At the outset, the letter of reprimand states: ". . . you furnished instruction and advice in language which you have characterized as leaving no doubt in Captain BROWN's mind as to what you *expected* to be done . . ." (emphasis supplied). I have never made that characterization, i.e. that my language left no doubt in Captain BROWN's mind as to what I *expected* to be done. My statement at the hearing was that I spoke in such a tone that I was certain that Captain BROWN knew what I would do if I were on duty and by the same token he knew what I *thought* he should do (emphasis supplied). The language of the letter of reprimand makes it appear that I was giving orders to Captain BROWN and thus *expected* them to be carried out. I never characterized my language as such.

5. In order for the punitive letter of censure to stand, the accused, (in this case, myself), must have committed an "offense" under the UCMJ. See paragraph 0102 (e) of the U.S. Navy JAG Manual and Article 15, UCMJ. The letter of reprimand does not refer to any specific offense listed in the punitive articles of the UCMJ, and, although it is recognized that a specific punitive article does not have to be cited, yet it is clear that the facts constituting the offense must

be set forth with sufficient clarity to allow me to ascertain what offense I have committed. In this case the letter is substantially defective in that neither I nor my attorneys can ascertain what punitive article has been violated.

6. Despite the foregoing, I assume in this appeal that I am being punished for a violation of Article 92 of the UCMJ, i.e. a violation of an order or regulation, viz, Article 13-3-4 of U.S. Coast Guard Regulations. That Article provides in pertinent part:

13-3-4 Succession to Command of a District

A. The district chief of staff shall act as district commander, unless the Commandant orders a different officer to duty as acting district commander, when there is a vacancy in that office, when the district commander is absent from the district office because of leave, sickness, or temporary duty outside the district, and when he is absent because of temporary duty within the district and the distance involved, communication and mail facilities, or period of time away from his office are such as to prevent the district commander from properly administering the district.

That Article is clearly a *grant* of power and authority to the Chief of Staff so that he may assume the duties, responsibilities and powers of the District Commander when the latter is absent from duty. It is not intended to prevent a District Commander from giving advice or guidance to the Acting District Commander when the latter seeks out that advice and guidance. Further, it seems clear that it amounts to direction to the Acting District Commander and all others in the Coast Guard, indeed, the District Commander himself, that the Chief of Staff is the person possessed of the powers and responsibilities of command until such time as the regularly-assigned District Commander returns to duty. It should be borne in mind that my sole contact with Captain BROWN consisted of a total of four telephone calls, i.e. one at 1:18 P.M., one at 3:20 P.M., one at 6:38 P.M. and the final one at 7:30 P.M. Each and every one of those calls was initiated by Captain BROWN and none of them lasted more than five minutes. I initiated no telephone calls or other inquiries into the case. To say that I thereby "infringed on the authority of the Acting District Commander who, under Section 13-3-4, Coast Guard Regulations, had succeeded to command during . . . [my] absence on sick leave," as the letter of reprimand states, is clearly erroneous and unjust. Indeed, how can one infringe on Captain BROWN's authority when he initiated all four telephone calls to ask for my views and recommendations. To hold me *criminally* liable for giving advice when it is sought after is just plain wrong and unjust.

7. In this case it is important to go back over the facts to assess what really happened. I have no real objection to the findings of the Board of Investigation in this case insofar as they pertain to me inasmuch as the Board heard a great deal of testimony and was acting under severe time limitations. However, I sincerely believe there are some errors in the inferences drawn by the Board which I shall point out as I continue.

The real issue is whether I was *criminally* wrong (the word seems harsh, but that clearly is the test in order for a *punitive* letter of reprimand to stand) in giving my advice and guidance to Captain BROWN under the circumstances that existed on 23 November 1970.

In determining whether I was criminally wrong in giving that advice the following matters are both relevant and material.

a. I was on 23 November 1970 at home recuperating from surgery which had been performed on 4 November 1970. Although I was not on medication, I was confined to my house and on doctor's orders limited to one trip downstairs per day.

b. I knew of the conference and the background of it.

c. Captain BROWN called me at about 1:18 P.M. and told me of the message from VIGILANT. I told him in essence that I felt we had to return the man if he defected. He voiced no objection to that procedure. He also told me that he had informed the Commandant at Washington, D.C., and that he had doubleheaded VIGILANT's message to the Commandant.

d. Captain BROWN called me again at 3:20 P.M. and informed me that he had talked to the responsible officers at Coast Guard Headquarters and told them of the situation. I assumed, and rightly so in my opinion, that he had also told Washington what my feelings on the subject were. Indeed, I also assumed that the Situation Reports (SITREPS) which are the reports required by Coast Guard Directives, especially COMDTINST 3123.11 and 3123.3C were being sent (copies attached). I might also add that it is clear that I could expect such action to be taken routinely since that was the regular procedure in the First District in the past and the Board recommended that Captain BROWN be tried by General Court-Martial for exactly that failure, i.e. failure to keep Coast Guard Headquarters informed of significant changes in the case as it progressed. Indeed, if I had issued "orders" to return the man, such orders would have been a significant change in the case, yet Captain BROWN apparently did not inform Headquarters of that fact. I can only assume that he did not inform Headquarters of my views since he did not consider them to be "orders" and that *he* had not yet decided what the course of action would be.

e. In the 3:20 P.M. phone call to me Captain BROWN unfortunately did not inform me of the legal advice he had received on this matter. Although it is true that he told me there was some disagreement on the staff, he did not inform me that the District Legal Officer recommended to him, *after research on the matter,* that the man be held and turned over to the State Department or Immigration Service. Since I have been District Commander at Boston, anytime I have gone against the advice of the District Legal Officer, I have always consulted with him personally before I did so. In such a case, if I persisted in my decision, he would usually suggest that he talk to the legal personnel at Washington before I acted and I cannot recall a single case where I acted against his advice on legal matters if he reported to me that Coast Guard Headquarters legal personnel agreed with his opinion. I am certain that if I knew of his recommendations, I would have told Captain BROWN to put CDR FLANAGAN on the phone and let me talk to him. This would at least have meant that CDR FLANAGAN would have known that I was aware of the case and it seems clear that if I went against his advice he would then have reminded Captain BROWN of the requirement to send the SITREPS required by current directives, thus informing Headquarters of the District's intentions in the matter.

f. Captain BROWN unfortunately failed to inform Commander FLANAGAN at any time on 23 November that he had ever talked to me or that I was ever aware of the case. The record makes it clear that at least in Commander FLANAGAN's view, Captain BROWN was making the decision as indeed Captain BROWN was required to do by the above-cited regulation. (See R-155, 156 Verbatim Transcript.)

g. In the 5:15 P.M. call to me by Commander EUSTIS, I received the call by default, i.e. because Commander EUSTIS could not reach Captain BROWN or Commander CURRY. I was reluctant to take the call but I knew that Commander EUSTIS wanted advice and had no one to turn to at the moment. At that time, i.e. at 5:15 P.M., I had told Captain BROWN of my ideas; I knew he had talked to Coast Guard Headquarters; and I had no knowledge of any further instructions from Washington, since if there had been any the RCC Controller, LT RYAN, should have known of them and have been briefed on them. He was on the telephone line as a third party while I talked to Commander EUSTIS.

Thus, I reiterated my original view of the situation to Commander EUSTIS. However, as soon as I finished the call, I told Lieutenant RYAN to be certain to contact Captain BROWN as soon as possible and inform him of my conversation with Commander EUSTIS. He assured me that he would. I specifically told him to inform Captain BROWN because I realized that I had, at that point, injected myself, and properly so in my opinion, between the Acting District Commander and the Commanding Officer of the VIGILANT. I submit that I had no alternative but to give some advice. The only reasonable alternative would have been for me to tell Commander EUSTIS that I could not advise him since I was not on duty. That alternative was not and is not acceptable to me. Indeed, I would be a sorry excuse for a flag officer of the Coast Guard if when one of my ship commanders called me for guidance or advice, I refused to talk to him and offer such views as I had on the ground that I was not on duty. In my mind, to follow that course of action would clearly have been grounds for charges to be preferred against me despite the fact that I was not on duty.

h. I received a third phone call from Captain BROWN at 6:38 P.M. In that call he told me that he was aware that I had talked with Commander EUSTIS and that he had just talked with Commander EUSTIS. He told me that he had told Commander EUSTIS to keep the defector in seclusion and ask the Soviet officers to leave VIGILANT so that he, Captain BROWN, could contact the Commandant for further advice. He told me that the only previous information he had received from the Commandant concerned what to do if the man jumped into the water. He did not tell me that Coast Guard Headquarters specifically said that they wanted to be kept advised of developments in the case. At that time Captain BROWN did not advise me of any significant change in circumstances from those existing at the time of the 3:20 P.M. call with the sole exception that he did say that he had been in further communication with Coast Guard Headquarters and that the only advice they gave was what to do in case the man jumped in the water.

i. Indeed, if my advice in the two earlier phone calls was taken as "orders" by Captain BROWN, it appears that he saw fit to countermand those "orders" in the course of his conversation with Commander EUSTIS since he expressly told the latter to place KUDIRKA in seclusion and ask the Soviet officers to return to their ship. He said to Commander EUSTIS: "This is a situation which is going to have to be resolved by the State Department." (See page 46 of the Board's Report.) In addition, of course, he told me that he had done so. It seems clear, then, that at that time Captain BROWN was exercising the powers and duties expressly granted to him by the above-cited regulation.

j. Thus, *insofar as I knew* during the 6:38 P.M. telephone call with Captain BROWN at the time I reiterated my former advice, the facts were as follows:

(1) The defector was now onboard the vessel.

(2) Captain BROWN had had further conversation with Coast Guard Headquarters and in particular RADN HAMMOND at Washington, D.C., since his 3:20 P.M. telephone call to me and had asked for specific advice as to what to do.

(3) The only advice that Captain BROWN received from Coast Guard Headquarters concerned what to do in the event the defector jumped into the water.

(4) The defector in fact had not jumped in the water, thus the Commandant's advice did not apply.

(5) Insofar as I knew, my recommended plan of action had been forwarded to Coast Guard Headquarters at Washington, D.C., via SITREPS and/or telephone conversations with

RADM HAMMOND and Captain DAHLGREN and was known by RADM HAMMOND and his staff.

(6) Coast Guard Headquarters had not objected to my recommendations.

In view of the foregoing it was my impression at that time that there was no significant change in circumstances that required any other action than what I had recommended at the outset. Accordingly, I reiterated to Captain BROWN my recommendation as to what should be done.

k. My next contact with the case occurred at 7:30 P.M. when Captain BROWN again called me at home. He told me that Commander EUSTIS was concerned for KUDIRKA's safety and that he (Commander EUSTIS) felt that his life was in jeopardy. In addition, he informed me that this was based on KUDIRKA's remarks to Commander EUSTIS. At that point it seemed reasonable to me that any man who had defected from the Russian vessel and who wanted to stay in the United States would claim that he was fearful of his life if he were returned. Thus, the only indication I had at that time that there was in fact any fear for the life of KUDIRKA was the statement of the Commanding Officer of the VIGILANT which in turn was based on statements emanating from KUDIRKA himself. In my opinion at that time I did not consider this unusual at all, i.e. that KUDIRKA would claim that his life was in jeopardy. Accordingly, I saw no reason to change the advice I had given Captain BROWN earlier.

l. As of the end of the 7:30 P.M. telephone call, I had no further contact whatsoever with the case. Specifically, at no time did I ever recommend nor was I ever advised that Soviet personnel were going to be used to return the defector to the Soviet vessel. In addition, at no time did I ever offer advice or recommendations on nor would I have condoned beating of KUDIRKA by either Coast Guard or Soviet personnel such as occurred. At the very most, I would have authorized adequate force by Coast Guard personnel to restrain KUDIRKA and take him in custody back to the Russian vessel.

8. I fully realize that there is a large body of opinion in the United States which feels that my recommendations and opinions in this matter were incorrect. I appreciate their viewpoint but I still believe that my view as to the ultimate decision, i.e. as to whether KUDIRKA had to be returned, was correct. I do agree that the decision, i.e. whether to return KUDIRKA, should have been made in Washington and that its implementation should have been accomplished in a controlled manner. The problem, of course, was that insofar as I knew at the time, Coast Guard Headquarters at Washington had been advised as to both the existing situation and my views on the matter and, despite a time interval of some seven and one-half hours, i.e. from approximately 1:00 P.M. until 7:30 P.M., had given no advice except the very narrow guidance as to what to do if KUDIRKA jumped in the water. In the absence of a decision by Washington, it appeared to me that Boston had to make the decision on its own.

9. In any event, whether my views and recommendations were correct or not, I submit that to have those views and make those recommendations under the circumstances that existed on 23 November 1970 was not a *criminal* act. Yet, that is precisely the test that must be met in the award of a punitive letter of reprimand under the authority of Article 15 of the Uniform Code of Military Justice. The Code itself states that punishment may be imposed for ". . . offenses . . ." Art. 15a, UCMJ, 10 USC §815. The Coast Guard Supplement to the Manual for Courts-Martial 1969 (Rev.) speaks only of punishment being imposed for ". . . offenses . . ." See §0101a, CG Supp, MCM (1969) (Rev.). See also U.S. Navy JAG Manual, §0101a. Thus, the punitive letter can stand only if my conduct in making my recommendations and giving advice to Captain BROWN was such as to render me a *criminal*. Clearly, my conduct was not of that nature.

10. Indeed, it would appear that any officer of the U.S. Navy faced with the same problem would more than likely have reached the same conclusion, absent advice from Washington—advice which neither Captain BROWN nor I received. I say this because I feel sure that he would have consulted U.S. Navy Regulations and found §0621 which states as follows:

0621. Granting of Asylum.

The right of asylum for political or other refugees has no foundation in international law. In countries, however, where frequent insurrections occur, and constant instability of government exists, usage sanctions the granting of asylum; but even in waters of such countries, officers should *refuse all applications for asylum* except when required by the interests of humanity in extreme or exceptional cases, such as the pursuit of a refugee by a mob. Officers shall neither directly nor indirectly invite refugees to accept asylum. (Emphasis supplied.)

It is true that a lawyer studying §0621 would probably realize that it speaks solely of diplomatic asylum, but I submit that any other seagoing officer, indeed even a flag officer, would not recognize the distinction. In fact, I am informed that most lawyers would not recognize the difference absent special expertise in the field of international law. My feelings in this regard are reinforced by the comments of the International Law Division of the U.S. Navy in their memorandum of law on the matter written on 2 December 1970, some nine days after the KUDIRKA incident. In that memorandum the International Law Division says that §0621 is the only guidance in the field, that it is "not sufficient" and that ". . . unless it is corrected, it is conceivable that a Naval officer might erroneously deny asylum in a situation of political/territorial asylum because of a misplaced reliance on the Navy Regulations." The same document goes on to state:

"The failure of article 0621 to address the question of territorial/political asylum must be corrected by a change to the

regulations or naval officers may be misled." (Emphasis supplied.) See Memorandum for the Judge Advocate General dated 2 December 1970 on Subject: Granting of Asylum by Officials of the Naval Service. (Copy enclosed.)

11. I hasten to add that I did not know of the U.S. Navy Regulation at the time I offered advice to Captain BROWN. I note the above-cited Regulation and the U.S. Navy memorandum solely to show that my views, advice, and recommendations were not so out of line with the action that any Naval commander might take as to make my conduct reprehensible enough to be considered *criminal.*

12. I also note that in a newspaper column in the St. Louis, Mo., *Post-Dispatch* on December 17, 1970, former Secretary of State Dean ACHESON is quoted as saying that regardless who made the decision, KUDIRKA would have to be returned. I enclose herewith a copy of that newspaper article as it appeared in the newspaper. Once again, I do not argue whether he is right or wrong in his analysis of the situation. However, I do submit that the fact that he, a former Secretary of State, feels that KUDIRKA would have to have been returned indicates that the views I held and advice and guidance I gave were not so reprehensible as to be deemed of a *criminal* nature.

13. In summary, my point is that at the most I am guilty of an error in judgment. Such errors in judgment have been made in the past by me and by others in places of responsibility and trust—and it seems fair to say that they will continue to be made, not only by military commanders but by high officials in the legislative, executive, and judicial branches of the Government. In the past, the persons who have made those errors have not been subjected to criminal sanctions —especially in a case where they were not acting for some private gain. I ask only to be judged by the same standard. Indeed, if the punitive letter in my case stands, it applies a totally different brand of justice to military officers from that which is applied to any other personnel of the U.S. Government, be they in the legislative, judicial, or executive branch. In this regard, I have yet to learn of any punish-

ment having been meted out to any personnel in the State Department as a result of this incident.

14. For the foregoing reasons, I request that the punishment in my case be set aside and that the punitive letter of reprimand be expunged from my military record despite the fact that I am being retired from the Coast Guard on 31 January 1971 after thirty-four and a half years of active service, five months prior to my scheduled retirement.

Respectfully,

W. B. ELLIS

Encl: (1) COMDT INST 3123.11
     (2) COMDT INST 3123.3C
     (3) Memorandum for The JAG dtd 2 Dec 70
     (4) Photo copy of St. Louis *Post-Dispatch* news article of Dec 17, 1970

The Secretary of Transportation

RADM William B. Ellis 1437, USCG
Post Office Box
Uncasville, Connecticut

Dear Admiral Ellis:

I have carefully reviewed your appeal of January 29 from the letter of reprimand issued you on December 23, 1970. I have also obtained the advice of the General Counsel on this matter, as I am permitted to do by Article 15. I conclude that the letter of reprimand is supported by the record of the board of investigation and that you were apprised of the offense which underlies the letter—namely, violation of Article 92 of the UCMJ.

The record indicates that your advice to the Acting District Commander was given and received as a command rather than as guidance and at a time when you were not on duty and could not, therefore, accept responsibility for the Coast Guard's actions. Thus, in violation of customs of the service you exercised command authority while not in command in derogation of a properly constituted authority.

Accordingly, your appeal is denied.

Sincerely,

/s/

John Volpe

APPENDIX I

Attempted Defection by Lithuanian Seaman Simas Kudirka

Report of the House Subcommittee on State Department Organization and Foreign Operations of the Committee on Foreign Affairs

CONCLUSIONS

Admiral Ellis and Captain Brown were spared court-martial proceedings and allowed to retire. Whether judicial process would have found either or both derelict in their performance and spared the Government the cost of their retirement is speculative.

Their relationship during this incident is a lesson in command. Either an officer is or is not in the chain of command. On November 23 Admiral Ellis was not and he knew it. Captain Brown knew it. It was his responsibility to exercise command no less than it was Admiral Ellis's not to inject himself even when his advice was sought. Admiral Ellis soon lost all sense of distinction between advice and orders. More significant, he gave advice and orders on substantive policy about which he knew nothing and cared less. He showed no disposition to urge Captain Brown to seek advice from Headquarters. At one point Captain Brown was wavering on what to do. In his 6 P.M. conversation with Lieutenant Ryan he said: "Look I think it might be preferred to keep that fellow on board the *Vigilant* and tell the *Vigilant* to go proceed to New Bedford." Admiral Ellis straightened him out.

Captain Brown had no confidence in the advice of his staff and ignored the order to advise Headquarters if the defector came aboard. He knew he was treading a dangerous course, but he did not care. In a conversation at 7:25 P.M. with Lieutenant Ryan as to whether Commander Eustis understood what he was to do these remarks were made:

> BROWN. What a lousy job.
> RYAN. And he's caught (Commander Eustis) in the middle.
> BROWN. No, he isn't.
> RYAN. Well, you are maybe. I don't know.
> BROWN. You bet your ever-lovin' bippy.
> RYAN. Yeah.
> BROWN. Hay [sic], uh, do you know how to knit?
> RYAN. Knit?
> BROWN. Yes.
> RYAN. No, sir.
> BROWN. K-n-i-t.
> RYAN. No, sir.
> BROWN. Maybe I oughta take that up.
> RYAN. What I meant—
> BROWN. I got my thirty in anyway [a reference to thirty

years service for retirement purposes].

In other words, he was saying: "I've got it made. What do I care for any human being." If this attitude is typical of high officials in the Coast Guard, God help America.

Commander Eustis was caught in an untenable position. He was ordered to use force but to avoid an incident. The situation on the *Vigilant* was such that one without the other was impossible.

In his view of the report of the Board of Investigation, Admiral Bender, Commandant of the Coast Guard, noted "that more aggressive action on the part of Coast Guard Headquarters might have altered the prosecution of this incident. Specifically, Coast Guard Headquarters might well have insisted on more definite guidance from State Department." He could well have added that his Headquarters should have made an initial decision (he has a legal staff) and that his Headquarters should have been more persistent in its communication with Boston. Instead of the routine "keep us informed" message, a clear directive not to return the defector until ordered by Headquarters would have forestalled the incident—assuming that Admiral Ellis would not overrule Headquarters.

The State Department also had a casual attitude about the situation. As in the case of Coast Guard Headquarters, a detailed knowledge of all the circumstances was not immediately necessary to state a basic principle of U.S. foreign policy. Whether a defector comes by land or sea does not alter the policy.

A reading of the many communications on the Kudirka case points up the need not only for aggressive action but for a refresher course in basic English for both Coast Guard and State Department officers.

One final point. As a nation we have pride and confidence in the reliability of our sophisticated communications equipment. If November 23 is a demonstration of its efficiency, we had better think of smoke signals or carrier pigeons.

SUPPLEMENTAL VIEWS

While we are in essential agreement with the subcommittee's report on the Kudirka case, we are reluctant to endorse those assertions which concern the subjective attitudes of Admiral Ellis and Captain Brown. We agree entirely that each of these officers bears a principal measure of responsibility for the outrageous mishandling of the matter, but we are not prepared to make speculative assessments of their motives.

> F. Bradford Morse
> William S. Mailliard
> Vernon W. Thomson

Notes

NOTES

Introduction

1. Information about Soviet fleet operations and the New England fishing industry was provided by William Gordon, Associate Director of the National Marine Fisheries Service (NMFS), Region Three in Gloucester, Massachusetts; Howard Nickerson, Resident Director of the New Bedford Seafood Dealers Association; and Robert Brieze, President of the New Bedford Seafood Producers Association. Also helpful was John D. Hebron's *Communist Ships and Shipping,* 1962; and articles in the *Standard-Times* of New Bedford dealing with fisheries and fishing.

2. *Boston Evening Globe,* July 13, 1971.

3. The *Standard-Times,* November 25, 1967.

4. The *Standard Times,* May, 16, 1966. For Soviet spying activities, see also February 9–10, 1969.

Chapter One

1. "Operation Keelhaul" was sanctioned by the American, British, and Swedish governments and remains a little-publicized aspect of Allied behavior immediately after World War II. At the insistence of Josef Stalin, the Allies turned back thousands of refugees to Soviet control—most of them at gunpoint. Hundreds committed suicide rather than go back. Congressman John Ashbrook (R–Ohio) as late as 1972 (92nd Congress, First Session) has tried to get public disclosure of all aspects of "Operation Keelhaul," but with little success. The government refuses to release the documents, even though the twenty-five-year statute of limitations is over, claiming it must also have the approval of the British, who also refuse to disclose the documents concerning this operation.

2. Although the meeting had been prearranged, the rendezvous was to be in international waters. In case of bad weather, the Soviets were to be escorted to safe anchorage nearer to land, as, indeed, they were later escorted out of territorial waters by the *Vigilant* "in accordance with long-standing practice" according to the words of a subsequent Coast Guard press release (Appendix C).

The message setting up the rendezvous reads as follows:

Message Nov. 11 received. Suggest meeting Nov. 23 at Flashing white buoy 9 miles south of Gay Head, Martha's Vineyard at Position 70–51W 41–12N, ETA 10:30 AM, 4:30 GMP. Party will depart your vessel same day. Coast Guard Cutter *Vigilant* WMEC-617, transporting party of 7–8, including Associate Regional Director Bill Gordon, who is heading U.S. delegation. *Vigilant* will stand by on 2 182 MHZ and FM-Channel 16. If weather conditions do not permit boarding in rendezvous area will move to lee of Martha's Vineyard. Observers also desire to board several trawlers.

Norris, Regional Director

3. Formal Coast Guard Board of Investigation, *Board Exhibit 18:* "Captain Fletcher W. Brown, Jr., Acting Commander, First Coast Guard District, letter 5921 of 5 November 1970 to Mr. Russel T. Norris reporting the participation of the USCGC VIGILANT in the fisheries meeting."

4. The letter is included as part of the record of *Hearings before the Subcommittee on State Department Organization and Foreign Operations of the Committee on Foreign Affairs, House of Representatives—Attempted Defection by Lithuanian Seaman Simas Kudirka,* pp. 33–34 [hereafter cited as *Hearings*].

Chapter Three

1. Zabiela's name came to light in testimony during Kudirka's reported treason trial in Lithuania six months after the incident. The testimony was smuggled out to correspondent Anatole Shub who revealed it in an article in the *Washington Post* on August 7, 1971. Though he did not refer to Zabiela in the article, the commissar's name is found in the copies circulated by *samizdat* ("self-publishing"), the Soviet literary underground. See PPC No. 679 (Chronicle of Current Events) "Notes by *samizdat* on the trial of the

Lithuanian S. Kudirka taking place in the city of Vilnius on May 17–20, 1971 (without the place and date, but probably: Vilnius, after May 5, 1971)."

Chapter Five

1. An excellent background account on Lithuania during World War II and after is Professor V. Stanley Vardy's (ed.) *Lithuania Under the Soviets, Portrait of a Nation 1940–1965,* 1965.

2. Kudirka's attitudes and quotes attributed to him in this chapter are found in the Russian language in PPC No. 679 (Chronicle of Current Events) "Notes by *samizdat* on the trial of the Lithuanian S. Kudirka taking place in the city of Vilnius on May 17–20, 1971 (without the place and date, but probably: Vilnius, after May 5, 1971). An article by Anatole Shub which quotes much of Kudirka's testimony is found in the *Washington Post,* August 7, 1971, p. 1, and in the *Boston Globe,* August 7, 1971, p. 1.

3. Order No. 001223, signed in Moscow by Deputy Commissar of the NKVD, General Ivan Serov, on October 11, 1939—a year before the actual takeover of the Baltic States—called for a massive purge of "socially dangerous elements *regardless* of concrete data concerning their anti-Soviet attitudes." (Emphasis in original.) See photostat of the document in *Lithuanian Bulletin,* 4: 17–35 (January, 1946).

4. I am particularly indebted for an account of Soviet fleet life from Miss Daina Palena of Boston, a former member of the Soviet fishing fleet from Riga, Latvia, who defected to the United States in 1969. Actually, she had tried to commit suicide by swallowing pills, but was rushed from her ship to a Staten Island hospital, where a former Latvian refugee happened to be one of the doctors on duty. The U.S. allows emergency cases from ships of foreign fleets to be brought to shore for treatment. The doctor spoke to Miss Palena when she came out of a coma and she asked for and received political asylum. The doctor used various medical ploys to keep her from the hands of Soviet functionaries who had come from the Soviet Mission in New York to claim her, while waiting for instructions from U.S. Immigration authorities.

5. Vytautas Miniotas, a Soviet Lithuanian journalist, prepared the article for *Laisve* (Freedom) (March 5 and 9, 1971), a Soviet-oriented paper published in the United States. Not a word about Kudirka appeared in the press in the Soviet Union.

6. The father and his son were Pranas Brazinskas, forty-six, and Algirdas, fifteen. Heavily armed, they boarded an Aeroflot flight in Batumi, near

the Turkish border, and diverted it to Trabzon, a Turkish city on the Black Sea. During a scuffle in which the pilot tilted the plane to throw the hijackers off balance, the older Brazinskas shot and killed a stewardess. He claimed later it was an accident caused by the plane's violent maneuvering. As of this writing the father and son are still on trial in Turkey for the shooting. The Soviets have demanded the return of Brazinskas and his son.

On November 9, a Lithuanian couple, Vytautas and Gražina Simokaitis, tried to commandeer a plane to Sweden, but were thwarted. Simokaitis, thirty-four, was sentenced to death and his pregnant wife to three years in prison as an accomplice. Widespread protest in the U.S. in December prodded the Soviets to reduce his sentence to fifteen years at hard labor. Simokaitis had refused clemency, because he and his wife had made a pact to escape from the Soviets or die.

Earlier—in June—eleven Baltic Jews had been arrested in Leningrad for plotting to escape to Israel via Sweden by hijacking a plane. Two of the dissidents were sentenced to death, but worldwide protests, including an appeal from Pope Paul VI, had also prodded the Soviets to reduce the sentence to fifteen years in labor camps. The other nine had also received fifteen years at hard labor.

Chapter Six

1. Interviews with Captain Brown on May 25, 1971, and June 22, 1972, in Gloucester, Mass. Tapes in my possession. Testimony of Captain Brown in *Verbatim Record of the Proceedings Conducted at The Transportation Systems Center, Cambridge, Mass. 1–4 December, 1970*, pp. 241ff. [Hereafter cited as *Proceedings, Cambridge.*] Testimony of Admiral Hammond in *Verbatim Record of the Proceedings Conducted at U.S. Coast Guard Headquarters, Washington, D.C., 8–10 December, 1970*, pp. 3 ff and 112 ff. [Hereafter cited as *Proceedings, Washington.*]

2. In addition to Captain Brown's reminiscences and his testimony before the board, the conversation is re-created from reminiscences of Admiral Ellis in a conversation with me in Beverly, Mass., on June 18, 1971—tapes in my possession—and his testimony before the board: *Proceedings, Cambridge*, pp. 260 ff; *Proceedings, Washington*, pp. 283 ff.

3. Testimony of the officers in *Proceedings, Cambridge:* Commander Flanagan, pp. 147ff., Commander Curry, pp. 159ff., and Captain Murphy, pp. 186ff.

Captain Brown maintained in interviews that all four officers, including himself, agreed the defector should be kept.

4. None of the officers reported this to the Board of Investigation, but Admiral Ellis said in an interview that Brown had mentioned it to him during one of their telephone conversations.

Chapter Seven

1. Captain Dahlgren's testimony is found in *Proceedings, Washington,* pp. 67ff.

2. Captain Webb's testimony is found in *Proceedings, Washington,* pp. 163ff.

3. Lt. Commander Seelman's account is found in the House subcommittee *Hearings,* pp. 97ff.

Chapter Nine

1. Formal Coast Guard Board of Investigation, *Board Exhibit 30:* "Stipulation of Testimony by Commander Smith, USCG, First Coast Guard District Communications Officer."

Chapter Ten

1. Interview with Admiral Ellis, June 18, 1971, Beverly, Mass. Tapes in my possession.

2. Killham's testimony is found in *Proceedings, Washington,* pp. 200ff.

Chapter Eleven

1. Admiral Hammond's suggestion to Captain Brown to tell the Russians that the defector was taken in "for medical treatment" and Killham's earlier statement to Captain Dahlgren that Kudirka could be picked up as a "mariner in distress" are wordplay (logomachy). According to Professor Louis F.E. Goldie, a noted scholar on international law teaching at the Naval War College at the time of the *Vigilant* incident, these wordplays amounted to legal fiction. In an article about the incident in the *Naval War College Review,* (May, 1971) entitled "Legal Aspects of the Refusal of Asylum by U.S. Coast

Guard on 23 November 1970," Goldie asked the pointed question: "How can Kudirka's standing as a distressed mariner be an improvement on that of being a political refugee?" p. 37.

2. *Proceedings, Cambridge,* p. 249 and *Proceedings, Washington,* p. 41.

Chapter Thirteen

1. Correspondence from Lt. Commander Pakos dated 13 September 1972 in my possession.

2. Account by Lieutenant Lundberg in conversation aboard cutter *Vigilant* April 5 and 12, 1971. Tapes in my possession.

3. Formal Coast Guard Board of Investigation, *Board Exhibit 46:* "Transcript of all telephone conversations recorded in RCC Boston from 1704 to 2046, 23 November 1970 along with seven additional pages for a total of forty-seven pages running up to 2329."

Chapter Fourteen

1. Account by Commander Eustis in conversations on Governor's Island, May 10, 1971, and June 20, 1972. Tapes in my possession.

Chapter Fifteen

1. Interview with Captain Brown in Gloucester, May 25, 1971. Tapes in my possession.

Chapter Sixteen

1. This telephone conversation was unrecorded, because it was not routed through RCC. It is re-created from interviews with Admiral Ellis and Captain Brown and from their testimony before the Board of Investigation.

2. Interview with Bob Couto in New Bedford, March 15, 1971. Tapes in my possession.

3. By the very fact of being Lithuanian, Kudirka had a solid claim to refugee status. Since the United States does not recognize the Soviet absorption of the Baltic States (see United States Department of State, *Status of World's Nations, Geographic Bulletin No. 2, 1969,* p. 1n), it also does not recognize Russian sovereignty over citizens of Lithuania. Once Kudirka was free from Soviet control, they technically could not demand him back in the eyes of the United States. This, of course, is a technical point aside from Kudirka's right to claim political asylum based on international law.

Atle Grahl Madsen writes in *The Status of Refugees in International Law:* "... a person cannot be expected to feel any loyalty or allegiance to the government of a state which has annexed his home country, irrespective of whether this is a result of war *(de bellatio),* threat of war, or to all appearances a voluntary *Anschluss* . . . There are several distinct groups of persons who have refused to submit themselves to the new regimes in their homeland and who, on this score, have won recognition as refugees. Thus, in the immediate postwar period, hundreds of thousands of Balts (Estonians, Latvians, and Lithuanians), Poles, and people from other Eastern European countries who were outside, or had managed to escape from, the area under Soviet domination refused to go back to their home countries and were eventually recognized as refugees by virtue of provisions of the Constitution of the International Refugee Organization . . ." pp. 78, 85, 259.

Chapter Eighteen

1. See Obolensky's account in House subcommittee *Hearings,* pp. 151ff.

Chapter Nineteen

1. In 1910 there occurred an incident in Marseilles, France, which was later referred to the Permanent Court of International Arbitration at the Hague and affirmed in international law the Territorial Integrity of a Receiving State. Although details of the incident were different from the *Vigilant* case, they did illustrate a principle applicable to Commander Eustis when he received the note accusing Kudirka of theft.

An Indian revolutionary by the name of Vinajak Damodor Savarkar was being transported by British authorities from England to India to face charges of "abetment of murder." The ship was to make a stopover in Marseilles, and

British authorities asked French authorities for assistance in Marseilles in the event that Savarkar escaped. Sure enough, Savarkar did escape, swam to shore, and was running along a dock when apprehended by a French police officer (brigadier).

The British asked for Savarkar back and the French officer, without consulting higher authority, gave Savarkar back to the British.

When the French government learned of this it protested the return before the Permanent Court of International Arbitration, claiming French territorial integrity had been violated and demanding the return of Savarkar to French control.

The Court made its ruling in 1911 saying that an "irregularity" had been committed. However, since the two countries had collaborated over Savarkar before the incident, and that "the case is not one of recourse to force or fraud," the British could keep Savarkar without going through the formality of giving him back to the French and asking the French government for him. See James Brown Scott (ed.), "Savarkar Case," *The Hague Court Reports,* 1916. See also Professor Goldie's discussion of the Savarkar case in "Legal Aspects of the Refusal of Asylum by U.S. Coast Guard on 23 November 1970" in *Naval War College Review* (May, 1971).

The key in this case for the *Vigilant* incident is the reference to "force or fraud." In an addendum entitled "International Law Aspects of Attempted Defection of Lithuanian Seaman at Martha's Vineyard" to its interim guidelines on defection policy, the State Department stated: "If . . . the cooperation of the United States was obtained by fraud, then the Soviet actions would constitute a breach of international law. In this connection it is noted . . . that 'the Soviet Master alleged that the defector had stolen $2,000 [sic] from the ship's fund.' If the decision to deliver the seaman to the Soviet ship was based on this allegation of theft, and such allegation was false, then the Soviet authorities would be guilty of a violation of international law, since their conduct would constitute fraud."

2. Interview with Alexis Obolensky, June 19, 1972, in Washington, D.C.

3. See his testimony in *Proceedings, Cambridge,* pp. 135ff., and *Board Exhibit 32:* "Statement of Witness Lt. Commander Paul E. Pakos, U.S. Coast Guard, USCGC VIGILANT, Executive Officer."

4. Interview with William Gordon, May 7, 1971, in Gloucester, Mass. Tapes in my possession.

Chapter Twenty

1. For Lieutenant Tritbough's testimony see *Proceedings, Washington,* pp. 136ff.
2. *Proceedings, Washington,* pp. 51 and 153.
3. For McGuire's testimony see *Proceedings, Washington,* pp. 226ff.
4. For Mainland's testimony see *Proceedings, Washington,* pp. 238ff.

Chapter Twenty-one

1. Interview with Robert Brieze, December 16, 1970. Tapes in my possession.
2. His meeting with Kudirka was recounted by Obolensky in an interview June 19, 1972, in Washington, D.C.
3. The ensuing conversation is according to Lieutenant Burke's testimony before the Board of Investigation. See *Board Exhibit 29:* "Stipulation of Lieutenant (jg) Burke's testimony, Board Exhibit 28, retyped for legibility."

Chapter Twenty-two

1. This portion of the phone patch was unrecorded, because it was made through the regular marine operator and not the Coast Guard Radio Station via RCC. However, both Captain Brown and Commander Eustis testified to its contents. *Proceedings, Cambridge,* pp. 233–235 and pp. 254–257. Also interviews with Captain Brown and Commander Eustis, cited earlier.
2. Seaman Maresca's testimony is found in *Proceedings, Cambridge,* pp. 38ff.
3. Ensign Hughes's testimony is found in *Proceedings, Cambridge,* pp. 48ff.
4. Interview with Commander Eustis, May 10, 1971, on Governor's Island. Tapes in my possession.

Chapter Twenty-three

1. Account by Lieutenant Lundberg who witnessed the scene, in an interview aboard cutter *Vigilant* April 5 and 12, 1971. Tapes in my possession.

2. Account by Lieutenant Lundberg in interviews cited above, and by John Burt in interview March 23, 1971, in New Bedford. Tapes in my possession. Witnessing the scene also (from the Captain's Cabin) were Robert Brieze, who gave his account in interviews December 16, 1970, and March 23, 1971, in New Bedford; and William Gordon, who gave his account May 7, 1971, in Gloucester. Tapes in my possession.

3. Seaman Santos's testimony is found in *Proceedings, Cambridge,* pp. 28ff., and *Board Exhibit 6:* "Statement of Witness Engineman Third Class D.R. Santos, U.S. Coast Guard, USCGC VIGILANT." Commissaryman Third Class Jabour's testimony is found in *Proceedings, Cambridge,* pp. 15ff.

4. *Ibid.*

5. *Ibid.*

6. *Proceedings, Cambridge,* p. 22.

7. *Ibid.,* pp. 203 and 141.

8. *Ibid.,* p. 54.

9. *Ibid.,* p. 203.

10. See Lieutenant Morehouse's testimony, *Proceedings, Cambridge,* p. 204.

11. *Proceedings, Cambridge,* p. 141.

Chapter Twenty-four

1. Interview with William Gordon, May 7, 1971, in Gloucester, Mass. Tapes in my possession.

2. Interview with John Burt, March 23, 1971, in New Bedford, Mass. See also *Proceedings, Cambridge,* pp. 52–53 and 202–204.

3. This phone patch was unrecorded, because it was made through the regular marine operator and not the Coast Guard Radio Station via RCC. Both Captain Brown and Lt. Commander Pakos testified to its contents. *Proceedings, Cambridge,* pp. 142 and 255–256.

4. In his article in the *Naval War College Review,* which is a composite of a series of lectures given at the Naval War College, Professor F.E. Goldie makes the following statement: "Thus, in considering the recent debacle, one should remember that since they had no extraterritorial rights here, the Russians were denigrating the territorial sovereignty and integrity of the United States. Without the consent of *Vigilant's* Commanding Officer to their

action, the Russians who arrested Simas Kudirka could be characterized as common criminals, kidnappers for example. Even with his consent, any excessive use of force that might have been brought to bear could not be made lawful merely by virtue of the commanding officer's invitation or nonintervention. It merely was an illegality aided and abetted by an officer of the U.S. Coast Guard. Let me repeat, Russian policemen have no extraterritorial status or privileges here in the United States except insofar as they may be granted them by the appropriate U.S. authorities. And this consent cannot condone what the Constitution and laws of the United States themselves prohibit." See his "Legal Aspects of the Refusal of Asylum by U.S. Coast Guard on 23 November 1970," *Naval War College Review* (May, 1971), pp. 34–35.

5. *Proceedings, Cambridge,* p. 40.

Chapter Twenty-five

1. Their telephone conversation was recounted by McGuire in a memo to his superior, Karl D. Ackerman, on December 5, 1970. The memo is one of the enclosures in the official State Department memorandum to the President on the "Attempted Defection by a Crew Member of the *Sovetskaya Litva.*"

2. See Mainland's testimony, *Proceedings, Washington,* pp. 238ff.

Chapter Twenty-six

1. *Proceedings, Cambridge,* pp. 70–71.

2. *Ibid.,* p. 38.

3. *Ibid.,* pp. 38 and 70–71.

Chapter Twenty-seven

1. Interview with Captain Brown, May 25, 1971, in Gloucester, Mass. Tapes in my possession.

2. In preparing an article for the Boston *Herald-Traveler,* a staff reporter checked with various military spokesmen and legal officers and found only

one recent case where a flag or general officer had been relieved. That case involved Major General Samuel W. Koster, who was relieved as Superintendent of West Point—but at his own request. He was involved in an investigation concerning the My Lai incident in South Vietnam. Koster, at the time, had been in charge of the Americal Division in Vietnam, and officers under his command were being charged with the massacre of more than 100 persons in My Lai. However, Koster was relieved of command only after being charged with dereliction of duty (covering up the incident). See "Flag Officer's Suspension Unprecedented," Boston *Herald-Traveler*, December 5, 1970.

Chapter Twenty-eight

1. The President and sole member of the Board of Investigation was Vice Admiral Thomas R. Sargent, III, the Assistant Commandant. Counsel appointed for the Board was Lt. Commander Jay M. Fidell, and Assistant Counsel for the Board were Lieutenant Billy W. Richardson and Lieutenant Donald A. Kopp. Admiral Ellis was represented by Captain Christopher S. Changaris and Commander Jerome Flanagan. Flanagan was allowed to represent Ellis, even though he was also to testify as a witness for the Board. Captain Brown was represented by Commander Lawrence J. Hoch, USCG (retired). Commander Eustis was represented by Commander James E. Brown, Jr., and Commander Norman B. Lynch.

2. The charges against Lieutenant Ryan centered on the phrase "case is being resolved" as opposed to "case has been resolved." It was soon evident from transcriptions of tapes that Ryan's information to Flag Plot implied the defector was being given back to the Soviets, or soon would be. Hence his designation as a party was dropped. Ryan was represented by Lt. Commander Nils Linfors, Jr.

Chapter Twenty-nine

1. Bender did not concur with the recommendation of issuance of a Commandant Instruction directing written confirmation of important orders given over the telephone, because the recommendation was "too broad in scope." He stated that existing instructions would be reviewed for necessary amendments.

2. For the two officers' accounts before the House subcommittee, see *Hearings before the Subcommittee on State Department Organization and Foreign Operations of the Committee on Foreign Affairs, House of Representatives— Attempted Defection by Lithuanian Seaman Simas Kudirka,* 1971, pp. 173ff.

Chapter Thirty

1. Letters filtering out of Lithuania to friends and relatives in the U.S. and Canada included guarded statements about him. Some said they saw him being led by security forces on a street in Vilnius, the capital. Others said he was dead. One letter to a family in Canada claimed he had died of kidney failure from the beating and that a new grave in a cemetery in Klaipeda bore the initials "S.K." But these were all rumors, each with its own mysterious source.

2. See footnote 6, Chapter Five.

3. PPC No. 679 "Notes by *samizdat* on the trial of the Lithuanian S. Kudirka taking place in the city of Vilnius on May 17–20, 1971 (without the place and date, but probably: Vilnius, after May 5, 1971)."

4. In May, 1971, nineteen-year-old Romas Kalanta, a member of *Komsomol,* the Communist Youth League, sat down in front of the Kaunas State Theater and burned himself to death in protest over the Soviet occupation of Lithuania. During his funeral a week later, thousands of persons jammed the streets shouting: "Freedom! Freedom! Freedom for Lithuania!" The Soviets had to send in special anti-insurgent police to quell the crowds. At least one militiaman was reported killed and hundreds of rioters were arrested. Their trials began in early fall of 1972. Two weeks after Kalanta's death a twenty-three-year-old worker identified only as Stonis stood on a roof of a building in the town of Varena, poured gasoline over himself, and lit it, then jumped off the building to his death. Stonis had gone to a fair with three friends where they raised the forbidden Lithuanian National Flag. His friends were arrested, but he escaped and killed himself the following day. On June 3, a sixty-year-old laborer named Andriuškevicius burned himself to death, and a fourth person, a sixty-two-year-old man named Zelišauskas, tried to burn himself as well, but was stopped by police. Dissident sources passing the information to Western correspondents in Moscow said both incidents were in protest over the Soviet occupation of Lithuania. See "Ordeal by Fire," *Time,* July 31, 1972, pp. 27–28, and United Press International dispatches: 052A Burn 7–6, July 6, 1972, and 055B Burn 7–5, Night Lead, July 5, 1972.

INDEX